Educational
Computing

Educational Computing

Learning with Tomorrow's Technologies

CLEBORNE D. MADDUX
University of Nevada, Reno

D. LaMONT JOHNSON
University of Nevada, Reno

JERRY W. WILLIS
University of Houston

ALLYN AND BACON
Boston   London   Toronto   Sydney   Tokyo   Singapore

Series Editor: Sean W. Wakely
Series Editorial Assistant: Carol L. Chernaik
Production Administrator: Annette Joseph
Production Coordinator: Susan Freese
Editorial-Production Service: Raeia Maes
Manufacturing Buyer: Louise Richardson
Cover Administrator: Linda K. Dickinson
Cover Designer: Suzanne Harbison

Copyright © 1992 by Allyn and Bacon
A Division of Simon & Schuster, Inc.
160 Gould Street
Needham Heights, Massachusetts 02194

Library of Congress Cataloging-in-Publication Data

Maddux, Cleborne D.
    Educational computing : learning with tomorrow's technologies /
Cleborne D. Maddux, D. LaMont Johnson, Jerry Willis.
        p.   cm.
    Includes bibliographical references (p.   ) and index.
    ISBN 0-205-13648-6
    1. Computer-assisted instruction—United States.   I. Johnson, D.
LaMont (Dee LaMont).   II. Willis, Jerry.
III. Title.
LB1028.5.M136   1992
371.3'34—dc20   91-42536
                                                                                      CIP

Printed in the United States of America

10   9   8   7   6   5   4   3   2   1   97   96   95   94   93   92

Credits

The credits appear on the page following the index. They should be considered an extension of the copyright page.

BRIEF CONTENTS

PART ONE An Introduction to Computers in Education   1

   1   Computers in Society and in Schools   3

   2   Type I And Type II Uses for Computers   21

   3   History and Hardware   43

   4   Issues and Trends in Educational Computing   75

PART TWO Specific Type I Educational Applications   93

   5   Drill and Practice, Tutorial, and Assessment Uses   95

   6   Computer-Managed Instruction and Telecommunications   115

   7   Administrative Uses of Computers   131

PART THREE Specific Type II Educational Applications   151

   8   Fundamental Computer Operations: Programming and Operating Systems   153

   9   Educational Simulations   173

   10   Word Processing in Education   193

   11   Computers as Prosthetic Aids   213

   12   Database Management and Spreadsheets   231

   13   Problem-Solving Software   251

   14   Logo: A Unique Computer Language   267

PART FOUR   Making Choices and Looking Ahead   291

15   **Evaluating Educational Software   293**

16   **The Future of Educational Computing   311**

Software Resources Appendix   327

Index   333

CONTENTS

Preface   xvii

PART ONE   An Introduction to Computers in Education   1

1   Computers in Society and in Schools   3

Computers in the Culture at Large   4

Education and Change   4
What Anthropology Tells Us about Change   5
The Role of Education in Cultural Change   5
Education as a Weak Force for Cultural Change   6
Anthropology and Computer Education   6
Computers and Values   6
The Values Underlying Educational Computing   7

Educational Computing Today   8
The Backlash against Educational Computing   9
The Negative Impact of Inflated Claims   10
The Precedent for Failure   11
Innovating in the Absence of Evidence   12
School Computer Uses and the Computer Backlash   14
How Computers Are Used in Schools   14
Some Comments on How Computers Are Being Used   15

Summary   16

Looking Ahead   17

Some Questions to Consider   18

Related Activities   18

Suggestions for Additional Reading   18

References   19

2   Type I And Type II Uses for Computers   21

Characteristics of Type I and Type II Educational Computing
   Applications   23

Type I Applications   24
Type II Applications   26
Examples of Type I and Type II Applications   27

Summary   39

Looking Ahead   40

Some Questions to Consider   40

Related Activities   41

References   41

3   History and Hardware   43

History and Hardware: Two Contexts of Educational Computing Today   44

A Bit of History   44

Computer Hardware Today   54
What Is Software?   54

The Hardware Aspects of a Computer System   56
Input Devices   56
The Central Processing Unit   61
Memory   62
Mass Storage   62
Networking   65
Output Devices   66

Summary   73

Looking Ahead   73

Some Questions to Consider   74

Related Activities   74

References   74

4   Issues and Trends in Educational Computing   75

Computer Literacy   76

Computer Equity   79

Computer Ethics   81
Violation of Copyright Law   81
Invasion of Individual Privacy   83
Unethical Entrepreneurship by Computer Educators   84

Labs versus Integration of Computers   85
Scarcity of Hardware and Software   85
Lack of Computing Expertise   86

Computer Networking   86

Computers and Problem Solving   88

Summary   89

Looking Ahead   90

Some Questions to Consider   91

Related Activities   91

References   91

PART TWO   Specific Type I Educational Applications   93

5   Drill and Practice, Tutorial, and Assessment Uses   95

A Brief History of Teaching Machines and Programmed Instruction   96
   Programmed Instruction, Teaching Machines, and Computers   100
   Drill and Practice and Tutorial Applications   102
   Early Computer Education Efforts   103
   What Research Says about Computer Learning   104
   Assessment Applications   105
   How Computers Are Used in Assessment   106

Summary   110

Looking Ahead   111

Some Questions to Consider   111

Related Activities   111

References   111

**6   Computer-Managed Instruction and
     Telecommunications   115**

Computer-Managed Instruction   116
   The Roots of CMI   117
   Trends and Issues Relating to CMI   120
Computer Telecommunications   122
   The Components of Computer Telecommunications   123
   Trends and Issues   126

Summary   128

Looking Ahead   128

Some Questions to Consider   128

Related Activities   128

Suggestions for Additional Reading   129

References   129

7   Administrative Uses of Computers   131

Supporting Management Tasks   133

The Automated Office   133
  The Computer as Document Processor   134
  The Computer as Record Keeper   135
  The Computer as Accountant and Business Manager   139
  Computer-Aided Time, Space, Vehicle,
    and Personnel Management   141
  Other Administrative Uses   142

Leadership Support Functions   143
  Electronic Mail and Teleconferencing   144
  Remote Information Databases   147

Summary   147

Looking Ahead   148

Some Questions to Consider   148

References   148

Software Products Cited in Text   149

PART THREE   Specific Type II Educational Applications   151

8   Fundamental Computer Operations: Programming and Operating Systems   153

Programming and Programming Languages   154
  Programming the First Computer   154
  Early Programming Languages   155
  High-Level Languages   156
  Educational Languages   160

Issues and Trends in Teaching Programming in the Schools   161
  Controversies in Teaching Programming   162
  Conclusions on Teaching Programming   165

Operating Systems   165
  What Is a Computer Operating System?   166
  Why Do We Need Operating Systems?   168
  What Is Essential to Teach about Operating Systems?   169

Summary   170

Looking Ahead   171
Related Activities   171
References   171

9   **Educational Simulations   173**

A Bit of History   174
Military Uses   175
Business Uses   175
Educational Uses   176
Why Are Simulations Used So Infrequently?   177
Why Do Students Find Simulations Appealing?   178
Advantages of Simulations   182
Potential Problems of Simulations   184
Using Simulations in the Classroom   186
Summary   189
Some Questions to Consider   190
Looking Ahead   190
References   190

10   **Word Processing in Education   193**

Word Processing: A Useful and Popular Tool   194
What Is Word Processing?   195
The Advantages of Word Processing   195
An Imaginary Typewriting Session   196
An Imaginary Word-Processing Session   196
Selecting a Word Processor   198
Word Processing in Schools   199
Ease of Production and Revision of Text   199
Word Processing and Cognitive Advantages   200
Word Processing and Social Advantages   202
Word Processing and Attitudinal Advantages   203
What about Keyboarding Skills?   203
Research on Word Processing in Education   204
Quality of Writing   204
Length of Compositions   205
Revisions   205
Attitudes   205
Interpreting Research on Word Processing   206

Idea Processors   206

Other Computer Writing Aids   206
Grammar Checkers   207
Spelling Checkers   207
Electronic Thesaurus   207

Specific Word Processing Systems   208

Summary   209

Looking Ahead   210

Some Questions to Consider   210

Related Activities   211

References   211

11   Computers as Prosthetic Aids   213

The Case for the Computer as a Prosthetic Device   214

General Types of Computer Prosthetic Devices   216
Speech Synthesis   216
Special Input Devices   217
Aids for the Blind   218

Hardware and Software for the Handicapped   221
Some Established Standards   221
Where to Go for Help   223

Issues and Concerns   225

Summary   227

Looking Ahead   227

Some Questions to Consider   228

Related Activities   228

Suggestions for Additional Reading   228

References   229

12   Database Management and Spreadsheets   231

Electronic Databases and Database Management Software   232
Managing Data with a Computer   233
The Electronic Database as a Type II Application   233
Database Management Software   234
*Database Management Systems and Databases
    for School Use*   236
*Common School-Oriented Database
    Management Systems*   237

Electronic Spreadsheets in Education   241
   The Electronic Spreadsheet   242
   Advantages of the Electronic Spreadsheet   243
   The Electronic Spreadsheet as an Educational Tool   246

Summary   248

Looking Ahead   248

Some Questions to Consider   249

Related Activities   249

Suggestions for Additional Reading   249

Software Products Cited in Text   249

References   250

13 Problem-Solving Software   251

The National Concern about Problem Solving   252

Where Should a Discussion of Problem Solving Begin?   253

What Is Problem Solving?   254

The Research on Problem Solving   255

Bloom's Taxonomy and Its Relevance
  to Problem Solving   257

Determining What to Teach   258

Commercial Problem-Solving Programs   259

Some Recommendations Concerning Problem-Solving Software   261

Summary   263

Looking Ahead   264

Some Questions to Consider   264

Related Activities   265

References   265

14 Logo: A Unique Computer Language   267

Historical Overview   268
  Logo's Roots   270

A Logo Advocacy Becomes Established   274

The Backlash against Logo   275
  Some Recommendations Concerning Logo   277

Specific Teaching Methods and a Sample Logo Lesson   280
  General Teaching Suggestions   280
  A Sample Lesson on Interactive Projects   281

Summary   286

Looking Ahead   287

Some Questions to Consider   288

Related Activities   288

Suggestions for Additional Reading   288

References   288

PART FOUR   Making Choices and Looking Ahead   291

15   Evaluating Educational Software   293

The Growing Body of Educational Software   294

The Quality of Educational Software   294

Why Is Much Educational Software of Poor Quality?   296

What Can Be Done about the Problem of Software Quality?   298
Short-Term Solution   298
Long-Term Solution   298

Finding Software Evaluations Written by Others   299
MicroSIFT   300
The EPIE Institute   300
Efforts of the Various States   301
Evaluations in Computing Magazines and Scholarly Journals   301
Formal Research Reports as Sources of Software Evaluations   301

Problems in Interpreting Software Evaluations Written by Others   302

Performing Your Own Software Evaluations   303
The Evaluation Process   303
Formal Evaluation Forms   304
Advantages and Disadvantages of Forms   307
Adapting Software Evaluation Forms   308
Obtaining Software for Evaluation   308

Summary   308

Looking Ahead   309

Some Questions to Consider   309

Related Activities   309

References   310

16   The Future of Educational Computing   311

Possibilities for the Future   314
Computers Themselves   314
Memory and Mass Storage   315

Telecommunications 317

Robots 317

Software 318

Prosthetic Devices for the Handicapped 318

Hypermedia, Interactive Multimedia, and Nonlinear Information 318

Summary 323

Some Questions to Consider 324

Related Activities 324

References 324

Software Resources Appendix **327**

Index **333**

PREFACE

Educational Computing is a book about an exciting experiment in education. The experiment involves making computers available to teachers and students in schools, and it is based on the idea that computing can be used to improve teaching and learning.

We are enthusiastic about the potential of improving teaching and learning with computers. It is this potential that makes the fledgling discipline of educational computing so exciting. If we are successful in using computers as tools to make available new and better ways of teaching and learning, we will have been responsible for creating a new discipline in education. Few professionals are fortunate enough to be at that pivotal place in history in which their actions determine the success or failure of a new discipline.

Today's educators are at such a pivotal point. In fact, we believe the future of educational computing depends primarily on the actions of those who will be practicing their profession during the 1990s. It is professionals in training, like you, who are exploring the vast potential of microcomputer technology, who will be called on to lead the way in integrating computing and teaching.

This book is intended to help prepare you to assume a leadership role in the new discipline of educational computing.

HOW THIS BOOK IS ORGANIZED

This book is organized into four parts. Part One is an introduction to educational computing. Chapter 1 addresses the role of computers in society at large and in schools in particular. Chapter 2 considers how computers can be used by educators to facilitate teaching in traditional ways or to make available new and better ways of teaching. Chapter 3 reviews the history of computing and provides a primer of computing equipment, and Chapter 4 considers issues and trends in educational computing.

Part Two describes and discusses Type I educational applications of computing, namely, those applications designed to make it faster, easier, or more convenient to continue using traditional teaching methods. Specifically, Chapter 5 covers drill and practice, tutorial, and assessment applications, Chapter 6 covers computer-managed instruction (CMI) and telecommunications, and Chapter 7 covers administrative uses.

Part Three addresses Type II educational applications, or those that make available new and better ways of teaching. Respectively, Chapters 8 through 14 address programming, educational simulations, word processing, the use of computers as prosthetic aids for the handicapped, database management and spreadsheets, the use of computers to teach problem solving, and teaching the Logo computing language.

Part Four is intended to help educators make intelligent choices about software options and provides a brief look at trends for the future. Chapter 15 considers evaluating educational software and Chapter 16 considers the future of educational computing.

ACKNOWLEDGMENTS

The authors extend thanks to the following reviewers whose contributions have enriched the text: Kim Burge, University of California at Irvine; Tom DeFranco, University of Hartford; Martin L. Harris, California State University at Sacramento; Gaylen Kelley, Boston University; Theodore Kellogg, University of Rhode Island; James Moseley, Wayne State University; Albert Nous, University of Pittsburgh; Penelope Semrau, California State University at Los Angeles; Frank Watson, University of Vermont.

Educational Computing

PART ONE

An Introduction to Computers in Education

IT IS ALWAYS DIFFICULT to decide how to introduce a topic. We have chosen to include four chapters in the introductory portion of this text. Chapter 1 deals with the role of computers in the society in general and in schools in particular. We begin by discussing how changes occur in society and in education and how this knowledge can be used by educational computing advocates. We also discuss what has caused the educational computing backlash and what we can do to help end this negative reaction. We then examine data on how computers have been used in schools in the recent past and we make recommendations about how such practices should be modified.

Chapter 2 presents the concept of Type I and Type II uses for computers. Type I uses facilitate traditional teaching methods, whereas Type II uses make available new and better teaching methods. Although there is nothing wrong with using good Type I applications in schools, we must ensure that we also adopt good Type II applications, since these are necessary to justify the considerable expense, effort, and enthusiasm needed to bring computers into schools. The Type I–Type II distinction is retained throughout this text because we believe it provides a useful way to think about educational computing and helps in making value judgments leading to intelligent choices about student computing experiences.

Chapter 3 includes a discussion of the history of computer development with an emphasis on prominent people and their historical roles.

The chapter also addresses function and operation of basic computer hardware.

Chapter 4 presents issues and trends in educational computing. We have elected to present these controversial issues at a relatively early point because we believe early awareness of controversies in the field will enhance understanding of the field as a whole. However, the reader is encouraged to return frequently to re-read portions of the chapter in light of knowledge gained from later study. Specifically, the chapter deals with issues related to computer literacy, computer equity, computing ethics, labs versus integration of computers, networking, and the teaching of problem solving. As we discuss these controversial topics, we attempt to provide many points of view, as well as our own related conclusions and recommendations.

1

Computers in Society and in Schools

GOALS AND OBJECTIVES

Goal: To understand why computers in education are at risk and to be aware of things to do to minimize that risk.

When you finish studying this chapter, you will be able to:

1. Compose a paragraph explaining why those who control formal education resist change until it is accepted in the culture at large.
2. Write a sentence defining *cultural lag*.
3. List at least two reasons why teachers sometimes oppose educational computi
4. Explain how unrealistic claims helped to fuel an educational computer backlash.
5. Identify educational movements other than those described in this chapter that illustrate the pendulum syndrome in education.

KEY TERMS

backlash
cultural lag
culture
efficacy

Logo
pendulum syndrome
software

This chapter is about the role of computers in society and in schools. It discusses bringing about educational change and how and why this sometimes works as we plan and sometimes does not. We begin by presenting information on change gleaned from *anthropology,* which is the study of humans and how they live. We include this discussion because we believe that many past innovations in education have partly failed because advocates have ignored what is known about change and how it is facilitated or hampered by events from inside and outside the education subculture.

The chapter then considers the ways that computers are being used in schools and why such applications have become widespread. We include some recommendations as to their use in this section.

The reader may wonder why we have chosen to make the chapter so problem oriented. It has been said that those who ignore history are doomed to repeat it. As we work to make educational computing succeed, we must learn from history and not repeat the errors of the past. If we consider the current status of education in general and educational computing in particular and how our past successes and failures have led to the current state of the art, we may discover clues to what we must do to succeed in the future.

COMPUTERS IN THE CULTURE AT LARGE

Even a casual observer of events in the United States during the 1980s would notice the rapid proliferation of computers in almost every walk of life. In fact, there are now many more computers in the United States than there are people.

Although computers are common in homes and schools, the incredible growth of the computer presence in the United States took place first and most dramatically in the business world. From video rental stores to fast-food restaurants to offices of all kinds, computers have become fixtures of U.S. business. In fact, when you compare the typical school environment to the typical business environment, it becomes apparent that schools have lagged far behind in implementing the use of computers.

EDUCATION AND CHANGE

Since many educators are vitally concerned with bringing about positive environmental/pedagogical change (such as the integration of computers and schooling), it is essential that we understand how change occurs, and how changes in our society and culture at large relate to change in our schools. The branch of social science that has intensively studied such changes is called anthropology.

What Anthropology Tells Us about Change

We believe there is much for educators in general and computer educators in particular to learn from anthropology. We are especially indebted to a classic and timeless book by George F. Kneller entitled *Educational Anthropology* (Kneller, 1965), and we recommend it to readers who become interested in the points we raise in this chapter.

We now turn briefly from our discussion of computing to consider some important knowledge about change. We pay special attention to the factors that contribute to the success or failure of changes in education.

The Role of Education in Cultural Change

Some anthropologists specialize in the study of **culture**, or the way of life shared by a given people, including both behaviors (beliefs, attitudes, and the like) and artifacts. Kneller points out that cultural anthropologists find that changes in the institutions of formal education, such as schools, typically occur after changes in the culture at large. Kneller also suggests that such cultural lag makes it unlikely that schools can lead the way as agents of cultural change (Kneller, 1965).

There are many reasons for this, but some of the most interesting and powerful reasons have to do with the purpose of formal education and who is chosen to control it. Kneller and many other anthropologists (for example, Webb & Sherman, 1989) assert that the primary purpose of schooling is to help transmit the way of life (the culture) of a people to their offspring. Partly because this is the purpose of education and partly because of the type of individual who is successful and honored, those chosen to control formal education are almost invariably those who are models of a specific way of life.

Consider the type of person most likely to be elected to a school board in our country. They are almost always model citizens. They tend to be successful, affluent individuals who have frequently distinguished themselves in business, hold traditional values and attitudes, and lead conventional lifestyles. Boocock (1980) describes school board members by comparing them with the general public: "By comparison with the general public, board members are disproportionately white, male, middle-aged, high in education, occupation, and income, and well established in their local communities" (p. 250). Underwood (1982) reported similar findings after conducting a national survey of school board members in the United States

Such individuals are ideal choices to control the cultural institution (school) whose primary purpose is to pass on the cultural heritage. They are ideal because they have a vested interest in preserving the status quo (the current culture) and in resisting change. For such citizens, the existing culture has led to success and prosperity, and they are therefore conservative in the largest sense of the word. (The *American Heritage Dictio-*

nary of the English Language defines the term *conservative* as "tending to favor the preservation of the existing order and to regard proposals for change with distrust.")

Education as a Weak Force for Cultural Change

There is yet another reason that formal education is incapable of initiating cultural change. Anthropologists have established that cultural change is not accomplished by any one cultural force such as formal education but by combinations of cultural forces exerted by institutions such as religion, mass media, the peer group, business, or various special-interest groups (Sarason, 1982). Formal education, by itself, is incapable of overcoming the momentum of these established and more powerful cultural forces.

This explains why the integration of computers in schools began to receive strong public support only after computers proved successful in business, government, and the military and in consumer goods such as appliances, toys, and automobiles.

Anthropology and Computer Education

We have seen how anthropology provides clues to why education was slow to bring computers into schools. In addition, and of more practical importance to computer educators, cultural anthropology provides clues that may be useful to those who plan the future advocacy of computers in education and to those who wish to maximize the effectiveness of their efforts.

Cultural Lag

Those who advocate the use of new technology in education should understand the concept of **cultural lag**. This term refers to the tendency for some elements of culture to change more rapidly than other elements. Specifically, in our culture, changes in technology commonly occur more rapidly than changes in values and attitudes.

One reason for this lag is that Americans resist changes in values more than changes in technology. It is revealing that individuals who dedicate themselves to changing technology may be called *inventors,* a term with highly positive connotations, whereas those who specialize in changing values or attitudes are often called *revolutionaries* or *malcontents,* terms with definite negative undertones.

Computers and Values

It would be a mistake for any educational computer advocate to assume that, since computers are a product of technology, they will be universally welcomed in schools by fellow teachers, school board members, or the general public. To understand why computers could be rejected, we must understand that successful technological change is always linked to the values a society endorses. For example, Kneller (1965) points out that the automobile enjoyed near instant success because it was linked to the accepted values of social mobility, private ownership, and the love of speed.

Those who seek to convince other educators that computers should be used in schools and that more resources should be devoted to their use should devote some thought to the values underlying computer technology. Some of these values appear to be widely endorsed in our society. For example, in the business subculture, where computing has enjoyed widespread success and approval, the computer can be linked to powerful values about work. These include beliefs about the desirability of (1) work speed, (2) work efficiency, (3) work power, and (4) the removal of human error from work activities.

The first three of these underlying values are accepted almost without argument by the business subculture. So, too, is the fourth, although computing will likely be opposed by labor if computers are seen as a possible replacement for a human worker. Even so, if computers are seen as increasing profit, they are then linked to the most powerful and universally approved value in the business world, and labor is not likely to be successful in blocking their integration.

The Values Underlying Educational Computing

Let us consider how the values of work speed, work efficiency, work power, and the removal of human error fare in education. The first three values are consistent with the values of most educators. Almost all teachers would welcome the opportunity to increase the speed, efficiency, and power of teaching and learning. But the removal of human error from work activities provides an area of possible conflict. If teachers believe that computers will replace them, they may reject the new technology, just as labor frequently rejects technology that threatens jobs.

A difference is that opposition by educators has the potential to be far more effective than the opposition of labor in the business world. Unlike business, in education there is no overriding profit motive to offset objections by labor. Even more important, the education subculture strongly endorses the value of preserving human interaction and involvement for its own sake. It is possible that educators will see computers not only as possible displacements for teachers, but also as dehumanizing the educational enterprise by limiting children's interactions with each other or with their teachers. If this attitude becomes widespread, strong opposition from within education will likely be encountered. Such fears contributed to the failure of teaching machines and programmed instruction, which were developed by B. F. Skinner and others during the 1950s and 1960s (Criswell, 1989).

Actually, fears that computers will replace teachers or that they will necessarily dehumanize education are unfounded. Computers are highly promising educational tools, but they do not have the ability or the potential to replace the teacher. Like other tools, such as pencils or books, they may modify the way typical teachers teach, but they cannot eliminate human teachers. Research has shown that computers can be used to increase or to decrease human interaction in education, but the teacher is the critical factor in determining how much human interaction will prevail.

Thus, educational computer advocates should take care to point out to teachers that the intention is to use computers to empower, not supplant, human beings in education and that research has shown that computers can be used to increase human interaction.

In addition to emphasizing the capacity of computing to increase the amount of human interaction in the classroom, it is equally important that we provide clear evidence that computing is accomplishing valuable educational goals. Those who control education (school administrators, school board members, and the general public) may be willing to ignore limited teacher opposition because such leaders value increasing the speed, efficiency, and power of teaching and learning. But if they are not convinced that computing can lead to the achievement of these and other goals and the consequent improvement of the school environment, they will not support the high cost of educational computing, especially if there is organized or widespread resistance from teachers. Thus, it is crucial that computer educators (1) make reasonable claims about what computers in education can accomplish and (2) provide evidence that promises about computing benefits are being fulfilled.

EDUCATIONAL COMPUTING TODAY

No one knows with certainty how many computers are being used in today's schools. The most comprehensive study available is already out of date, but that research can provide some valuable clues to educational computing trends, even though the actual numbers reported are probably no longer accurate. This research was conducted by Henry J. Becker (Becker, 1983a, b, c, d; 1984; 1986a, b, c; 1987, 1988) at the Center for Social Organization of Schools at Johns Hopkins University.

In 1983 and again in 1985, Becker surveyed 10,000 teachers and principals in over 2,300 elementary and secondary schools. One of the most striking findings of these surveys was that the number of instructional computers in schools grew tremendously between 1983 and 1985.

For example, Becker (1986a) reported that the 1985 survey revealed the following:

1. The number of instructional computers in use in schools quadrupled from about 250,000 to over one million.
2. Three-fourths of those schools that had not previously used computers began to do so.
3. The percentage of elementary schools with five or more computers jumped from 7% to 54%.
4. The percentage of high schools with 15 or more computers increased from 10% to 56%.
5. The typical high school with computers increased from 5 machines to 21 machines.
6. The typical elementary school with computers increased its holding from two computers to six computers.
7. During the 1984–1985 academic year, about 15 million students and 500,000 teachers used instructional computing in schools.
8. By the spring of 1985, there was approximately one computer for every 40 children in the schools.
9. Ninety percent of U.S. school children attend schools with at least one instructional computer.

It is apparent that the availability of microcomputers in schools increased dramatically between 1983 and 1985, and every indication is that this trend has continued from 1985 to the present. In fact, during the 1985–1986 academic year, state departments of education reported that schools spent $550 million for computer hardware and $130 million for software. Many authorities believe that by Spring 1988 there were more than two million instructional computers in schools. Officials at IBM predict that the total number of instructional computers will grow to five million by 1993 (McCarthy, 1988).

A more recent study was completed in 1988 by the U.S. Office of Technology Assessment (OTA) for the U.S. Congress (Office of Technology Assessment, 1988). This study was intended to be an in-depth report on the past, present, and future impact of technology in education. The report concluded that virtually all schools in the United States have at least one instructional computer and that there is approximately one computer for every 30 students.

The Backlash against Educational Computing

Examining statistics on the growth of school computer usage might lead us to conclude that all is well with the budding discipline of educational computing. Indeed, there is cause for computer advocates to rejoice. The increase in the numbers of computers in schools has been exciting and encouraging. However, there are accompanying problems. One of the most troubling developments has been the recent **backlash** of opinion against educational computing.

This backlash can be seen in a number of anti-educational-computing articles that have appeared in a variety of newspapers, magazines, and scholarly journals. For example, a recent *Wall Street Journal* headline proclaimed "Computers Failing as Teaching Aids," and a recent entire issue of the prestigious *Teachers College Record* was devoted to scholarly articles questioning the efficacy and advisability of using computers in education.

The Negative Impact of Inflated Claims

We believe and have often written (see Maddux, 1987) that an important cause of the educational computer backlash is the extravagant and unrealistic claims often made about the benefits of various computer applications in education.

Obviously, we are educational computing advocates. We believe that the computer's potential as a teaching and learning tool is unprecedented in the history of attempts to integrate electronic innovations into education. We also believe that advocates must keep their enthusiasm under control and refrain from making unsubstantiated and unlikely claims. Lavish claims about the effects of computing in schools have contributed to the educational computing backlash. The following excerpt concerning teaching the **Logo** computer language is an excellent representative of such claims:

> *Logo makes possible: number, letter, and color recognition; symbol association; directionality; decision making; following instructions; memory recall; spatial awareness; sequential thinking; creativity; computer awareness. Furthermore, teachers report that young children who use Logo develop an improved self-image, pay attention to detail, have a capacity for both divergent and logical thinking, have improved decision making, spelling, math, and communication skills and have developed an awareness of the computer as a tool. . . . These outcomes are found at both ends of the exceptional child spectrum, the gifted as well as the educationally handicapped. (Judd, 1983, p. 20)*

We cannot imagine any educational innovation that could possibly live up to such inflated claims. Such promises set up unrealistic expectations that have a way of coming back to haunt the incautious innovator. This happens when those who control resources eventually (and inevitably) begin to demand evidence that expenditures have been worthwhile. When they realize that most promises have gone unfulfilled, they may quickly change from advocates to opponents of the innovation. The danger, of course, is that the resulting backlash may be so severe that the innovation is abandoned.

This common cycle could be termed the educational **pendulum syndrome**, which is familiar to all educators and has afflicted past educational innovations in general (new math, assertive discipline, new grammar, open classrooms, team teaching, and the like) and electronic innovations in particular. The pendulum phenomenon involves a cycle of unrealistically optimistic expectations followed by disappointment, disillusionment, and massive curtailment or outright abandonment. Slavin (1989) has pointed out that education seems particularly susceptible to the pendulum syndrome.

The Precedent for Failure

No one should doubt that educational computing could fail; the precedent for failure exists in abundance in the history of past efforts to integrate electronic technology and education. Eight- and 16-millimeter film, teaching machines, educational television, and numerous other electronic innovations have suffered from the well-known and dreaded pendulum syndrome in education.

None of these innovations has lived up to initial expectations. They did not revolutionize teaching and learning. When educators and others began to realize that a major impact was not being made, the resulting backlash against the innovation was destructively strong and widespread. A few of these innovations, such as 16-millimeter film and educational television have made small contributions and continue to enjoy limited use. Criswell (1989) says, "Educational television is available today, but its popularity has been eclipsed by many factors, including CBI [computer-based instruction]. Like movies and textbooks, educational television does not allow for active participation on the part of students and teachers" (p. 5). Cuban (1986) reviewed all available surveys on the use of instructional television in schools and commented that in most schools students spend more time going to and coming from the bathroom than watching televised lessons. Other innovations, such as teaching machines, have been completely abandoned. Spitzer (1987) makes reference to the cyclical nature of events in this new discipline.

Although there is some danger that educational computing could suffer the same fate as some of the now abandoned innovations described above, computers enjoy a great advantage not shared by educational television, film, or overhead projectors: Computer programs can be made highly interactive. We believe the interactive nature of computing has the potential to make educational computing successful where other electronic innovations have been unsuccessful.

Innovating in the Absence of Evidence

Although extravagant claims are a prime cause of the pendulum syndrome, they are not the only cause. Another contributing factor is the tendency for teachers and administrators to implement sweeping changes long before researchers establish (or even begin to address) their **efficacy** (efficiency). Why this happens is difficult to determine, and it would be easy to confuse cause and effect. However, we believe that one reason practitioners institute changes before the changes are proved to be beneficial is that the education subculture provides no efficient mechanism for the translation of research findings into practice.

In other professions, such as medicine, this mechanism is provided by professional journals and preservice and inservice (continuing) education. However, relatively few teachers subscribe to professional journals, and the most popular of these journals are not those that present or interpret educational research. Inservice courses in education are rarely research oriented, usually because they are designed by practicing teachers who avoid such an orientation. Preservice courses are sometimes research oriented, but all too often teachers in training dismiss research evidence as worthless.

We believe that most teachers do not value research because teacher trainers have been unsuccessful in convincing students of the practical value of theory. Indeed, most teachers, even after the completion of a master's degree, seem to categorize knowledge into that which is *practical* (useful in the real world of public education), and that which is *theoretical* (useful only to write down as answers for tests in college education and psychology courses).

Such a categorization represents a false dichotomy, since theory and practice are actually inseparable. What is done in the classroom (practice) depends almost totally on how the teacher chooses to look at the world (theory). Therefore, a theory underlies and determines every action in every sphere of our lives.

By this reasoning, it is impossible to function without theory. Our only choice as teachers is to make use of either conscious theories or subconscious theories. It is important that our theories be conscious ones so that we can be constantly thinking about them, evaluating them, and revising them by applying logic and new knowledge.

The atheoretical or practical teacher drifts blithely along, disregarding and sometimes deriding educational and psychological theory. However, his or her every action is dictated by a theory (or, more likely, by bits and pieces of many, often conflicting theories) whose very existence is unknown to that teacher.

Those who believe in the false dichotomy of theory and practice frequently argue that they have no need of theory because they "use what works." Maddux (1988) has addressed the argument that theory is not needed:

> *There are many problems with this, not the least of which is how, in the absence of a theory of learning, one can determine that learning is taking place! But even if we ignore this paradox, there are other, formidable difficulties. For example, if we attempt to operate without theory, how do we choose what* might *work in the beginning? And when it quits working, how will we know what to try next? Available answers to these questions will sound familiar because we have lived with them for years in education. Without conscious theory (a) we may rely on experts to tell us what to do, (b) we may use what is currently popular, (c) we may resort to trial and error, or (d) we may simply continue doing what we've always done in the past, whether it "works" or not. (p. 3)*

Professionals in any field would likely reject the above alternatives. In fact, we do not believe a true profession can be built around such arbitrary decision making. Without conscious theory, practitioners are forced to rely completely on methods and materials, and teachers become mere technicians instead of professionals.

This brings us back to the question of why practitioners adopt some innovations before they are thoroughly tested and shown to be advantageous and persist with others that research has shown to be ill advised. We believe the phenomenon is directly related to the devaluing of research, as discussed above.

Unfortunately, when educational innovations are implemented, they are frequently those that are passed from teacher to teacher by word of mouth and those that are given wide media exposure. These forms of communication tend to produce inaccurate and exaggerated information, and often they nurture unrealistically optimistic expectations about the benefits to be derived from the innovation. As such innovations spread, they begin to require more and more time and money. School boards, legislators, administrators, and politicians begin to take notice and demand evidence that the innovation is succeeding. The media cover these demands, and the federal government and other granting agencies begin to fund research studies on the efficacy of the educational innovation. Since the early claims concerning benefits were overly optimistic, the results of efficacy research often show the innovation to be less beneficial than originally claimed. Because such studies are timely, findings are often reported by the media in the fashion of an exposé. Too often, the result is abandonment of the innovation, even though it may actually be moderately successful and highly promising.

There are several positive things teachers can do to counter the backlash against educational computing:

1. We have already discussed the importance of avoiding making unrealistic and unsubstantiated claims.
2. We should all be suspicious of anyone who makes lavish claims for any computing application, and we should demand evidence from software manufacturers and others who make such claims.
3. Teachers and teachers in training should strive to maintain an open mind concerning the relationship of theory to practice, and they should demand that professors and those who present inservice programs demonstrate how theory is related to practice.
4. Teachers and teachers in training should recognize that useful theories are forged and refined by research; they should therefore read the research reports of others and encourage and participate in research projects in their own classrooms.

School Computer Uses and the Computer Backlash

We have seen how unrealistic claims fuel the pendulum effect in education and add to the educational computing backlash. Another powerful contributor to the backlash is the poor way in which computers are sometimes used in schools. This is partly due to difficulty in locating excellent educational **software** (the instructions that make computers perform specific tasks), a problem that we will explore in depth in future chapters. Poor usage is also due to poor decisions made at the classroom, school, or district level, a topic we will now address.

How Computers Are Used in Schools

The most recent research on this topic is already antiquated. Credible data come from the survey we referred to earlier conducted by Henry J. Becker at Johns Hopkins University. Some of the most surprising findings included:

1. Mean number of hours of use per microcomputer in elementary schools was 15 hours per week. In middle schools and secondary schools, means were 20 and 23 hours per week, respectively.
2. At a typical computer-using school, more than one-fourth of the student body used computers at least once in a given week. However, the average time for elementary students was 35 minutes a week. In secondary schools, the average time was 90 minutes per week.
3. In elementary schools, when more computers were acquired, more students were included in the computer program, but the mean time per student was not increased.

4. Means of 10% of elementary teachers and 27% of secondary teachers were viewed as "expert" in one of four computing applications (using some instructional programs, knowing about a wide variety of programs, using word processing or other professional tools, and writing computer programs).

5. Across all grade levels, about one-third of all computing time was spent on drill and practice and tutorial programs, about one-third on programming, and one-third on other applications. Only about 16% of computing time was spent on word processing.

Some Comments on How Computers Are Being Used

The data in point 1 show that at the time of the survey computers were receiving only light usage (an average of 15 hours per week in elementary schools). This is somewhat surprising, since many school administrators report that their most important instructional computing problem is obtaining enough computer hardware. Although scheduling problems probably make it unlikely that available computers will be used for the entire school day, we suspect that lack of computing expertise is a more powerful factor in light usage. Therefore, we recommend that teachers and administrators strive to balance their concern for hardware and software acquisition with a concern for adequate training of instructional personnel.

With regard to the average amount of time spent by each student in a computer-using program, we believe that 35 minutes per week is clearly inadequate. This works out to an average of only 7 minutes per day per student. Then, too, 35 minutes is probably an overestimate of actual time spent computing, since data were gathered from school schedules. As all experienced teachers know, a scheduled time of 35 minutes frequently results in considerably less actual time spent by students.

We view limited instructional time as one of the most serious problems in the field. As with books, microscopes, canvas and paint, or any other tool, mere exposure to computers is not educationally valuable. We doubt that anyone would expect students to learn to read, use a microscope scientifically, or create an oil painting in 7 minutes per day.

It may be possible to achieve some relatively trivial educational computing goals in 7 minutes per day. We might, for example, be able to develop some rudimentary computer familiarity, improve rote skills such as recognition of sight vocabulary or number facts, and dispel any fear of computing. However, we do not believe 7 minutes per day can make a contribution to relatively more important and exciting educational goals, such as teaching transferable problem-solving skills, fostering creative writing skills, improving self-concept, or dispelling negative attitudes toward mathematics. We recommend that elementary students work with computers for a minimum of 30 minutes per day.

The findings related to the percent of teachers viewed as computing experts points up another serious problem. Only 10% of elementary teachers and just over 25% of secondary teachers were perceived as being expert. Those are very low percentages, especially when low-level skills such as "using some instructional programs" and "knowing about a wide variety of programs" were two of the four categories defined as constituting expertise.

These findings have obvious implications for inservice and preservice education. More and more universities are offering courses in computer education, and some states even require such courses prior to certification. We believe better preservice and inservice computer education is essential.

The figures on types of educational computing applications in current use are also interesting. As we reported above, about one-third of all computing time was spent on drill and practice and tutorial programs, about one third on programming, and one-third on miscellaneous applications. We will discuss drill and practice software and the arguments for and against teaching programming in later chapters. We believe there are good reasons to teach both of these applications. We would, however, prefer to see considerably more than the present 16% of time spent on word processing because we believe it to be one of the most powerful and advantageous applications of computers in education.

SUMMARY

Educational computing is an exciting new discipline whose fate will depend on how today's teachers in training use computers in their own classrooms in the future.

Computers were a success in business before they were implemented in education. This occurred because changes in education are always preceded by changes in the culture at large. Cultural anthropologists tell us that education cannot change culture, although the reverse is common. Changes occur first in the culture at large because in every culture formal education is controlled by leaders who are conservative. These leaders resist changes in formal education until the changes have become well accepted in other cultural institutions. Then, too, changes in the general culture are brought about not by any one institution, but by the combined influence of several.

Anthropologists also tell us that changes in technology are accepted more readily than changes in values. However, all technological innovations are linked to values. To be successful, these underlying values must be endorsed by a society.

Computer advocates need to understand cultural change if they are to be successful. Teachers should be assured that computers cannot replace them, but they can empower them and their students. It should also be emphasized that computers can be used to increase, rather than decrease, human interaction in the classroom.

Educational computing advocates must also help establish and disseminate evidence that computers are helping to meet realistic goals. They can do this by making only reasonable claims about the value of computing, reading the research of others, participating in research studies, and telling parents and others about this research.

The number of computers in schools in the United States has increased markedly since 1983 and continues to grow. There may be nine million instructional computers in schools by 1992. However, there is a backlash against educational computing. A major reason for this backlash is that many computing advocates make unrealistic and unsubstantiated claims about what computing can accomplish. These claims are almost always detrimental in the long run when leaders realize that the rosy promises they made are unlikely to be fulfilled.

The overly optimistic promises are part of the educational pendulum syndrome, in which educational innovations undergo a cycle of unrealistically optimistic expectations followed by disappointment, disillusionment, and massive curtailment or outright abandonment. This syndrome occurs for many reasons, including the fact that education has no efficient mechanism for the translation of research into practice. The university could serve as that mechanism, but most teachers do not appreciate the practical value of theory and research. Therefore, innovations are frequently endorsed before they are validated by research, and practices are frequently continued long after research has shown that they are ill advised.

Research has revealed some problems in school computer usage. Each computer is used for only a small portion of the school day, students in computing programs are given very little time to use a machine, few teachers have the computing knowledge they need to integrate computers into their teaching, and powerful applications such as word processing are underused. In addition, a recent government report concludes that the resources being allocated to instructional computing must increase beyond present levels if we hope to provide students with anything more than spotty access.

LOOKING AHEAD

Now that the reader has been exposed to some of the problems in implementing educational changes as well as some general information about the state of the art in educational computing, the next chapter presents an explanation and a rationale for classifying educational computing applications. The classification system is dichotomous (containing two categories), and its purpose is to help educators to understand their options and to choose applications that will maximize the human and computer resources at their disposal. We believe this system (involving the classification of applications as either Type I or Type II) will help us make the choices that have the best likelihood of avoiding the problems presented in this chapter, thus ensuring the success of the educational computing movement.

SOME QUESTIONS TO CONSIDER

1. In your opinion, what is the most encouraging trend in computer use identified in the chapter? Why?
2. What is the most discouraging trend? Why?
3. What do you think would be the most important single step a teacher could take to help avoid the educational pendulum syndrome in educational computing?
4. Do you agree that Americans resist changes in the culture of values more than changes in the culture of technology? Give an example.

RELATED ACTIVITIES

1. Locate an article in a popular magazine about the use of computers in schools. Do you think the authors would judge it to be extravagantly optimistic, realistic, or overly pessimistic? Why?
2. Interview a local teacher and/or administrator concerning his or her views on educational computing.
3. Interview a local businessperson concerning his or her attitude about computers in business.

SUGGESTIONS FOR ADDITIONAL READING

Collis, B. (1988). *Computers, curriculum, and whole-class instruction: Issues and ideas.* Belmont, CA: Wadsworth.

Kinzer, C. K., Sherwood, R. D., and Bransford, J. D. (1986). *Computer strategies for education.* Columbus, OH: Merrill.

Rothman, S., & Mosmann, C. (1985). *Computer uses and issues.* Chicago: Science Research Associates.

Weizenbaum, J. (1976). *Computer power and human reason.* New York: W. H. Freeman.

REFERENCES

Becker, H. J. (1983a). School uses of microcomputers: Reports from a national survey. Johns Hopkins University Center for Social Organization of Schools, Issue No. 1, April.

_____. (1983b). School uses of microcomputers: Reports from a national survey. Johns Hopkins University Center for Social Organization of Schools, Issue No. 2, June.

_____. (1983c). School uses of microcomputers: Reports from a national survey. Johns Hopkins University Center for Social Organization of Schools, Issue No. 3, October.

_____. (1983d). School uses of microcomputers: Reports from a national survey. Johns Hopkins University Center for Social Organization of Schools, Issue No. 4, February.

_____. (1984). School uses of microcomputers: Reports from a national survey. Johns Hopkins University Center for Social Organization of Schools, Issue No. 5, June.

_____. (1986a). Instructional uses of school computers: Reports from the 1985 national survey. Johns Hopkins University Center for Social Organization of Schools, Issue No. 1, June.

_____. (1986b). Instructional uses of school computers: Reports from the 1985 national survey. Johns Hopkins University Center for Social Organization of Schools, Issue No. 2, August.

_____. (1986c). Instructional uses of school computers: Reports from the 1985 national survey. Johns Hopkins University Center for Social Organization of Schools, Issue No. 3, November.

_____. (1987). Instructional uses of school computers: Reports from the 1985 national survey. Johns Hopkins University Center for Social Organization of Schools, Issue No. 4, June.

_____. (1988). The impact of computer use on children's learning. Johns Hopkins University Center for Research on Elementary and Middle Schools, April.

Boocock, S. S. (1980). _Sociology of education: An introduction_ (2nd ed.). Boston: Houghton Mifflin.

Criswell, E. L. (1989). _The design of computer-based instruction._ New York: Macmillan.

Cuban, L. (1986). _Teachers and machines._ New York: Teachers College Press.

Judd, D. H. (1983, March/April). Programming: An experience in creating a useful program or an experience in computer control. _Educational Computer,_ pp. 20–21.

Kneller, G. F. (1965). _Educational anthropology: An introduction._ New York: Wiley.

McCarthy, R. (1988). The network story: What's available/How they're used. _Electronic Learning,_ 7(4), 24–30, 62.

Maddux, C. D. (1987). Educational computing: A Sunday morning assessment. _Computers in the Schools,_ 4(2), 53–56.

Maddux, C. D. (1988). _Logo: Methods and curriculum for teachers._ New York: Haworth Press.

Office of Technology Assessment (1988). _Power on! New tools for teaching and learning_ (Publication No. 052-003-01125-5). Washington, DC: U.S. Government Printing Office.

Sarason, S. B. (1982). *The culture of the school and the problem of change* (2nd ed.). Boston: Allyn and Bacon.

Slavin, R. E. (1989, June). PET and the pendulum: Faddism in education and how to stop it. *Phi Delta Kappan,* pp. 752–758.

Spitzer, D. R. (1987). Why educational technology has failed. *Educational Technology,* 27(9), 18–21.

Underwood, K. E. (1982). Your portrait: School boards have a brand-new look. *American School Board Journal,* 69(1), 17–20.

Webb, R. B., & Sherman, R. R. (1989). *Schooling and society.* New York: Macmillan.

2

Type I and Type II Uses for Computers

GOALS AND OBJECTIVES

Goal: To understand the differences between Type I and Type II educational computer applications and how this categorization can be helpful in designing and implementing appropriate educational programs.

When you finish reading this chapter, you will be able to:

1. Write a paragraph describing why Type I applications alone cannot be expected to establish educational computing as a revolutionary teaching tool.
2. List the five characteristics shared by most Type I software.
3. List the five characteristics shared by most Type II software.
4. Describe the characteristics of SemCalc that qualifies this software as a Type II application.
5. Name the types of Type II software that you see as most useful and tell why.

KEY TERMS

administrative software
assessment software
backlash
computer-managed
  instruction
computer simulations
database management

drill and practice software
electronic spreadsheets
expert systems
graphics software
higher-order thinking skills
Logo
meta-analysis

presentation software
problem-solving software
programming languages
prosthetic aids
telecommunications
  software

tutorial software
Type I
Type II
word processing

We have stated that we believe the computer has the potential to become education's single most useful teaching and learning tool. Today's microcomputers are amazing technological achievements. However, the value of any tool does not depend solely on the qualities of the tool itself. If the tool is to be useful, a necessary (but not sufficient) requirement is that the tool's users must choose to apply the tool to important tasks. Equally crucial is the requirement that the problem chosen to be solved be consistent with the particular solution upon which the tool's design is based. A third requirement is that the cost of the tool not be disproportionately large compared to the seriousness of the problem it addresses.

The hammer, for example, is an extremely successful tool. It is used primarily for the important task of driving nails into wood, a necessary step in achieving larger goals, such as the building of houses and other expensive buildings. The hammer is so successful a tool that almost everyone owns or has access to one. But the hammer would probably not have succeeded if it had first been used merely to prop doors open. Although the hammer could function as a door stop, it is not well suited for this purpose, and its cost is excessively great compared to the minor problem it would solve.

Although we doubt that anyone is employing a microcomputer as a door stop, we believe that some educators may not be devoting enough careful thought to the kinds of teaching and learning tasks to which the microcomputer tool can best be applied. These educators do not gain the full educational value of computing, and they contribute to the **backlash** (negative reaction) against educational computing.

The success or failure of educational computing is closely tied to the value judgments we must make about educational practices and computer applications. In a sense, the primary purpose of this book is to help provide educators with a sound rationale for making such value judgments. All other goals and objectives are subordinate to this end.

In the course of making value judgments about educational computing, we have found it helpful to categorize computing as Type I, or Type II applications. We define and discuss these terms in the following section. The rest of the chapter is devoted to a discussion of characteristics of typical Type I and Type II software, followed by examples of each type.

CHARACTERISTICS OF TYPE I AND TYPE II EDUCATIONAL COMPUTING APPLICATIONS

Some educational applications of computing are designed to make it easier, quicker, or otherwise more efficient to continue teaching the same things in the same ways we have always taught them. We have called these **Type I** applications. **Type II** applications make available new and better ways of teaching.

It is obvious from these definitions that we place a higher value on Type II applications than on Type I applications. However, Type I applications should not be completely avoided. There is certainly nothing wrong with making traditional teaching easier, faster, or otherwise more efficient. In fact, good Type I computer applications are useful and convenient, and can and should play an important educational role. (They are best used to release the teacher from a variety of mundane and repetitive teaching tasks so that more time and effort can be devoted to more important, more complex, and more creative teaching.)

However, Type I applications by themselves, no matter how well done, cannot justify educational computing to media critics, other educators, school board members, legislators, or the public at large. Type I uses are insufficient because educational computing is too expensive to devote entirely to relatively trivial problems.

Although dollar costs continue to decline, computer hardware and software still require substantial financial investment. The less obvious and probably more significant expense is in terms of the time, effort, and enthusiasm of teachers and students. Teachers and students have a limited supply of these ingredients to invest in teaching and learning. If the time, effort, and enthusiasm of either group are devoted to materials and methods that are inefficient or that can only achieve goals of relatively limited importance, such materials and methods are not likely to receive lasting support.

Therefore, although excellent Type I applications are to be supported and encouraged, we believe that a balanced, successful educational computing program requires the development and use of both Type I and Type II applications.

Unfortunately, Type II applications are very difficult to develop and test, and thus Type I educational applications are far more common. Many observers have pointed out that Type I software such as drill and practice materials far outnumber other applications (Collis, 1988; Roblyer, Castine, and King, 1988). The 1988 study conducted by the Office of Technology Assessment (1988) revealed that over 10,000 commercial programs are available and that most of this software provides rote drill (15%), skills practice (51%), or tutorials (33%). The report concludes that software aimed at developing **higher-order thinking skills** (problem solving, critical thinking, and the like) is scarce and more expensive and more difficult to produce. The report also speculates that software producers may emphasize Type I software because they are less sure that Type II software will be a commercial success.

In the following section, we present the characteristics of Type I and Type II computer applications. As you read about these characteristics, you may wonder why we have found it necessary to create yet another categorization system, when categories such as drill and practice, simulations, and applications, already exist. The Type I/Type II system, however, differs from these other systems in that it embodies an educational value judgment, while traditional categorizations are merely descriptive. The Type I/Type II system is based on a commitment to finding new and better ways of teaching, instead of simply facilitating existing methods. Then too, the Type I/Type II system can be applied to yet to be developed educational software, while traditional categories may not be appropriate for future applications. Finally, we have talked about this system and published articles about it for a number of years. An educational computing journal even featured the system on its cover (*The Computing Teacher*, February, 1987). Many teachers have told us that the Type I/Type II categorization has provided a useful way of thinking about possible computer applications in education.

Type I Applications

Although Type I applications vary considerably, below are listed some characteristics they usually share:

1. *Type I applications generally stimulate relatively passive involvement on the part of the user*. The involvement we are referring to here is intellectual involvement. Type I applications generally do not require a high degree of intellectually active involvement. Although users are usually required to respond in some way, the responses generally do not involve higher-order, complex cognition.

We believe that intellectual passivity has played a major role in past failures of electronic innovations in education. Educational television is an interesting case in point. Although there is nothing about educational TV itself that encourages or requires only passive user involvement, network television fare has conditioned children to be intellectually passive viewers. We have noted that our own children are frequently unable to recall what they have just viewed on network television. It is not surprising that children who have become accustomed to network viewing fare tend to adopt the same passive viewing style even when presented with more intellectually stimulating material.

Fortunately, the nature of computers and computing encourages more active user involvement than does other electronic media. Very little software has been written that would allow the child to simply turn on the computer and then sit back while the machine does all the work. Virtually all educational software, even the poorest Type I software, requires some user involvement. Children must hit the space bar, type YES, answer questions, or otherwise make choices at various points in the program. However, Type I applications require less active intellectual involvement relative to that required by Type II applications.

A good example of Type I software is any one of the many programs designed to drill children on math facts. Typically, problems are generated at random and displayed on the computer screen. The user types the answer and the computer checks the user's response and provides some feedback about correctness. Most programs keep a record of the number of correct and incorrect responses and provide that record on demand or at the conclusion of the program. Figure 2.1 is an example of such a program.

Such drill and practice programs (often called CAI, or computer-assisted instruction) can be highly useful and have a valuable role in educational computing. The point we are trying to make is that, although we would use Type I programs, they are not by themselves important enough to justify the time, effort, and money required to implement

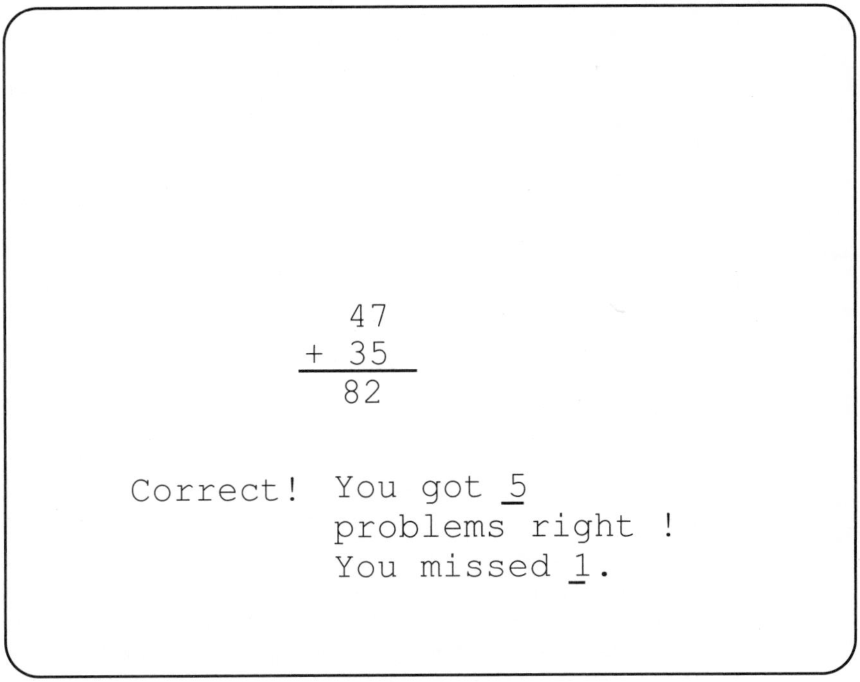

```
              47
          +   35
          _____
              82


   Correct!  You got 5
             problems right !
             You missed 1.
```

FIGURE 2.1   Example of drill and practice software.

computers in schools. Although it is important that children learn their math facts, and the computer is an efficient way to provide math fact drill and practice, other noncomputer activities are less expensive and almost as efficient as the computer application.

2. *With Type I applications, the software developer predetermines almost everything that happens on the screen.* The user may vary his or her answers or even make choices about difficulty level or speed of presentation, but the majority of what happens on the screen is predetermined by those who plan and develop the software. In the math example cited above, the programmer decided where the problems would be placed, how the machine would respond to correct and incorrect answers, and all other aspects of program execution. Virtually the only time that control is passed to the user is when the program pauses and waits for an answer to be entered from the keyboard.

3. *In Type I applications, the type of interaction between user and machine is predetermined by the developers of the software, and the contribution of the user must conform to a highly limited repertoire of acceptable responses.* With math drill and practice software, for example, the only time the user plays a role is when the machine stops and waits for an answer. At that point, the only acceptable response is a single number.

4. *Type I applications are usually aimed at the acquisition of facts by rote memory.* Once again we emphasize that drill and practice to develop rote memory can be very important. We find fault with such applications only if they are the only educational computing applications used.

5. *With Type I applications, everything the software is capable of doing can usually be observed in a very short period of time, frequently in 10 minutes or less.* The math drill and practice software described above may be capable of generating problems at several difficulty levels using more than one computational process. The student can usually sample everything this software is capable of doing in 5 minutes or so

Type II Applications

Type II applications of computing make new and better ways of teaching and learning available to teachers and students. If use of the computer improves teaching or learning and if it would be impossible (or extremely difficult) to teach or learn in this manner without the use of the computer, then the application in question is most likely a Type II application.

Type II applications, like Type I applications, vary considerably. However, some characteristics are shared by most Type II applications. Generally, these characteristics are in contrast to those listed for Type I applications:

1. *Type II applications generally stimulate relatively active intellectual involvement on the part of the user.* A good example of a Type II application is the use of word processing to teach or to improve skills in composition. Compare the degree of intellectual involvement needed to compose a passage with the involvement needed to respond to a Type I drill and practice program, such as the math facts software described above.

2. *With Type II applications, the user, rather than the software developer, is in charge of almost everything that happens on the screen.* In fact, with many (but not all) Type II applications, the user is furnished with a blank screen and a powerful way to put various contents on that screen. Such is the case with word processing, for example.

3. *In Type II applications, the user has a great deal of control of the interaction between user and machine, and there is an extensive repertoire of acceptable user input.* For example, in word processing, the user determines when (or whether) to invoke the spelling checker, the thesaurus, and various editing aids such as global searches, replacements, and block moves. By contrast, a Type I math fact drill and practice program controls both the schedule and the type of user interaction allowed.

4. *Type II applications are usually aimed at accomplishing more creative tasks than are Type I applications.* Writing a narrative passage using a word-processing package is obviously a more creative task than learning the multiplication facts.

5. *With Type II applications, it generally takes many hours of use before the user has seen everything that the specific software is capable of doing.* Because of this characteristic, it is difficult to find useful and reliable published reviews of Type II software, but it is relatively easy to find good reviews of Type I software. Unfortunately, staff writers and others who prepare software reviews for computer magazines are frequently not regular users of the software they review. In fact, they are often totally unfamiliar with the software when they begin their review, and they rely on what they find out through using the software for a few minutes before beginning to write. This may work well with Type I software, but it may take days, weeks, or even months of use before a user can take advantage of all features of a Type II application such as word processing.

Examples of Type I and Type II Applications

Type I applications make it easier, quicker, or otherwise more efficient to continue teaching the same things in the same ways as we have always taught them, but Type II applications make available new and better ways of teaching. When classifying a specific piece of software, the characteristics given for each type in the preceding discussion above should be used only as aids. Final determination about the category depends on adherence to one or the other of these definitions. Another aid to classification is the fact that certain kinds of educational software tend to fall consistently into one or the other category.

Typical Type I Software

Drill and Practice Software   Software designed to allow the user to practice a skill that has already been acquired is called **drill and practice software**. This software may drill the student on math facts, sight vocabulary, parts of speech, names of the 50 states, or any other skill dependent primarily on rote memory. Figure 2.1 depicts an example of drill and practice software.

One of the authors once wrote a drill and practice computer program for a learning disabled adult who had obtained a job as a management trainee in a supermarket. The job required the trainee to learn a code number for every vegetable sold in the produce department. The program, written in the Logo computer language, randomly chose the name of one of the 75 vegetables, displayed the name on the screen, and required the trainee to type in the code number. Alternatively, the trainee could elect for the computer to display the code number. The trainee's role then was to type in the name of the vegetable that corresponded to the code number. The program kept track of right and wrong answers and then provided a summary of performance.

This program represents a Type I application. The most important indicator of category is that the software makes it more efficient to practice the number/name associations in a highly traditional manner. The drill strategy employed is the same as what would probably be used if the skill were practiced with off-computer activities, that is, presentation of half the desired association followed by the user supplying the other half.

In support of Type I classification, note that the program has all five of the common characteristics of Type I software discussed previously: (1) relatively passive user intellectual involvement, (2) predetermined control of most of what happens on the screen, (3) predetermined interaction between the user and computer and a highly limited repertoire of acceptable user responses, (4) a goal of acquisition by rote memory, and (5) all capabilities of the software evident after only a few minutes of operation.

The vegetable drill software (1) required only that the trainee associate a vegetable name with a number or a number with a vegetable name; (2) employed a predetermined scheme for problem placement, answer placement, reinforcement, and the like; (3) limited acceptable user responses to either a vegetable name or a number typed in at strictly defined, limited, and predetermined points in program execution; (4) was aimed entirely at the acquisition of the rote association of specific numbers with specific vegetable names; and (5) had such limited capability that everything it was capable of doing (displaying numbers and accepting vegetable names or vice versa) could be seen in only a few minutes.

Tutorial Software   Whereas drill and practice software is designed to provide a way to practice a skill that has already been learned, **tutorial software** is designed to teach the skill in the first place. Figure 2.2 shows a tutorial program designed to teach keyboarding skills.

Most available tutorial software falls into the Type I category, although there is really no reason why Type II tutorial software could not be written. (It would be Type II if it used new and better methods of teaching the material, methods that would not be possible without the computer.) Other examples of Type I tutorial programs include any of the commercial programs available to tutor students in preparation for taking the Scholastic Aptitude Test and the programs intended to orient users to the use of a specific computer or specific software. These tutorial programs, like most such programs, take the user through a series of steps by emulating traditional methods of lecture, demonstration, and student trial activities, and most could be easily transported into workbook format without significantly changing the overall methodology or diminishing the effectiveness of the instruction.

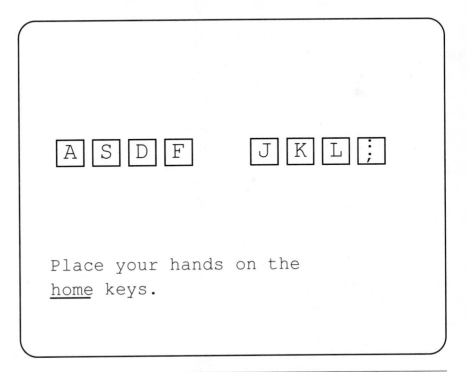

FIGURE 2.2   Example of a tutorial program designed to teach keyboarding skills.

Assessment Uses **Assessment software** seems to be growing in popularity. This class of software is designed to (1) administer, (2) score, (3) summarize, and/or (4) interpret the results of standardized tests. The first three of these functions represent Type I applications by definition, since they are intended to make it more convenient, more accurate, or less time consuming to administer a test that was originally developed for noncomputer implementation. (Some characteristics of Type I or Type II applications are difficult to apply to this class of software because such characteristics were developed for use with educational software designed for direct teaching. As always, the final determination of category depends not on consistency with the characteristics, but on adherence to the definitions of Type I or Type II applications.)

Some of the fourth type of assessment software, that designed to interpret the results of standardized testing, is in a class by itself. This kind of software is intended to be Type II software. If successful, this software would be classified as Type II since it is intended to make the judgments of the most knowledgeable experts in a field available to anyone who has access to a computer and the software.

Software intended to perform this function falls into a category known as **expert systems**. Expert systems have not yet fulfilled their initial high expectations. Most authorities agree that no expert systems have yet been developed that do an acceptable job of emulating the judgment of educational or psychological experts.

Administrative Uses Administrative applications include software for producing, calculating, coordinating, or compiling registration information; attendance records; graphics; student grades; room, teacher, or school schedules; mailing labels; budgets; filing; or other secretarial tasks to aid administrative activity. Figure 2.3 depicts one screen from a piece of **administrative software** designed to help teachers create different test formats.

It should be obvious from this discussion that the use a piece of software is put to can determine whether the application falls into the Type I or Type II category. For example, although word processing used properly to teach composition skills is a Type II application, word processing as a secretarial substitute for typewriting is a Type I application.

Computer-Managed Instruction **Computer-managed instruction** (CMI) is a mixed bag of applications designed to perform tasks or combinations of tasks such as organizing student data, monitoring student progress, testing student mastery and prescribing further instruction or remediation, recording student progress, and selecting the order of instructional modules to be completed.

We do not think the term computer-managed instruction is a good one, because only human beings, not computers, can be managers and

```
What kind of test do
      you want to make?


    a.   multiple choice
    b.   matching
    c.   short answer



    Type a, b, or c and press
    Return.
```

FIGURE 2.3   An example of administrative software designed to help teachers create different tests.

because no direct instruction takes place. Regardless of terminology, CMI should probably be considered a Type I application, for it is usually used to make it more efficient to teach something as it has always been taught.

Typical Type II Software

Word Processing   The use of **word processing** to teach written composition is a Type II application because it makes possible the teaching of composition in a way that is not possible without the use of the computer. The ease of revision made possible by word processing cannot be duplicated with noncomputer activities. Although researchers are still attempting to determine exactly which student writing achievement outcomes are most favorably influenced by instruction employing word processing, there is little doubt that word processing results in more positive achievement gains than traditional instruction. Researchers have also found that student attitudes toward writing are improved following instruction using word processing. Since both student achievement and attitude are favorably influenced and since word processing takes the drudgery out of the composing and revising process, Roblyer, Castine, and King (1988) have made the excellent point that it would be sufficient if effects on student achievement were only equal, rather than superior, to traditional instruction. Roblyer (1988) subjected word processing research to **meta-analysis**, a statistical technique that permits analyzing the collective results of a number of individual research findings. She concluded that word processing is one of the most potentially powerful uses of microcomputers for instruction.

In addition to conforming to the definition of Type II software, word processing also possesses all the characteristics common to applications in this category: (1) relatively active intellectual involvement, (2) user control of almost everything that happens on the screen, (3) user control of interaction with the machine and an extensive repertoire of acceptable user input, (4) focus on creative instead of rote tasks, and (5) many capabilities that require hours, days, or even weeks to view fully.

In our previous discussion of the characteristics of Type II software, we used word processing as the example. Therefore, we will not provide an in-depth discussion of how word processing conforms to all of these characteristics at this time. Suffice it to say that composing a written passage using word processing requires a high level of intellectual involvement, places the user in charge by providing a blank screen and a powerful way to place whatever text the user chooses on that screen, and is a highly creative act. In addition, full investigation of a word processor's capabilities cannot be accomplished in a few minutes; it may require days or weeks. Figure 2.4 shows an example of text prepared using WordPerfect 5.1 (© WordPerfect Corporation 1990), the most popular word-processing package currently available.

Two related Type II applications are the use of spreadsheet and database management software. **Electronic spreadsheets** are accounting ledger sheets that allow the user to create complex displays consisting of rows and columns of numbers. Electronic spreadsheets greatly simplify accounting tasks because of the ease of changing individual entries and all related entries. This is important, since entries in accounting ledgers are highly interdependent. Because of this interdependence, changing a handful of numbers may require the revision of thousands of other entries, since complex formulas may be used involving specific entries that are then used to calculate other entries. For example, if one entry represents the wholesale cost of a raw material used in the manufacture of a certain product, a change in this number requires changing numerous other numbers, such as tax paid on each item, percentage of profit, and commissions to be paid to salespeople.

Electronic spreadsheets allow the user to enter formulas that are then used to calculate other entries. When the user changes any of the involved entries, the program automatically and almost instantaneously changes all affected entries. Thus, managers may pose complex hypothetical business scenarios that can be answered with only a few key-

```
COURSE  DESCRIPTION:

   Uses  of  microcomputers  in  education,  microcomputer
operations,  hardware/software  selection,  word  processing,  and
Logo.  Applied  outcomes  applicable  to  the  classroom  for  teachers
seeking  a  practical  knowledge  of  how  to  operate  and  use
microcomputers  in  education.

GOALS:

   Students  will  acquire  an  awareness  of  how  small  computers
can  be  used  in  education.

   Students  will  learn  introductory-level  skills  needed  to  use
microcomputers  in  schools.  Entry  level,  hands-on  expertise  will
be  acquired  in  (a)  word  processing,  (b)  Logo,  (c)  PILOT  (d)
BASIC,  (e)  software  evaluation.

   Students  will  become  aware  of  major  issues,  trends,  and
controversies  in  the  field  of  educational  computing.
```

FIGURE 2.4   An example of text prepared using WordPerfect.

strokes. These same scenarios might require dozens of accountants days, weeks, or even months to analyze without the help of computers. Figure 2.5 shows a portion of a spreadsheet that has been used to enter student grades. The spreadsheet automatically totals the points earned and, in the final column, assigns a grade based on a user-entered formula.

Spreadsheets can also be used for a variety of teaching tasks. These would be classified as Type II uses for the same reasons that word processing is so classified.

Database management software is another Type II application somewhat similar to word processing and electronic spreadsheets. Database management software allows the creation of an electronic filing system. Once data are correctly entered, the user can then search the data for all cases conforming to some predetermined criteria or combination of criterion.

For example, a social studies class might research data about tropical rain forests. Once the data are found and entered in the data base, it is then possible to search the file for all cases of tropical rain forests that conform to some criterion (such as all rain forests between certain latitudes, or with a given range of annual rainfall, or with certain flora or fauna).

	Q		R		S	T		U
Book	Reaction	Term	Paper	Final	Exam Total	Points	Final	Grade
	10				0	10		5
	10		19		88	334.50		2
	10				90	311.50		2
	10		18		94	349.50		1
	7				46	218.50		4
	10				78	261.50		3
	10		17		90	360		1
	10		14		78	302.50		2
	10		17		88	341		1
	10		18		86	339.50		2
	10		20		82	348		1
	10		20		92	348		1
						82.50		5
	10				80	301		2
	10				84	312		2
						0		5
	10		15		82	318.50		2
			5		88	310		2
	10		20		72	300.50		2

FIGURE 2.5   A portion of a spreadsheet that has been used for storing, summing, and calculating grades.

Programming Languages   Controversy continues over the issue of whether or not there are cognitive benefits to be gained by teaching a **programming language** to children and, if so, what these benefits are.

Although final determination of category depends on the resolution of this controversy, we believe for two reasons that computer programming should be considered a Type II activity. First, benefits are involved in learning to program (although we feel these benefits have been exaggerated by some advocates). Second, these benefits are unique to computer programming and are not easily available through noncomputer activities. In addition, programming a computer possesses all the characteristics unique to Type II applications: (1) programming requires a high level of intellectual involvement as the user attempts to supply the code to accomplish some task; (2) the user is completely in charge of determining what will happen on the screen, since a computer language, like a word processor, provides a blank screen and a powerful way to enter and revise whatever code the user chooses; (3) the user is in charge of the interaction with the computer and there is great flexibility in and an extensive repertoire of acceptable user input (all commands provided by the specific language); (4) programming is a highly creative problem solving act; and (5) the full capabilities of a programming language cannot be viewed in only a few minutes. Figure 2.6 shows a short program written in the **Logo** computer language.

Simulations   **Computer simulations** make available experiences that are too expensive, too dangerous, or otherwise unavailable to students. Thus, simulations are Type II applications almost by definition.

```
TO ; :COMMENT
END

TO AGE
NOW.DATE
BIRTHDATE
AGE.DAYS
AGE.MONTHS
AGE.YEARS
GIVE.AGE
END

TO NOW.DATE
; [ESTABLISHES CURRENT DATE]
PRINT [] CT
PR [ENTER CURRENT MONTH (1-12)]
MAKE "M FIRST RL
PR [ENTER DAY OF THE MONTH (1-31)]
MAKE "D FIRST RL
PR [ENTER PRESENT YEAR (4 DIGITS)]
MAKE "Y FIRST RL PR []
END

TO BIRTHDATE
; [ESTABLISHES BIRTH DATE]
PR [ENTER MONTH OF BIRTH (1-12)]
MAKE "M1 FIRST RL
PR [ENTER DAY OF BIRTH (1-31)]
MAKE "D1 FIRST RL
PR [ENTER YEAR OF BIRTH (4 DIGITS)]
MAKE "Y1 FIRST RL PR []
END

TO AGE.DAYS
; [ESTABLISHES AGE IN DAYS]
MAKE "AD :D - :D1
IF :AD < 0 [MAKE "AD :AD + 30 MAKE "M :M - 1]
END

TO AGE.MONTHS
; [ESTABLISHES AGE IN MONTHS]
MAKE "AM :M - :M1
IF :AM < 0 [MAKE "AM :AM + 12 MAKE "Y :Y - 1]
END

TO AGE.YEARS
; [ESTABLISHES AGE IN YEARS]
MAKE "AY :Y - :Y1
END

TO GIVE.AGE
(PR [YOU ARE] :AY [YEARS,] :AM [MONTHS, AND] :AD [DAYS OLD!]
END
```

FIGURE 2.6   An example of a *Logo* program to calculate age from date of birth.

Some of the most sophisticated and complex simulations have been developed for use by the military. Examples of these simulations are any of the complex computer flight simulators currently in use. The cost and safety advantages of flight simulators over actual flight are obvious. A single actual flight in a modern jet fighter is dangerous and costs thousands of dollars for the fuel alone. The same flight in a jet simulator is completely safe and involves only the cost of the computer and software, which can be used for years. In addition, flight simulators make it possible for trainers to systematically confront trainees with a wide variety of flight conditions, such as severe weather, equipment malfunctions, and attack by enemy planes or ground weapons.

Generally, educational simulations are not as well developed as are highly complex and sophisticated simulations like flight simulators. Nevertheless, we believe that simulations represent one of the most exciting potentials in education.

Although scarce, some excellent educational simulations are available. Examples include controlling the ecology of a small pond, designing a machine for a factory, managing the fossil fuel reserves of the United States, leading a wagon train across the Oregon Trail, controlling osmosis in a living cell, and operating a hot dog concession at high school football games for a year. (Sunburst Communications markets many excellent educational simulations.)

In the cell membrane example, users are shown minimum and maximum concentrations of substances that can move into and out of a cell by osmosis. The user acts as the cell membrane and can thus increase or decrease concentrations as the cell "lives." When this simulation is started, concentrations vary due to cell metabolism, and the user must adjust these concentrations to keep them within acceptable limits. Care must be taken, because allowing one substance to diffuse into the cell can have unexpected and potentially catastrophic effects on concentrations of other substances. The user attempts to keep the cell "alive" as long as possible. This software makes an experience available that is not available in real life due to the small size of the cell and to the difficulty in controlling exactly what will diffuse across the cell membrane in a real laboratory.

Most of the qualities of typical Type II software are present in simulations. In the cell membrane simulation, for example, (1) active intellectual involvement is required for the user to avoid altering one concentration in such a way that another reaches a lethal level, (2) the activity requires creative manipulation of concentrations to keep everything within acceptable levels, and (3) the simulation is complex enough that a user would probably never see all possible combinations requiring all possible solutions.

Two characteristics of most Type II software may not be applicable to some simulations. For example, in many simulations, most of what happens on the screen is predetermined by the software developer instead of the user (although it could be argued in our example that the manipulation of the various concentrations is completely controlled by the user). In addition, the developer of the simulation predetermines the nature of the interaction as well as acceptable responses. (Again, it could be argued that the user- chosen concentrations in the cell simulation can range over an extremely wide numerical continuum. Still, the user is restricted to numbers alone, and they must fall within the predetermined acceptable range.) Therefore, these two common qualities of Type II software do not seem to apply to educational simulations.

In conclusion, we believe that simulations are one of the most exciting and promising applications in educational computing. We will devote Chapter 9 in this book to this exciting potential.

Problem-solving Software   **Problem solving software** is a relatively new educational application. At least two types of software could fall into this category. The first is based on the assumption that there are universal or generic problem-solving skills that can be learned in one domain and then transferred to other domains.

Educators who accept this assumption might use a piece of software by Sunburst Communication called The Incredible Laboratory (© Sunburst Communications, Inc., 1984, 1985, 1986). (This software depicts a list of imaginary chemicals that the user can choose to add to a beaker. Each ingredient produces a specific feature in a monster that is supposedly produced by the chemical mixing. In addition, the chemicals can be combined to form other results. The user is required to use trial and error and the process of elimination to deduce the effect of each chemical as well as the effects of combining chemicals.)

The underlying assumption of those who advocate the use of this and other similar software is that trial-and-error and process-of-elimination skills are generic problem-solving strategies. Advocates also believe such skills, learned while using The Incredible Laboratory, will transfer to other situations such as those found in mathematics, social studies, and daily living. The assumption of transferrability of generic problem-solving skills is open to question, and more will be said about this kind of software in Chapter 13.

Another problem-solving software just emerging is designed as a problem-solving tool in the same way that a calculator is designed as a tool to assist in solving calculation problems. The software is designed to focus attention on or to clarify specific skills or concepts needed for problem solving within a single domain. (Remember that the first type of problem-solving software described was aimed at teaching generic problem-solving skills that would transfer to other domains.)

An example of this second type of problem-solving software is Judah Schwartz's semantic calculator (marketed as SemCalc by Sunburst Communications and available for use with a variety of microcomputers). SemCalc is designed to be used by students as they work through written word problems in mathematics.

SemCalc was developed because much research has shown that many students do not learn to solve arithmetic word problems. In support of this position, research has shown that many children who have difficulty solving word problems in math develop a rote computational habit. In other words, when they encounter a word problem, they seize upon the numbers in the problem and perform computations with those numbers without proper regard to the rationale for selecting that computational process. SemCalc is designed to encourage the user to focus on number referents instead of solely on the numbers themselves. (If a problem refers to "5 miles," "5" is the number and "miles" is the referent.)

SemCalc uses a modified spreadsheet approach in which the child enters numbers in one column and their respective referents in an adjacent column. Eventually, the child selects a computational process such as addition or subtraction. The computer program poses a series of questions that requires the child to focus on and then consider the referents and whether or not the computational process selected will yield an answer with a sensible referent. For example, if the child instructs the program to add 5 inches to 7 feet, the program first askss if inches and feet can be converted to a common referent. If so, the program then performs the calculation and lists the answer using the new referent. (If the user asks the program to add 5 oranges and 7 grapefruit, he or she will be asked to fill in the following blank: "Oranges and grapefruit are both _____ ." The program then performs the addition and lists the answer as 12 fruit.)

If the user indicates that no common referent exists, he or she is asked if it is possible to convert one of the variables to the referent category of the other variable. For example, if the user enters 5 inches and 7 feet, the program will ask if feet can be converted to inches or inches converted to feet. If the user indicates that this is possible, he or she is asked to choose the direction of conversion and is then prompted for conversion information ("How many inches in a foot?" or "How many feet in an inch?"). The program then performs the conversion, calculates the answer, and lists both the number and the referent of the answer.

The jury is still out on the efficacy of software such as The Incredible Laboratory. It is doubtful that there is a set of generic problem-solving skills, the mastery of which will automatically transfer to other subject domains; but there is some indication that there may be problem-solving skills that are similar and that there are teaching strategies that can be used to facilitate transfer from one domain to another. We will deal more fully with this issue in Chapter 13.

SemCalc would be classified as Type II software because it makes it possible to teach mathematical word problems in a way that is not possible without the use of the computer. In addition, the software has all of the characteristics of Type II software, in the same way that word processing does.

Computers as Prosthetic Aids   One of the least controversial computer applications is the use of **prosthetic aids**. Examples include computer-generated synthetic speech used for a variety of purposes. For example, text-to-speech synthesizers can accept text entered at the keyboard and convert it to speech. This application can be invaluable for handicapped individuals who have communication disabilities. A more sophisticated application for use with hearing impaired or aphasic children can convert unintelligible speech to synthetic speech, print, or both.

Other applications in this category include special input devices that allow physically handicapped individuals to use a computer. For example, devices exist that permit computer input via head, chin, tongue, or eyebrow movement for use by individuals with limited movement capabilities. Large-print word processors and braille word processors are available for use by visually impaired individuals.

Such applications would obviously be considered Type II applications, since they make learning possible for individuals who could not participate without the use of the computer.

Graphics Software, Presentation Software, Telecommunications Software, and Other Software   **Graphics software** is designed to enable users to draw pictures (graphics) on the computer screen. **Presentation software** can be used to help teachers and others make presentations using a variety of media. **Telecommunications software** enables more than one computer to be linked. These types of software, as well as other yet to be developed types, have the potential to be Type II software if they are used in such a way that the user is given the ability to learn in new and better ways.

SUMMARY

Microcomputers have the potential to revolutionize teaching and learning. However, if the computer is to be successful in education, it must be used to solve important educational problems.

We have found it helpful to classify educational computing applications as either Type I or Type II. Type I applications make it easier, quicker, or otherwise more efficient or more convenient to continue teaching the same things in the same ways as we have always taught them. Type II applications make available new and better ways of teaching.

Type I applications are much more common than are Type II applications, probably because Type I applications are much easier to develop. Both Type I and Type II educational applications are useful, but

Type I applications alone will not convince lawmakers, school board members, taxpayers, and others that educational computing benefits are worth their cost.

Type I and Type II applications have very different characteristics. Type I applications (1) call for relatively passive user intellectual involvement, (2) employ screen events that are largely predetermined by the software developer, (3) call for developer-determined interaction between user and machine, (4) are aimed at rote memory, and (5) can be completely reviewed in a short period of time.

Type II applications usually share all or most of the following characteristics: (1) they require relatively active user intellectual involvement, (2) they place much of the control of what happens on the screen in the hands of the user, (3) they give the user control of the interaction between user and machine, (4) the goal of the application is the accomplishment of relatively creative tasks, and (5) many hours of use are required before the user experiences everything the software is capable of doing.

Examples of Type I applications include drill and practice applications, tutorial uses, assessment software, administrative uses, and computer managed instruction (CMI). Examples of Type II software include word processing, spreadsheet and database management software, programming languages, simulations, problem-solving software, and computers as prosthetic aids for the handicapped.

LOOKING AHEAD

You should now be gaining an appreciation for the wide variety and different types of educational software that are available. We have purposely presented an introduction to software before beginning our discussion of computer hardware. We have done so because we believe that educational computing issues are much more closely tied to software than to hardware, and we believe that teachers should devote most of their time and effort to investigating and evaluating software.

Computer software must be run on computer hardware, and knowledgeable teachers must be familiar with both. Therefore, the next chapter is devoted to an introduction to computers and peripherals (equipment that can be plugged into a computer). To be complete, this introduction must also deal with the history of computers and computing, and so Chapter 3 deals with history as well as hardware.

SOME QUESTIONS TO CONSIDER

1. Why do you think some tools in education are successful, whereas others never catch on?

2. Which Type I educational application do you think is the most potentially useful to you? Tell why.

3. Which Type II educational application do you think is the most potentially useful to you? Tell why.

4. Do you think Type II applications will ever completely replace Type I applications? Tell why or why not.

RELATED ACTIVITIES

1. Go to your College of Education microcomputer laboratory or a retail store that sells computer software and ask someone who works there to demonstrate a piece of educational software.

2. After viewing the software, tell whether you think it is Type I or Type II software and why you think so.

REFERENCES

Collis, B. (1988). *Computers, curriculum, and whole-class instruction: Issues and ideas*. Belmont, CA: Wadsworth.

Office of Technology Assessment (1988). *Power on! New tools for teaching and learning* (Publication No. 052-003-01125-5). Washington, DC: U.S. Government Printing Office.

Roblyer, M. D. (1988, September). The effectiveness of microcomputers in education: A review of the research from 1980–1987. *T.H.E. Journal*, pp. 85–89.

_____, M. D., Castine, W. H., & King, F. J. (1988). Assessing the impact of computer-based instruction. New York: Haworth Press.

___3___
History and Hardware

GOALS AND OBJECTIVES

Goal: To understand the history of the development of computers, with particular emphasis on the conceptual and technical developments that brought us the modern personal computer.

When you finish reading this chapter, you will be able to:

1. Draw parallels between the way a music box and a computer operate.
2. Describe the contributions made by computer pioneers such as Blaise Pascal, Charles Babbage, and Herman Hollerith.
3. Explain the lag between the concept of computer in the nineteenth century and the production of computers in the twentieth century.
4. Describe the contributions of Alan Turing and George Boole to the development of computers.
5. Trace the evolution of the computer from vacuum tubes to integrated circuits and explain the improvements at each step.
6. Describe the first general-purpose digital electronic computer and the way it was used.
7. Describe the structure of an integrated circuit (IC) and explain how and why it was invented.
8. List the three most prevalent computers in education today and indicate the level of education where they are most often used.
9. Define the term software; compare and contrast educational and application software.
10. List the major components of a computer system and explain what they do.

KEY TERMS

Ada Lovelace	IBM-compatible computer
Alan Turing	integrated circuit
Analytical Engine	laser disc
applications software	laser printer
binary system	local area network
bit	megabyte
Blaise Pascal	memory
byte	microprocessor
CD–ROM	mouse
Charles Babbage	near letter quality
CPU	pixel
Difference Engine	program
disk drive	RAM
dot matrix printer	ROM
draft quality	scanner
educational software	semiconductor
ENIAC	Steven Jobs
George Boole	Steven Wozniak
Grace Hopper	

HISTORY AND HARDWARE: TWO CONTEXTS OF EDUCATIONAL COMPUTING TODAY

The history of computing is both long and short. It is short in the sense that modern electronic computers were not even invented until the 1940s. However, the field has a long history because many of the concepts that underlie modern computing have been around for centuries (Willis, Johnson, & Dixon, 1983). The first half of this chapter presents some of the concepts that underlie electronic computers.

A BIT OF HISTORY

One of the earliest ancestors of electronic computers is the music box. The sound from a music box is created by a slowly rotating drum with small metal pins protruding from it. As the drum revolves, the pins catch on extensions from the box's sound board and then flip back as the drum continues rotating. This relatively simple process can be used to create music boxes that play very complex, very beautiful compositions.

The important point to remember is that the music box builder deals with only two options when it comes to placing pins on the drum:

put a pin in or don't put a pin in. When you have only two choices you have a **binary system**. The binary number system has only two digits, 1 and 0, and it uses these two digits to build larger numbers. The music box builder converts binary 1's and 0's into pins on a drum (that is, 1 = pin, 0 = no pin). Today, computer designers convert binary numbers into electrical signals (1 = on, 0 = off). The basic principle is the same. The music box builder and the modern computer designer both build complicated patterns from simple ones. Inside the computers you will use in your classroom everything is expressed in patterns of 1's and 0's.

While the music box is one ancestor of the computer, it is not the only one. During the seventeenth, eighteenth, and nineteenth centuries, several scientists including John Napier, **Blaise Pascal**, Gottfried Leibnitz, and **Charles Babbage**, invented mechanical aids for solving simple mathematical problems (Evans, 1981). The devices of Pascal, Leibnitz, and Babbage all used intermeshed gears to represent the basic mathematical operations of adding and subtracting. On these machines, adding numbers involved turning gears that in turn caused other gears to rotate. The answer to the problem was then read from indicators attached to the gears. The most ambitious of these devices, the **difference engine** of Charles Babbage, was so complex that it required gears more precise than could be produced in the nineteenth century.

The early, gear-driven calculating devices are most accurately considered as direct ancestors of modern adding machines and calculators rather than computers, because the machines performed one type of task, calculating, in a specified pattern. Computers, on the other hand, can be programmed or given instructions to perform many different types of tasks.

In spite of his difficulties in actually building the difference engine, the English mathematician Charles Babbage is generally considered the father of computing (Evans, 1981), because he also designed the **analytical engine**, a device that could be programmed or instructed to perform a variety of computational tasks. Babbage was assisted by **Ada Lovelace**, the daughter of the poet Lord Byron and a theoretical mathematician in her own right. Her contribution to the development of computing was acknowledged in the 1970s when a new computer language, Ada, was named after her.

Unfortunately, like the difference engine, the analytical engine was never successfully constructed by Babbage, although the concepts upon which it was based were sound. Babbage intended to use cards with holes punched in them to tell the analytical engine what to do. He borrowed the idea from a French silk weaver, Joseph Jacquard, who had invented a weaving machine that created very complex tapestries by following instructions on stiff cards with holes in them. Different patterns of holes produced different patterns on the tapestry. The cards with holes in them are a link back to our music boxes and a link with the punched cards that were used for many years to provide data to computers. All these use a binary number system; the codes created by different binary patterns are used to provide instructions and data to a machine. Thus, the music box, the loom, the analytical engine, and a desktop computer are all based on the same concept. Different results are produced by different instructions. These machines can all be programmed.

The reason that computers are relatively young, therefore, is not the complexity of the concepts used to create them. It was the problem of manufacturing them that held back earlier efforts. Babbage's analytical engine was to be a huge assemblage of metal rods, wheels, and gears run by a steam engine. The precision possible at that time was simply not good enough to allow the design to work properly. Charles Babbage died in 1871, and in 1876 an American engineer named George Grant demonstrated a difference engine that worked. Grant, in fact, actually sold a number of machines, which he called rack and pinion calculators.

As the nineteenth century ended, the precision required to produce reliable mechanical calculators became available. It was also at this time that American technology began to equal and even exceed European

FIGURE 3.1 Swedish industrialist George Scheutz built this version of Babbage's Difference Engine.

technology. An American named Herman Hollerith developed a machine that greatly simplified the work on the 1890 Census (Figure 3.2). Hollerith used a system that punched holes in cards to represent different types of census information. Hollerith's Tabulating Machine Company eventually became International Business Machines (Willis, 1983). In the first half of the twentieth century, researchers continued to work on mechanical computers in the tradition of Babbage. For example, Vannevar Bush, a professor at MIT, built and demonstrated a differential analyzer in 1930 (Bitter, 1989). It was large, had many gears, and used electric motors. It worked and could be reconfigured (reprogrammed) to perform many different types of calculating work. Bush's machine was the first to use electricity not only to turn the gears, but also to store data. His machine could store numbers or quantities as electricity in one part of the system. Because memory, the ability to store data the computer will use later, is an important aspect of any electronic computer, Bush is considered by some to be the father of the electronic computer.

Bush's mechanical computer is a direct descendant of Babbage's analytical engine, but the day of the gear-driven computer was almost

FIGURE 3.2   The Hollerith Tabulating Machine.

over. Other scientists decided to explore the possibilities of an electronic computer. (Much of the historical information in this section was taken from two excellent publications, T. R. Reid's (1985) book on the invention of the integrated circuit, *The Chip*, and Steven Levy's (1984) book on the development of the hacker ethic, *Hackers*, and from personal interviews.)

Konrad Zuse, a German engineer, and Howard Aiken, a Harvard math professor, both built hybrid, part mechanical and part electronic machines in the period between 1930 and 1945. These hybrid computers were never widely used in Germany or the United States. The future belonged to fully electronic computers. Although there is some controversy over the title, many consider the still secret British computer called Colossus the first special-purpose, electronic digital computer. Digital computers are on/off devices. In computers On and Off are generally referred to as 1 and 0, and all data inside digital computers consist of patterns of 1's and 0's. Colossus was developed by a secret team of scientists that included **Alan Turing**, a mathematician who made several contributions to the theoretical concepts of computing.

Turing was one of several pioneers who came to understand that binary math could be the basis of powerful computers (Hodges, 1983). He suggested that an on state in the computer be designated a 1 while an off state be designated a 0. Turing believed that machines could be designed so that they would follow instructions and by following those instructions they could solve all sorts of mathematical problems. This came to be known as a **Turing machine**. Turing's contributions to computing are somewhat surprising, because few of the instructors who taught Turing thought he had much intellectual potential, and he twice failed the entrance exam to the college he wanted to attend. After earning a Ph.D. in mathematics from Kings College of Cambridge University, Turing joined a crack team of scientists who developed Colossus. The team used Colossus to crack German Enigma military communication codes during World War II.

Another major contributor to the intellectual and conceptual stew that led to the development of modern computers was John von Neumann (Goldstine, 1972). Born in Budapest and educated at several major European universities, he published a scholarly treatise at age 18.

Both von Neumann and Turing believed that binary numbers should be the basis of computers. At first glance it is difficult to see how a machine that can deal with only two states, on and off (or 1 and 0), could accomplish anything important. Fortunately, more than 100 years earlier another British mathematician, **George Boole**, had developed a complete algebraic system of logic that used only two digits, 1 and 0. Boole, who came from a poor family, never attended college (Boole, 1972). His love of mathematics led him to write a number of poems, including one called "Sonnet to the Number Three." Boole came to believe that human reasoning could be boiled down to sequences of decisions that had yes or no answers. His major book, which was published in 1854, was titled *The Laws of Thought, on Which Are Founded the Mathematical Theories of Logic and Probabilities.* A complex system of logic that brings everything down to a series of yes or no decisions was not very appealing, although several contemporaries, including a mathematician named Charles Dodgson, did appreciate Boole's work. In a book written under a pen name, Dodgson created many characters who viewed their world with yes–no, this or that logic. Dodgson's pen name was Lewis Carroll and his books were *Alice in Wonderland* and *Through the Looking Glass.*

Early computer theorists, who needed a system of logic for a machine that could only deal with two states, on and off, found Boole's logic essential to their work. The offbeat logic system of a nineteenth-century shoemaker's son who did not even graduate from high school made electronic computers possible.

The leap from obtuse theory to electric circuits was made by George Shannon, a graduate student at MIT (Reid, 1985). He completed a master's thesis in 1937 that used the yes–no, true–false of Boolean logic to wire electrical switching circuits. Shannon expressed Boolean logic with elec-

FIGURE 3.3   John von Neuman is pictured here with one of the computers he helped develop.

trically operated mechanical relays. Less than a decade later others would create a computer by expressing Boolean logic with vacuum tubes. Smaller and smarter computers would then be built, first with **transistors**, and then with integrated circuits. The medium of expression varies from one computer generation to another, but the fundamental logic in each generation of computer is George Boole's logic.

The first general-purpose, electronic digital computer was **ENIAC**, which was built in America (Evans, 1981). ENIAC, or Electronic Numerical Integrator and Calculator, was developed by J. P. Eckert and J. W. Mauchly at the University of Pennsylvania during World War II. It was a huge machine with thousands of vacuum tubes that were only moderately reliable, but ENIAC set the stage for greater things to come. The initial idea was to develop a device that could both determine artillery shell trajectories and predict the weather. Within a few years the machine was being used for a variety of business and government applications.

Because ENIAC was developed during a war, it was used for military applications such as calculating artillery shell trajectories. Before ENIAC, the tables used by artillery officers were hand calculated by teams of workers who might spend months or even years computing the tables for just one type of armament. Although ENIAC generally operated for just a few minutes before one of its vacuum tubes burned out and had to be replaced, it reduced the time needed to calculate the tables to a few hours or minutes. That was a tremendous accomplishment. One member of the team of operators who kept ENIAC going was **Grace Hopper**, a young Naval officer. One day, while trying to find the source of a problem, she found a bug caught between two electrical contacts. She removed the bug and ENIAC began operating again. Computer programmers today still use the term *debugging* when they look for errors in a computer **program**. Hopper, who later became Admiral Hopper, continued her naval career and is one of the American pioneers of computer use.

ENIAC was the beginning of the age of computers. Over the next two decades a number of developments helped bring us from boxcar-sized computers like ENIAC to computers the size of a book. The first of these developments was the transistor, which was developed in 1947 (Evans, 1981). It made modern computers practical because of its dependability, small size, and low power requirements. Transistors replaced vacuum tubes as the building blocks of computers, and the computer age was underway. Transistors were the first widely used solid-state, **semiconductor** components. The term solid state refers to the fact the electrical activity in a transistor takes place in a solid (in the first transistor the solid was specially treated germanium; today silicon is used in most solid-state devices). In the vacuum tubes that transistors replaced, the electrical activity occurred across a vacuum created inside a glass tube when certain metal elements were heated. The term *semiconductor* refers to elements that can be made to behave as either insulators or conductors.

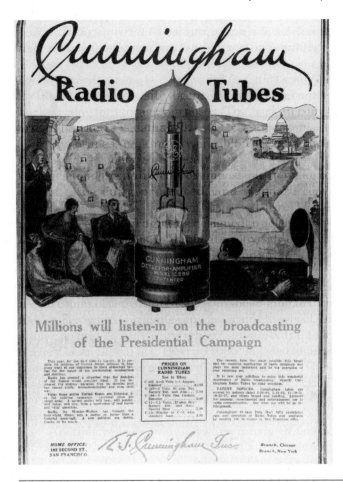

FIGURE 3.4   Tubes like this one were used in ENIAC.

Since 1947 several major advances in semiconductor technology have produced smaller and smaller components that do more and more. The most important of these advances is the development of the **integrated circuit** or IC (Figure 3.5). By 1958, transistors had revolutionized the electronics industry. However, during manufacture each component in a transistorized electronic circuit had to be connected to other components. In a large computer, this meant millions of connections. The connections were generally made by hand, which meant they were expensive and there were errors.

In the summer of 1958 a young engineer who had been working for his new employer for only a few months developed a solution to the connection problem (Reid, 1985). Employees at the large Texas Instruments research center in Dallas, Texas, generally took their vacation at

FIGURE 3.5   Integrated circuits like these two made personal computing possible.

the same time each summer, but Jack Kilby was so new to the company he did not have any vacation days. Kilby thus found himself working alone in the laboratory while everyone else was on vacation.

When his colleagues returned from their vacations, Kilby presented his design for the first crude integrated circuit. He had found a way to make different sections of the same small sliver of a semiconductor element called silicon work as resistors, capacitors, and transistors. An IC, often called a *chip*, thus contains many transistors, resistors, and capacitors in a circuit enclosed in a single small case. The production of chips can be automated, which means the interconnections between the different components inside the chip do not have to be made by hand. ICs solved the interconnection problem, and soon manufacturers all over the world were producing billions of chips each year.

Kilby, a tall Kansan who attended the University of Illinois after he failed the entrance examination for MIT, also invented one of the first new products that used ICs, the pocket calculator. He shares the credit for inventing the IC with Robert Noyce, a Ph.D. from MIT.

Large scale integrated (LSI) circuits followed soon after ICs with hundreds and then thousands of components packed into a single chip.

Large scale integration, followed by very large scale integration (VLSI) and ultra large scale integration, enabled designers to put the equivalent of large rooms and then buildings full of 1950s-era vacuum tube circuits on a tiny sliver of silicon smaller than a penny. These LSI, VLSI, and ULSI circuits are the foundation of personal computers today. VLSI and ULSI technology made computers affordable and thus accessible to individuals, and it is the reason you can put a computer on your desk instead of building a large room to house it.

Another computer revolution occurred in 1971 when Intel Corporation produced the first **microprocessor** IC. These computers on a chip are what made personal computers possible. In 1974, the first microcomputer kit was advertised nationally. In 1977 and 1978, several companies, including Tandy/Radio Shack and Apple Computer Company, began selling assembled computers. These personal computers were designed so that the buyer could unpack the system, plug it in, and begin using it. Tandy/Radio Shack and Apple Computer still manufacture popular computers that are widely used in business and education.

FIGURE 3.6   Apple Computer co-founders Steve Wozniak and Steve Jobs are on the left. Both left the company several years ago. On the right is John Scully, former president of Pepsico, who now heads Apple.

Tandy/Radio Shack was a thriving corporation when it built its first computer, the TRS-80 Model One. Apple Computer Company, on the other hand, was the brainchild of **Steven Jobs** and **Steve Wozniak**, two California "hippies" who were friends in high school (Levy, 1984). Wozniak's homemade computer became the Apple computer and the two Steves began Apple Computer Company in a garage. Jobs raised money by selling his Volkswagen van (a considerable sacrifice for a California boy living near the beach) and Wozniak sold his Hewlett-Packard programmable calculator. The original Apple computer could be purchased through the mail for $666.66. Soon after the first Apple computer was ready for sale, Wozniak began work on a new and better computer, the Apple II, which was demonstrated at a Homebrew Computer Club meeting in December 1976. Although the current versions are much more powerful than the original, Apple Computer Corporation is still selling Apple II computers. Neither of the company's two founders is with the company today, but Apple Computer Corporation is the only one of the original personal computer companies that is still a major force in the field.

Personal computers today are a far cry from the ENIAC computer that occupied 3,000 cubic feet of space, used 140,000 watts of power, weighed 30 tons, and had 18,000 tubes, 70,000 resistors, and 10,000 capacitors.

COMPUTER HARDWARE TODAY

Today, several hundred companies manufacture personal or minicomputers. However, in schools today only three major series of computers are in widespread use: the Apple II, the Apple Macintosh, and **IBM-compatible computers**. There are several different Apple II models, at least six different versions of the Apple Macintosh, and hundreds of IBM-compatible computers. The term *IBM-compatible* means the computer works like models made by IBM. Several hundred companies including Tandy/Radio Shack, Dell, Texas Instruments, NEC, Zenith, Compaq, and Hyundai make computers that work like computers produced by IBM.

What Is Software?

A computer will not do anything until it has a program (a set of instructions) to follow. Two types of software are in common use in schools today.

Commercial Educational Software
Tens of thousands of **educational software** programs are available to-

day that teach everything from basic reading readiness skills to college-level physics. These programs cost as little as $10 for a simple program to as much as $30,000 for a complete math or science curriculum for an elementary school. A few of these programs are outstanding examples of quality software, but a great many are so poorly conceived and executed that they are simply not worth their purchase price.

Applications Software

Many of the uses of computers in schools do not call for educational software. A word-processing class, for example, could use one of the popular word-processing programs such as Microsoft Word or WordPerfect or other such **applications software**. An English literature class might use the database management features of Microsoft Works or AppleWorks to create a file of information on the social and political conditions when great poets or novelists wrote their best works. A drafting class can use computer aided design (CAD) software and an accounting class can use electronic spreadsheets like Lotus 1 2 3 or SuperCalc.

All the uses mentioned above, and many others, can be accomplished with commercially available programs used in homes, offices,

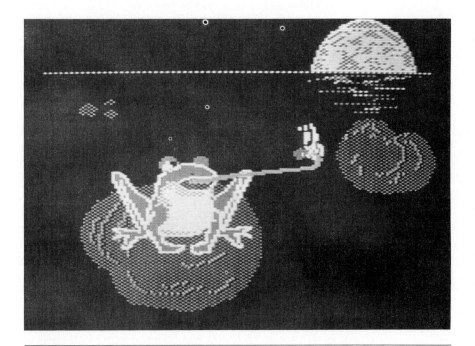

FIGURE 3.7   Many educational programs, such as Operation: FROG from Scholastic, make extensive use of graphics.

and factories everyday. Excellent applications software, software that helps you accomplish a particular type of task, is available today.

THE HARDWARE ASPECTS OF A COMPUTER SYSTEM

Software is one aspect of a computer system. The other aspect is the hardware, the physical components of a computer. The final section of this chapter deals with the features that are most important when the computer is used for educational applications.

Input Devices

Although keyboards are the most widely used input device, there are many others.

Keyboards

The primary method of getting information and instructions into the computer is the keyboard. Keyboards, like wines and steaks, are subject to a great deal of personal preference. There are, however, some generally agreed upon points that differentiate a good keyboard from a bad keyboard. Some early personal computers had "doomsday" keys on their keyboards. If pressed, a doomsday key will cause the computer to erase everything in its memory. Few current models have "doomsday" keys. Some computers do have *pseudo-doomsday* keys. When pressed, these keys give the impression that something terrible has happened. The daughter of one of the authors called him from her college dorm room late one night to say she was afraid she had lost a paper she was writing for her Writing Fiction class. She was using a Tandy 1000 computer, which is IBM compatible, and the machine had frozen. She could see part of her paper on the screen, but nothing she did had any effect on the computer. She had called and asked for help as a last resort before pulling the plug and starting over. Some models of the Tandy 1000 have a key named HALT that is just above the ENTER key. When you press the Halt key, it freezes the computer. Nothing is erased or destroyed, but nothing will work until you press the HALT key again. Then everything works normally. This key, because it is so near the ENTER key, can be pressed accidentally without even knowing it. That is poor keyboard design. Poorly placed keys are problems on the keyboards of many popular computers.

Some keyboards also emit a relatively loud click each time a key was pressed, something that can be distracting in a class where 20 or 30 students are furiously typing away. Some computers, including the Apple Macintosh, allow you to select whether you want to hear a click or beep each time a key is pressed.

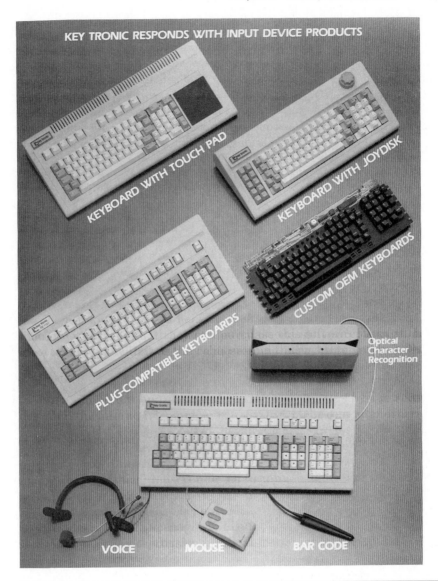

FIGURE 3.8   Key Tronic manufactures many different types of computer keyboards.

On the positive side, some computers come with more keys than others. There are, for example, 10 to 15 *function keys* on some keyboards. These keys can be assigned to different tasks by different programs. Function keys make it easier to use some programs. Some keyboards also have separate keys for common functions, such as moving the cursor on the screen, while the cursor control keys on other models are used to

FIGURE 3.9   Several companies produce special keyboards for children.

perform other functions as well. Keys that must be used for more than one purpose are not as convenient.

Alternative Input Devices
A significant number of educational programs work best with input devices other than the keyboard. Some computers have no provisions for connecting input devices such as joysticks, while others provide connections for several types of input devices.

Joysticks and game paddles, which are required to play many computer video games, are one type of alternative input device. Several companies manufacture large, oversized keyboards with specially labeled templates that make using some programs much easier for young children. Also growing in popularity are graphics tablets that allow you to create color graphics on the screen of the computer by drawing with a stylus on the surface of a special tablet that can sense when and where the stylus is moved.

Light pens, which are used to touch the screen to make choices or enter data, and touch-sensitive screens are two input devices that are not popular today. However, another device, the **mouse**, is becoming very popular. A computer mouse is a palm-sized device with small wheels or a ball on the bottom. As the mouse is moved over the surface of a desk or table, the cursor (a blinking spot of light on the screen that tells you where text you type will be entered) also moves. On computers like the Apple Macintosh, the mouse is standard equipment. It controls the

FIGURE 3.10   Many computer-aided design (CAD) programs accept input from light pens.

movement of the cursor and is also used to give the computer commands. The mouse is one reason why it is very easy to learn to use the Macintosh.

On other computers, such as the models from IBM, mouse input devices are optional. However, the computer mouse is fast becoming a very desirable input device, even if you are using an IBM-compatible computer. Some programs even require the use of a mouse.

Trackballs

Recently, a new type of device, called a trackball, became available. It has a large ball in a stationary housing. As you roll the ball, the cursor moves on the screen. Trackballs can take the place of joysticks and computer mice, but they are not widely used today. Because they don't move about the desk, trackballs require less desktop space.

Scanners and Card Readers

An optical **scanner** is a device that scans a sheet of paper and converts what it sees into signals that are sent to a computer. In schools, scanners are used for a variety of purposes. Multiple-choice tests can be scored with a scanner if students enter their answers on a special sheet. Attendance data, the daily lunch count, semester grades, and many other types of data can also be entered into the computer from a scanner if teachers use special sheets to collect the data. Several companies also

FIGURE 3.11   A computer mouse can have one, two, or three buttons.

FIGURE 3.12   This hand scanner can scan graphics or text and covert the input to data the computer can process.

sell card readers that can be connected to personal computers. Card readers can also be used to score tests and input routine information such as attendance data.

Optical scanners can also be used to convert an image on a page to a computer graphic. For example, photographs for the school newspaper could be scanned and converted to electronic images. Some scanners can also be used as optical character readers (OCR). OCRs can read the text printed on a page and convert it to computer data.

The Central Processing Unit

The **CPU**, or central processing unit, is the heart of a computer system. Although most CPU integrated circuits are smaller than an Oreo cookie, they have as much electronic capability as components manufactured a few decades ago that would have filled a large building. Using advanced microelectronic techniques, manufacturers can cram millions of circuits into tiny silicon chips that work dependably and use less power than an electric razor. There are several manufacturers of CPU chips. Intel makes the 80286, 80386, and 80486; Motorola makes the 6800 and 68000 chips. All CPU chips operate in essentially the same way, but there are many real differences among the various chips used in computers today. For example, different chips run at different speeds. Newer CPU chips can also handle larger amounts of memory.

Memory

The central processing unit in a computer is the brain of the machine, but it cannot do everything. It must have the support of several other types of integrated circuits that perform special functions. One very important type of specialized IC is memory. You need memory in your computer for three reasons. First, the computer must have some instructions built in so that it can start itself when you switch on the power. Manufacturers generally put the instructions the computer needs to get started in **ROM**, or read-only memory integrated circuits. The data in ROM cannot be changed by the user. They are permanent.

All computers also have another type of memory, random-access memory (**RAM**). When you want the computer to run a program that is stored on a disk, you must load that program into the computer's memory (RAM). In addition, programs such as word processors and student record management software need memory to store data, such as the daily attendance data or that report you are writing. Programs and data are stored in RAM.

Computer memory is divided into **bytes**. One byte can hold the code for one character. The memory capacity of computers is usually expressed in K. One K of memory is enough to store 1024 characters. The IBM-compatible computer one of the authors used to write this chapter had 640K of RAM, which is general-purpose memory. The word-processing program and the operating system software that were loaded when the author was ready to write took up approximately 380K. That left 260K of RAM available to hold this chapter. It is only about 48K long, which means there was plenty of room. Most modern computers can use millions of bytes of RAM. The term meg or **megabyte** refers to 1024K of memory.

Mass Storage

When you turn the computer off, anything stored in general-purpose memory (RAM) will be erased. It is there only as long as the power is on. You thus need some means of storing programs and data outside the memory of the computer. The first personal computers in schools used some type of cassette recorder to store data and programs. Cassettes were cheap, but slow and generally unreliable. Fortunately, most computers in schools today use **disk drives** for storage.

Disk drives are fast and reliable, and even the least expensive models store over 150K of data on a flexible round platter of Mylar called a floppy disk. Many computers in schools today use 5 1/4-inch disks, but most new models use 3 1/2-inch disks which are housed in a sturdy, rigid plastic case. Standard 3 1/2-inch drives store 720K on each disk; high-capacity 3 1/2-inch drives store 1.44 meg.

In addition to the floppy disk drives mentioned already, there are many models of hard disk drives that work much faster than floppy

FIGURE 3.13 The disk drive on the left is an old 8" model. The next three are 5 ¼" models that were popular in the 1980s. Most computers today use 3 ½" models like the two on the right.

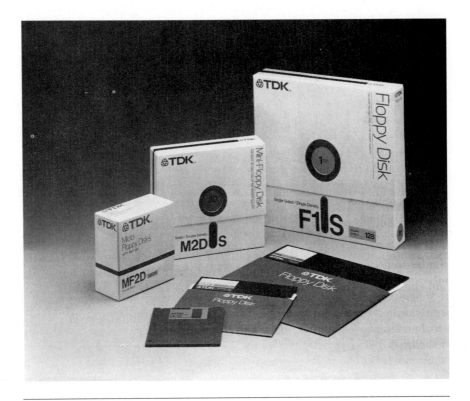

FIGURE 3.14 Floppy drives store data on floppy disks. Three sizes, 8", 5 ¼", and 3 ½" are shown here.

disks, store millions of bytes of data, and, unfortunately, cost two to fifty times as much as floppy drives. Computers equipped with hard disk drives are much more convenient to use.

There is also a new type of mass storage that has become very important to educational computing. **CD-ROM** storage, which is short for compact disk read-only memory, is a method of storing data on a small disk like those used in compact disk players for music. With current technology it is possible to store billions of bytes of data, both text and graphics, on one compact disk. Several publishers of encyclopedias, for example, provide their entire set of encyclopedias on one or more CD-ROM disks. The electronic versions of these encyclopedias can be searched by entering keywords into the computer. The computer then searches the CD-ROM for relevant information and the pages of the encyclopedia appear on the screen of the computer. CD-ROM are also used to store graphic images, databases of information, and much more. When you do a computer search for information at your college or university library, you are probably using a computer with a CD-ROM drive attached to it.

CD-ROM drives are beginning to be used in education today as is another type of storage device, the **laser disk.** Laser disks are much

FIGURE 3.15   With the cover off, you can see the metal platters where data is stored on this hard disk drive.

FIGURE 3.16   CD-ROM drives like this one are at work in many schools and libraries today.

larger than CDs, and they are generally used to store video images such as movies. Although video disk systems can be used without a computer, they are increasingly being connected to computers to provide interactive video instruction. For example, IBM's PALS program, a computer-assisted system for teaching adults to read, uses a laser disc to deliver instruction. A special video monitor displays computer-generated text and graphics, as well as video and sound from the laser disk. In some colleges of education, a computer-controlled laser disk system displays scenes from a classroom on the screen and stops occasionally to allow a teacher education student to make a decision about what should be done next. Once the decision is made, the computer plays a scene from the video disk that shows the result of the decision. The educational uses of both CD-ROM and laser disk players are likely to increase considerably in the near future.

Networking

Many schools with Apple or IBM-compatible computers in their computer labs have connected their computers through a **local area network** or LAN. LANs make it possible for teachers, administrators, and students

FIGURE 3.17   Laser disc players are used to deliver multimedia computer-controlled instruction in many schools.

to communicate with other users through *electronic mail* systems, to share data between computers (including large mainframe and minicomputers), and to share expensive peripherals such as printers, high-capacity disk drives, and special output devices such as graphics plotters.

Output Devices

Two types of output devices are in common use, video monitors and printers.

Video Monitors

The most common input device for a personal computer is a keyboard, and the most common output device is some sort of **video display**. The terms *video display*, *monitor*, and *CRT* (for cathode ray tube) all refer to the same thing. Getting signals from the computer to a video screen involves two major components, the video circuit in the computer and the display itself. This section focuses on the displays available today, but you should also be aware of the role of the video circuits in your computer. These circuits determine what you can display on your screen and the quality of the display. The most important factors in the video output from personal computers are briefly described here.

Text display format is the most obvious factor in a video display. Most video systems today can display 24 lines of 80 characters on the screen. Higher-quality displays can produce characters in different formats, such as italicized and bold, in different sizes, and in different colors. Computers like the Macintosh have several different display fonts. If you want text displayed in Old English script, it is available.

Color options are another desirable feature. Many computers can output information in only one color (monochrome), while others can display text and graphics in many different colors. Amber and green monochrome monitors produce less eye fatigue with prolonged use than black and white monochrome monitors. Other things being equal, the computer with color capability is more desirable. Many educational programs use both color graphics and text.

The third factor that determines the performance of a video monitor is graphics modes. Most personal computers have at least some ability to display graphics. They can display figures, graphs, game boards, diagrams, and illustrations as well as text.

You may read advertisements that describe the graphics features of a computer in terms of **pixels**. A computer, for example, might have a

FIGURE 3.18   Many programs generate graphics that are displayed on a color monitor.

graphics mode that is 280 by 192 pixels. This means that the computer can divide the screen into 280 rows and 192 columns. Each point where a row and column intersect is called a pixel or picture element. A pixel is like one tiny square on a sheet of graph paper. The computer is capable of controlling whether a tiny rectangle of light is displayed at that point or not. The larger the number of pixels a computer can control, the finer the graphics the computer can display. On most computers the number of different colors that can be displayed simultaneously on the screen decreases as you move from low to medium to high resolution. However, more expensive high-resolution systems allow you to use more colors than less expensive systems with the same resolution.

Many computers can be configured with any of several different types of video display systems. The lowest-quality color video display for an IBM-compatible machine, for example, is a color graphics adapter (CGA) system. Even better are enhanced graphic adapter (EGA) systems and very enhanced graphic adapter (VGA) systems.

Printers

After the video monitor, the most popular output device for a computer is a printer. There are several different types of printers on the market today and over 500 different models. Four characteristics differentiate one printer from another: speed, quality of print, range of characters and graphics elements that can be printed, and printing method. Printers work at speeds that range from around 10 to well over 500 characters a second. You can buy a slow printer that produces high-quality output or a fast printer that produces low-quality output for under $400. For a computer lab where students complete assignments, a fast printer that produces readable but not necessarily high-quality output is preferred over a high-quality printer that is very slow. It can be very frustrating to realize 5 minutes before the class ends that the printing your students just began will take 15 minutes to finish. On the other hand, you want the printer used to produce correspondence to parents and other local education agencies to produce high-quality output. If you only have enough funds to buy quality or speed, quality may be more important here.

The third characteristic of printers, the range of characters and graphics elements that can be printed, can also be very important. Printers that will be used in a lab where standard word processing will be taught may be required to do no more than print standard text in one or two sizes. On the other hand, a lab that will be used for classes in art, drafting, physics, chemistry, or desktop publishing may need a printer that can produce a wide range of graphics. The type and range of characters and graphic elements you want a printer to produce depend on the way the material will be used.

The fourth characteristic, printing method, has an influence on the other three. Most printers today are dot-matrix models. They produce

FIGURE 3.19 Millions of dot matrix printers like this one from Seikosha are in use today.

characters by knocking the ribbon into the paper with a series of wires in the print head. **Dot matrix printers** are generally fast, from 80 to 500 characters a second, and even the least expensive models (about $150) produce readable print and graphics. The characters are made up of tiny dots of ink on the paper. Mediocre dot-matrix print is often called **draft quality** while better, but not perfect, print is called *correspondence quality*. The best quality of print is called **near-letter quality** or *letter quality*. More expensive dot-matrix printers generally produce higher-quality print. Some models have several print modes. For general use, dot-matrix printers are probably the best choice where budgets are limited. For example, Apple's ImageWriter and IBM's ProPrinter models are excellent dot-matrix printers that produce good- to high-quality text as well as graphics.

The second most popular printing method is *solid character impact*. These printers produce solid characters that generally cannot be distinguished from the characters printed by an office typewriter. Most use *daisy wheel print mechanisms*. The output of these printers looks very good, but there are several disadvantages. First, these printers are rela-

FIGURE 3.20   Daisy wheel printers produce characters by knocking the petals on this wheel against the paper.

tively slow when compared to dot-matrix models. Second, they generally have very limited, if any, graphics capabilities. Third, because they are relatively complicated to build, they generally cost more than dot-matrix models with similar speed and print quality characteristics. Daisy wheel printers are not as popular today as they once were.

The third widely used print method is *ink jet*. Ink jet printers produce characters on paper by spewing out minute droplets of ink that hit the paper in the pattern of the characters you want to print. Thus far, most ink jet printers have had one or more of the following disadvantages: they are expensive, prone to get out of adjustment, messy, or slow. Some ink jet printers have one major advantage—the ability to print in color. (There are color dot-matrix printers as well.) Ink jet printers are rarely used in schools today except for special applications (for example, the software a drafting teacher uses may work best with a particular ink jet printer, or the graphics software used to produce overheads for presentations may be designed for use with an ink jet printer). The same is true of another special-purpose output device, the plotter. A plotter is a device that can be used to draw figures and graphs under the direction of a computer.

The final printing method to be discussed is laser technology. Several companies, including Apple and Hewlett-Packard, produce **laser**

FIGURE 3.21   Color ink jet printers like this one from Sharp can produce outstanding color graphics.

printers today. They combine the technology of a copy machine that uses dry ink power (toner) with a laser beam that draws an image of the page on a photosensitive drum in the printer. Laser printer output approaches the quality of a typesetting machine. Laser printers can produce

FIGURE 3.22   This laser printer from Ricoh is sold in North America under several brand names.

text in a wide range of sizes and styles and they can produce high-quality graphics, even photographs that have been scanned. Laser printers are the foundation of a new use of computers, desktop publishing. Many books, newsletters, magazines, brochures, and reports are desktop published today. Laser printers combine high-quality output with speed. The only drawbacks are the cost of the printer, five to fifty times that of a dot-matrix printer, and the cost of printing. The per page cost of printing is higher with a laser printer than on a daisy wheel or dot-matrix printer.

Laser printers are beginning to appear in school computer labs today and in administrative offices. Where the extra cost of purchasing and using a laser printer can be justified, they are very desirable. High school journalism programs, for example, are beginning to use laser printers because they allow students to produce a high-quality student newspaper. In fact, the cost of publishing a student newspaper can be reduced by as much as 20% to 40% by desktop publishing the paper on a laser printer if the school has normally paid a printer to typeset the

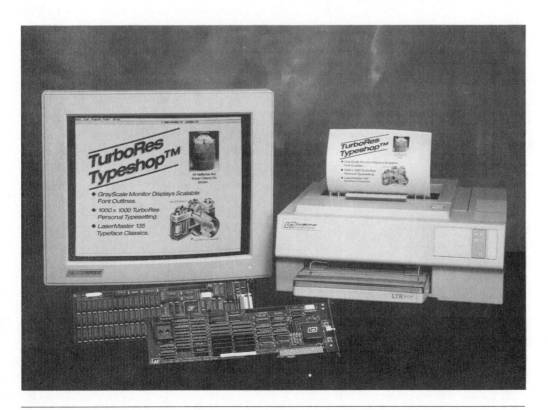

FIGURE 3.23   High-resolution graphics video system and laser printers make desktop publishing possible.

paper. Typesetting costs, which are very high in many sections of the country, can be completely eliminated, and students receive better training because they are involved in more steps in the process. The same laser printer can be used for student and teacher handbooks and other documents.

SUMMARY

The concept of a computer, a mechanical device to compute, was developed through the work of Pascal, Leibnitz, Babbage, and Hollerith. The last two designed mechanical "computers," but the technology of the nineteenth century was not advanced sufficiently to make their production possible. What nineteenth-century minds envisioned, twentieth-century technology produced. The impetus of World War II led Alan Turing and others to develop Colossus, a computer designed to crack German codes. The computers of the 1940s were huge because their major components were vacuum tubes. The development of the transistor in the late 1940s revolutionized the electronics industry, but it was the invention of the integrated circuit in 1958 that permitted the development of the microcomputer. This led to the production of computers that could be purchased and used by individuals and schools.

Today, educators are most likely to encounter three types of personal computers in schools: Apple II, Apple Macintosh, and IBM PC-compatible. The software available may be classified into two categories: educational and applications software. The hardware of computing is the machine itself and its peripherals. These usually consist of input devices such as keyboards and computer mice, the CPU that is the heart of the computer and the memory that supports the CPU, mass storage devices such as floppy and hard disk drives, network hardware, and output devices such as monitors and printers.

LOOKING AHEAD

This chapter completes the introductory material on computers and the use of computing technology in education. In Chapter 4 you will begin to explore in detail the uses of technology in education. Chapter 4 begins that exploration with a discussion of the major issues and trends. In the 1980s, many people believed that a revolution in education could be achieved if only we could get enough computer hardware in the schools. Equipment is certainly needed, but the material in Chapter 4 and those that follow supports the assertion that equipment alone is not enough. Used improperly, technology can actually retard the development of quality education programs.

SOME QUESTIONS TO CONSIDER

1. Compare the application of basic research, such as George Boole's system of logic to the development of computer technology, to the application of basic research in fields such as psychology to education. Are there parallels in the way basic research finds its way into practice?
2. If the transistor and integrated circuit had not been invented, what roles would computer technology play in education today?
3. If CD-ROM and laser disk technology was as widely available and inexpensive as overhead projectors, how might they be used to support instruction in K–12 schools? In colleges and universities?

RELATED ACTIVITIES

1. Check the library at your school for books on the history of computing. The lives of pioneers like George Boole, Charles Babbage, Ada Lovelace, Alan Turing, Steven Wozniak, and many others provide very interesting reading.
2. Check recent issues of general interest computer magazines like *PC World*, *PC Magazine*, and *MacWorld*. What hardware topics are "hot" today? Are some aspects of computer hardware about to change drastically?

REFERENCES

Bitter, G. (1989). *Microcomputers in education today*. Watsonville, CA: Mitchell Publishing.

Boole, M. (1972). *A Boolean anthology*. New York: Association of Teachers of Mathematics.

Evans, C. (1981). *The making of the micro: A history of the computer*. New York: Van Nostrand Reinhold.

Goldstine, H. (1972). *The computer from Pascal to von Neumann*. Princeton, NJ: Princeton University Press.

Hodges, A. (1983). *Alan Turing, the enigma*. New York: Simon & Schuster.

Levy, S. (1984). *Hackers: Heroes of the computer revolution*. Garden City, NY: Doubleday.

Reid, T. R. (1985). *The chip*. New York: Simon & Schuster.

Willis, J. (1987). *Educational computing: A guide to practical applications*. Scottsdale, AZ: Gorsuch/Scarisbrich Publishers.

Willis, J., Johnson, L., & Dixon, P. (1983). *Computers, teaching, and learning*. Beaverton, OR: Dilithium Press.

__4__

Issues and Trends in in Educational Computing

GOALS AND OBJECTIVES

Goal: To become aware of issues and trends in educational computing and the arguments used to support and refute the various positions surrounding these controversial topics.

When you finish studying this chapter, you will be able to:

1. Write a paragraph describing what reports such as *A Nation at Risk* had to do with interest in computer literacy.
2. Write a paragraph describing what is wrong with insisting that computer literacy skills are prevocational skills.
3. Tell how stereotypical attitudes could result in computer inequity.
4. Describe hard mastery and soft mastery of computers and tell what these concepts have to do with equity.
5. Tell why networking almost always results in a reduction of the total pool of available software.

KEY TERMS

backup copy	computer literacy
computer ethics	computer networking
computer equity	computer virus

computing entrepreneurs
copy program
copy protected
curriculum integration
database management
hacker
hard mastery
local area network
management system
national economic
  necessity

network manager
panacea
prevocational necessity
site license
soft mastery
software piracy
spreadsheet software
technology gap
word processing

There is no lack of topics for inclusion in a chapter on issues and trends in educational computing. There are many hotly debated issues. At times, the controversial nature of the field can cause practitioners to feel a bit unsettled or insecure. At the same time, however, the presence of many unanswered questions as well as the evolving nature of theory and practice in educational computing creates an environment of great excitement and vitality.

The purpose of this chapter is to introduce the reader to some controversies in educational computing. Specifically, we will discuss issues and trends related to computer literacy, computer equity, computing ethics, labs versus integration of computers, networking, and the teaching of problem solving.

COMPUTER LITERACY

One of the most hotly debated issues in educational computing has been centered around the concept of **computer literacy**. The controversy involves several subissues such as (1) how the term should be defined, (2) how important computer knowledge and/or skills are to learners now and in the future, and (3) what knowledge or skills should make up computer literacy.

The origin of the term computer literacy is unclear. One of the first people to use the term was Andrew Molnar of the National Science Foundation. Molnar (1978) suggested that the next great crisis in education would be related to computer literacy. Although it is difficult to separate cause from effect, two related phenomena took place in the early 1980s that helped convince many educators and noneducators that computer literacy deserved a place in the school curriculum. The first of these events was the publication of formal reports of the findings of a number of commissions whose charge was to study and critique American education. Most of these reports were highly critical of schools and in cluded the teaching of computer knowledge and skills (computer literacy) in their list of recommended educational reforms. (One of the most highly publicized of these reports was *A Nation at Risk*, published in 1983 by the National Commission on Excellence in Education.)

The second related event was the inclusion of this same recommendation in reports by numerous educational organizations such as the *National Council of Supervisors of Mathematics*, the *National Council of Teachers of Mathematics*, and the *National Council for Social Studies* (Riedesel and Clements, 1985). For the next five years or so, the professional journals were full of the debate about how to define literacy (see, for example, Anderson, Klassen, & Johnson, 1981; Luehrmann, 1981; Moursand, 1983). This debate produced little, if any agreement on definition. In fact, Tinker (1984, p. 2) has observed that "Everybody wants it but nobody knows what it is." Bramble and Mason (1985) make the excellent point that difficulty with a definition of computer literacy is to be expected, since even in the traditional sense, experts in language arts have failed to make literacy a clearly defined concept.

Although the debate concerning the definition of computer literacy produced little consensus, it did produce a number of interesting definitions. Riedesel & Clements (1985, p. 14) present a list of various definitions of computer literacy, and interested readers are referred to their excellent review.

By about 1984, most educators had accepted the idea that computers should have a place in the curriculum. The controversy then became whether literacy should be learning about computers or learning how to use computers. From 1984 until 1990, the debate narrowed somewhat. Advocates of each position argued among themselves about specific content or skills to be taught. This debate has been particularly keen among those who believe that computer literacy should involve teaching learners to use computers. Some such advocates asserted that all children should be taught to program computers, while others maintained that programming is a waste of time and that children should be taught to use programs written by others.

An excellent review and analysis of the debate about computer literacy was written by Kelman (1984). Kelman suggests that the two most common rationales for computer literacy are (1) computer literacy as **prevocational necessity**, and (2) computer literacy as **national economic necessity**. According to Kelman, both are based on flawed assumptions.

The assumption underlying the prevocational argument is that computers will continue to pervade the workplace and that, therefore, workers of the future will need to know progressively more about computers and how they work. However, Kelman maintains that, as computers become easier to operate, workers will need to know less about how they work. He points out that we are surrounded by electric motors, but we need to know little or nothing about them in order to use them.

The national economic necessity argument, according to Kelman, is that computer literacy skills should be taught in order to ensure that the United States does not lose its competitive economic edge among the nations of the world. According to this rationale, the United States suffers from a **technology gap** relative to other developed nations such as Japan and some Western European countries. Kelman (1984) denies that such a gap exists, since new technological advances and inventions still come predominantly from the United States. Foreign countries sometimes do a better job of applying new discoveries, but Kelman suggests that their success is due to differences in (1) national economic policies, (2) industrial practices, and (3) the cost of labor. Kelman concludes by endorsing the suggestion by Watt (1981) that computer literacy should be viewed as analogous to literacy in one's native language. Specifically, says Kelman:

> *Students should learn to use the computer for word, data, and number processing from their earliest possible years in school. They should also have the opportunity to use the graphics and sound capabilities of the computer to explore their creative urges. Moreover, teachers should provide opportunities for students to use computers in problem-solving and decision-making situations. At times, this may include programming a computer. At other times, it may not. (p. 16)*

By the late 1980s, most computer advocates had concluded that literacy should be both learning about the computer and learning to use the computer. However, there is still considerable disagreement about whether children should be taught programming skills and, if so, what computer language should be used. To date, if a trend has been established, it is probably one of de-emphasizing the teaching of programming. Recent definitions are similar to Hoelscher's (1986): "Literacy is learning about what computers can do, becoming familiar with various types of software, and gaining some exposure to programming languages" (p. 23).

We tend to agree with those who emphasize that all students should be taught to use the computer as a tool. **Word processing** (using the computer to replace a typewriter), **database management** (electronic filing), and **spreadsheet software** (electronic accounting) are valuable tools to aid learning in content areas such as math, science, and social studies. Another reason for teaching children about such applications is that they have proved to be significantly useful in the culture at large. Software such as word processing, spreadsheets, and databases have proved their worth in a variety of environments, and we believe that children should become familiar with the concepts upon which they are based and have some practice with specific examples of each.

We support the importance of literacy primarily because computers now occupy an increasingly prevalent and important niche in our culture. Therefore, knowledge about computers, as well as basic computer skills, is part of the common intellectual heritage that educators are charged with transmitting.

COMPUTER EQUITY

There has been concern about the issue of equity almost since computers first began to be brought into schools. Ever since the late 1970s or early 1980s, some educators have thought computers in schools could act to widen existing gaps between rich and poor, male and female, black and white, handicapped and nonhandicapped, haves and have-nots.

In general, equity issues arise (1) because access to computers varies from school to school, and (2) because many people hold stereotypic attitudes about who should operate computers (Vockell and Schwartz, 1988).

The problem of access is due primarily to the way public education is funded in our country. With few exceptions, school districts are small, locally organized entities with clearly defined geographic boundaries. Most of the money to finance schools is obtained by collecting property taxes on homes and businesses located within the district. Since the amount of tax assessed depends on the value of the property being taxed, it is obvious that districts with valuable homes and businesses within their borders collect more taxes than districts containing less valuable property. Thus, there are poor districts and rich districts. Obviously, rich districts are much more likely to be able to afford a quantity of high-quality computer hardware and software than are poor districts. If computer skills lead to improved learning and if computer education is more accessible to students in rich districts than to those in poor districts, then computer education could perpetuate and exaggerate existing educational and related inequities.

Research has shown that **computer equity** is a real problem in our nation's schools. Wealthier schools are much more likely to have computers than are poorer schools, and they tend to have more computers. There is also some evidence that low-income minority schools tend to use their computers differently than do nonminority schools in low-income areas. Specifically, the minority schools tend to provide drill and practice for below-average students, while Anglo schools of comparable means use computing to teach programming to above-average students.)

The problem of stereotypic views about who should operate computers in what ways has resulted in inequities related to gender or to the presence of a mental or physical handicap. Research has shown a clear tendency for *girls to use computers less often than boys and to use them differently* (Vockell and Schwartz, 1988). Boys are more likely to use science and math applications and girls are more likely to use the computer exclusively as a word processor. Handicapped students are more likely to be given drill and practice software to develop rote abilities, while gifted students are more likely to be taught more creative, Type II uses.

Problems of sexual stereotyping or stereotyping because of handicapping condition will be easier to correct than will problems of unequal access. The latter problem is related to the larger issue of unfair educational funding policies. Poorer districts should seek grants from the federal government and from other sources to help obtain funding. Such districts should also seek partnerships with business and industry and enlist parent—teacher organizations to assist with fund drives (Bitter, 1987). However, we believe that school finance policies themselves are largely inequitable and that fiscal reform will be necessary before the problem of unequal access to computing can be completely solved.

Stereotypic attitudes must be recognized before resulting practices are likely to be changed. The concept of computer equity should include the handicapped and should imply access to appropriate uses of computers based on individual needs, rather than simply equal physical access (Maddux and Cummings, 1987). Educators should give thought to how handicapped students (and all others) are using the computer, rather than simply counting the number of handicapped users. Handicapped students should be given the same access to Type II applications (such as word processing and programming) as are nonhandicapped users, and the use of drill and practice software should be limited for all users.

Turkle (1984) categorizes computer mastery as **hard mastery** or **soft mastery**. Hard mastery is more typical of males and is characterized by a desire to bend the computer to the will of the user. It is systematic, planned, objective use. Many females, on the other hand, tend to work toward soft mastery, which is more impressionistic, artistic, and subjective. Both styles should be encouraged and rewarded.

Bitter (1987) suggests that stereotyping can be minimized by (1) making sure that the use of computers is not limited to higher-level mathematics courses, which tend to be dominated by nonhandicapped, white, male students; (2) preventing after-school computer clubs from becoming male hangouts by limiting the use of arcade-type shoot-'em-up games; and (3) establishing clubs specifically for females (p. 84).

Computer equity issues are far from solved. However, there does seem to be a growing realization that the problem exists, as well as a willingness to take steps to solve it. We must continue to work on this problem. It will be bitterly ironic indeed if a potentially revolutionary learning tool like the computer, which has the ability to greatly empower users, instead results in intensifying existing societal inequities.

COMPUTER ETHICS

Computer ethics has recently become an issue of concern to educators. This has been a natural development. As technology empowers human beings, new behaviors become possible, and ethical questions about these behaviors are bound to arise. This phenomenon is not unique to computer education; it occurs whenever technology makes possible new ways of behaving. Ethical dilemmas related to new technology are also occurring in medicine, where organ transplants and sophisticated life-support systems have sparked debates about many issues related to these new techniques. In biology, the ability to create new organisms or modify existing ones through genetic engineering has created new ethical dilemmas.

In education, there has been concern about a variety of computing behaviors. Bear (1986) lists 24 different ethical issues, including such topics as copyright law and issues, computer crime and abuse, freedom of information, hacking, vandalism, video games, the cashless society, and classroom computing rules. He suggests that computer ethics is a topic that has been neglected in introductory college textbooks about educational computing. However, Kinzer, Sherwood, and Bransford (1986), in their introductory text, include a chapter entitled Ethical Issues and discuss the quality of software, ethical uses of software including unauthorized copying, equity issues, and computers and personal privacy.

We have surveyed a number of textbooks and articles and have found that most ethical topics can be placed into one of the following four categories: (1) violation of copyright law, (2) invasion of privacy, (3) unethical entrepreneurship by educators, and (4) lack of equitable access to computers. We discussed equity in an earlier section of this chapter.

Violation of Copyright Law

This issue is straightforward: *It is illegal to make unauthorized copies of a copyrighted computer program.* Software is protected under the U.S. Copyright Act of 1978. The law makes it a crime to copy any program that has been copyrighted, except to make one archival or **backup copy** for storage.

Unfortunately, teachers have a poor reputation for software honesty. Estimates are that from 10% to 50% of software used in schools are illegal copies (Mandell and Mandell, 1989).

In the past, some teachers have taken the position that violation of the copyright law is moral as long as unauthorized copies are made for use in teaching children in schools. The law, of course, recognizes no such exemption for educators, and the courts will not accept such a defense.

It is difficult to understand why some educators take this position. Most teachers would not suggest that stealing goods from a department store is moral as long as the thief passes the goods on to a student! Just as the theft of a coat deprives the maker and middlemen of a fair return on their efforts, illegal copying of software to avoid purchasing multiple copies deprives the developer and middlemen of a fair return on their efforts.

Violations of copyright are sometimes referred to as **software piracy**. Piracy should be avoided for a number of reasons, including the fact that it is illegal. Teachers who engage in illegal acts in the classroom are sending a covert message to students. As we have suggested (Maddux and Cummings, 1987b), students learn by example, not by memorizing rules. Standards for ethical behavior cannot be taught by lecturing or preaching and must be modeled. If students realize their teachers are stealing software, they can be expected to act similarly.

In fairness to educators, copyright violations sometimes occur due to ignorance. Therefore, we present the following list of illegal behaviors that have taken place in schools:

1. *Purchase of one copy of a program, followed by unauthorized copying of the software for simultaneous use on a number of computers.* This is illegal, unless the company has issued a **site license**. Such a license permits the purchaser to make multiple copies or to perform multiple boots. This latter option is described in the next section.

2. *Purchase of one copy of a program, followed by multiple booting of the program for simultaneous use on a number of computers.* This illegal technique is possible if the software is so designed that the entire program is loaded into memory and it is not necessary for the computer to read anything from the diskette while the program executes. It is then possible to load the program first into computer A, remove the diskette, place it in computer B, load the program into computer B, and so on. However, unless the software license gives the user this right, multiple loading is as illegal as making unauthorized copies.

3. *Copying a program purchased by one lab for simultaneous use in another lab.*

4. *Purposely placing a copy of a copyrighted program on an electronic bulletin board so that users can download a copy of the program.* This activity could result in thousands of illegal copies, and there have been several court cases involving such activity.

5. *Loaning a copy of a copyrighted program to a friend, knowing that the friend intends to make unauthorized copies of the software.*

6. *Knowingly allowing anyone to use your personal or school computers to make unauthorized copies of copyrighted programs.*

7. *Placing copyrighted programs on a hard disk drive and allowing it to be downloaded for simultaneous use on a number of computers.*

However, there is a situation in which copies may be legally made in the absence of a site license. You are permitted to make a single backup copy for storage purposes. The backup copy is handy in case the original diskette is damaged.

Sometimes, making a workable copy is a problem, because many software developers guard against piracy by using a variety of technical schemes to make it difficult or impossible to make copies. Such software is said to be **copy protected**, and standard copying techniques will generally not be successful with this software. However, various companies produce **copy programs** designed to defeat these protection schemes. Use of copy programs to duplicate copyrighted software is legal only if the copies are for storage purposes and are not made in order to avoid purchasing additional copies.

Sometimes, children will bring copy programs to school to make illegal copies of copyrighted software belonging to the school. Most schools have rules against bringing copy programs to school. If a teacher knowingly allows a child to copy copyrighted software, the teacher becomes an accessory to an illegal act. Harris (1985) suggests four steps that educators can take to help guard against illegal copying. These include warnings issued to teachers and students, disciplinary action taken if violations are discovered, storage of software in secure areas, and close supervision of students.

Another reason that software piracy in education should be discouraged is that piracy causes software to be sold at inflated prices. Just as shoplifting drives up the price of consumer goods by passing the cost of thefts on to purchasers, so the price of software is driven up by piracy. In addition, widespread educational software piracy can cause software houses to decline to enter the educational market, thus exacerbating the problem of scarcity of high-quality educational software.

Invasion of Individual Privacy

Invasion of privacy refers mainly to inappropriate use of bulletin boards or unauthorized access to various types of information accessible through computer networks. We have all read stories about **hackers**, or individuals who gain unauthorized access to computers and information stored thereon. Recently, a hacker made headlines by gaining access to a national computer network and installing a program (improperly called a **computer virus**) that damaged software on computers used by other users of the network.

Electronic bulletin boards have also been abused. Mandell and Mandell (1989) refer to some of these problems:

> *Some people have misused bulletin boards by placing notices about access codes to corporate computers, describing instructions for building weapons, posting information about crimes or illicit sex, and inserting programs that destroy the user's software . . . . Before that first telephone call is made, school personnel should formulate guidelines for bulletin board use. (p. 251)*

Another problem related to privacy is the tendency to regard anything displayed on a computer screen as public information. Although most people, including students, would never pick up and read a document lying on someone else's desk, many people do not hesitate to read someone else's computer screen. As word-processing and other tool software becomes more and more common, we must extend the courtesy of privacy from written documents to material displayed on computer screens.

Unethical Entrepreneurship by Computer Educators

A relatively new development is the growing number of educational computer experts in public schools and in higher education who have become **computing entrepreneurs**. This includes activities such as (1) selling computer hardware and software to students, parents, school districts, or the general public; and (2) traveling with software or hardware salespeople and helping them sell a specific product to educational entities such as public schools.

Almost everyone would agree that teachers should not attempt to sell products to their own school districts or to the parents of children they teach. Some educators, however, argue that as long as they avoid these pitfalls they can ethically sell computer products or services to others. We outlined our objection to this concept in an earlier article:

> *We contend that salesmanship and scholarship are totally incompatible. As teachers or consultants we are constantly compelled to make recommendations concerning computer products and services. It flies in the face of common sense to assert that an objective assessment and recommendation could be made by anyone who stands to gain from the success of a particular product or service. An entrepreneur is not qualified to impartially judge his, or a competitor's product. (Maddux and Cummings, 1987b, p. 32)*

We have the same problem with computer educators who are hired to travel with salespeople and aid in the attempt to sell computer products and services to school districts. Such educators are hired in order to exploit academia's tradition of objectivity. Prospective buyers will probably assume that such educators have conducted a disinterested, scholarly evaluation of the product or service being peddled and are providing an honest, unbiased endorsement.

We have no problem, however, with computer educators who sell their consultant services to school districts, as long as these consultants do not stand to gain from a purchase of goods and services that they recommend. The difference is that a true consultant who has nothing to gain from his or her recommendations is able to make straightforward, disinterested recommendations.

LABS VERSUS INTEGRATION OF COMPUTERS

To date, the most common educational arrangement has involved placing all computers in one room (a computer laboratory) and assigning one or two teachers to teach children computing skills and knowledge. This is a necessary first step in computer education because of the scarcity of hardware and software and because so few teachers have the computer expertise needed to do a good job of teaching.

We believe, however, that the eventual, long-term success of computer education depends on widespread use of computers as teaching and learning tools in individual classrooms (**curriculum integration**). We agree with the observation that pencils would never have become useful educational tools if students had been allowed to use them only in "pencil labs."

We therefore support curriculum integration as a logical and necessary long-term goal for computer educators. However, we think a call for curriculum integration is, at present, somewhat premature for most districts because of two critical problems: (1) scarcity of computer hardware and software in most schools, and (2) lack of computing expertise by the majority of the nation's teachers.

Scarcity of Hardware and Software

The most recent survey revealed that the ratio of computers to students is approximately 1 to 30 (Office of Technology Assessment, 1988). Other studies have shown that the vast majority of school computers are located in labs and that there are usually only one or two different classrooms in a school that contain any computers at all. Thus, the only way that even one computer could be placed in every classroom would be to dismantle all computer laboratories in the nation and redistribute the hardware and software that has been located there. Obviously, such a move would be impossible due to political, legal, and financial considerations. Given the current scarcity of hardware, widespread curriculum integration must await better funding for educational computing.

Lack of Computing Expertise

Before curriculum integration can become feasible, the average teacher must acquire basic computing skills, as well as the more advanced skills needed to use the computer to teach their disciplines to children. However, the OTA document (Office of Technology Assessment, 1988) reports that only half the nation's teachers report that they have ever used a computer, and the number who say they use computers regularly is much smaller.

This problem occurs because of a lack of effective preservice and inservice training among public school teachers in the various disciplines. The OTA document reports that the vast majority of teachers have had little or no training in the effective use of technology and asserts that this lack of training is the single most important reason that technology's potential is largely unexploited. The report goes on to show that only 18 states currently require preservice technology training.

Computing hardware and software are scarce commodities in schools. Until this situation can be improved, the way to make the best use of a scarce resource is by centralizing that resource in a central computer laboratory. Then, too, until computer preservice and inservice are more widely implemented, distributing hardware and software to untrained teachers would probably result in thousands of pieces of expensive hardware gathering dust in the back of teachers' closets.

COMPUTER NETWORKING

Computer networking involves the electronic linking of two or more computer systems. For schools, the most common arrangement is the creation of a **local area network** (LAN) in which all or most of the instructional computers in a building are linked to a common hard disk drive containing software to be used by students. In such classroom or building networks, the linkage is by cable, although telephone lines or even satellites can be used when greater distances are involved. For example, the Maryland State Department of Education has installed a satellite network to allow all school districts in the state to copy (download), via satellite, any computer courseware in the state's central collection (Lillie, Wallace, & Stuck (1989).

Recently, networking has become something of an educational fad. Eltoft (1989) has referred to this tendency as well as the tendency to believe that networking is a **panacea** (magical solution):

> *Networking is used as a buzz word that implies increased performance and connectivity. The unfortunate truth is that having a network is not always better than not having one. . . . Networking in and of itself is neither inherently good or bad. (p. 22)*

Networking in educational settings is definitely growing in popularity. Apple Computers Incorporated reports that by 1988 there were 20,000 school installations of its AppleTalk network, and IBM has predicted that within 5 years networking in schools will be primarily responsible for increasing the ratio of computers to students from the present 1 to 30, to 1 to 5.

The important thing to remember about networking (and about any computing application) is that there are both advantages and disadvantages. Networking of microcomputers increases the complexity of the computing environment. Whenever complexity is increased, new problems will be introduced. For some districts, the problems encountered will be well worth the capabilities acquired. For other districts, the trade-off will not be advantageous and networking, in its present state of the art, is not a viable alternative.

The most common educational application of networking involves linking microcomputers to a central hard disk drive containing educational software. Frequently, a **management system** is also supplied by the vendor. The management system keeps track of students' progress through individual software packages, makes decisions about when students should repeat individual items or whole packages or move on to new ones, and provides students with feedback and reinforcement. The management system may also provide printed reports or charts of progress.

As you might suspect, such a system requires extensive development and must be customized to meet the specific needs of each educational environment where it is installed. Developers who provide networking systems must customize the management package so that it works with all software the district wishes to use. This is no small task, and the total price tag for such a system may be $30,000 to $40,000 or more.

If commercial software is to be used, someone must obtain site licenses from the owners of such software. This must be an ongoing process, since new software constantly becomes available. Unfortunately, while site licenses are becoming more common, some software developers still do not issue them or charge prohibitively high prices for them.

These issues highlight a major networking problem: networking almost always results in a reduction of the total pool of software available to schools. There may also be a reluctance to examine and adopt new software as it becomes available. Thus, networking may contribute to maintaining the status quo.

Another problem is that, during the development of the management software, many educational decisions must be made. For example, someone must decide on the criteria for repetition of units or entire software packages, the type and schedule of reinforcement to be provided, and numerous other philosophical and theoretical issues. This can be a real strength if it leads to school district personnel working closely with network vendors. When this occurs, it can be highly productive, since it causes teachers to ask themselves important pedagogical questions. However, if network vendors make these decisions themselves, it can result in poor educational decisions and an abdication of the rights and responsibilities of educators.

Another problem is network maintenance. We recommend that no school adopt networking unless someone knowledgeable can be designated as the network system manager. This teacher should devote at least half-time to network maintenance (full time would be preferable). The **network manager** serves as liaison between the school and the network vendor, reports problems to the vendor and solutions to teachers, arranges for new software to be incorporated on the network, negotiates changes in the management system, sees to it that network documentation is complete and up to date, establishes rules for network access, maintains network security, conducts and supervises network inservice education, and handles many other technical and educational details.

Although we have emphasized networking problems, we do not want to leave the impression that we are opposed to networking. When properly implemented and supported, networking can be highly advantageous. Although initially expensive, networking can save money on both hardware and software and can greatly increase access to both. In addition, networking can be highly motivating to both teachers and students. Some networks permit users to interact with each other, sometimes over long distances, and this can be interesting and rewarding. In addition, as new, better, and more economical databases become available, networking can greatly increase the breadth of experiences for teachers and students, especially those in rural settings.

COMPUTERS AND PROBLEM SOLVING

Educators have long been concerned about finding strategies to teach problem-solving skills. There has been a recent resurgence of interest in this topic, perhaps as a result of widespread criticism about the effects of modern schooling. Many select panels have criticized American education on the grounds that students are not learning thinking skills, critical thinking skills, or problem-solving skills.

Perhaps because of these developments, a rapidly growing body of commercial software purports to teach problem-solving skills. We will deal more fully with such software in Chapter 13. However, we believe a few words of explanation are necessary at this point.

To understand the issues involved in attempting to teach problem-solving skills, we must look at some research results. Psychologists and others have conducted many studies in their search for general problem-solving skills and methods to teach these skills. Unfortunately, the search for teachable, general, automatically transferable problem-solving skills has not been highly successful. Researchers have found that problem solving is relatively domain specific. That is, when children learn problem-solving skills in history, these skills do not automatically transfer and become available when students think about problems in physics.

Fortunately, however, there is some preliminary evidence that the teacher can do things that will increase the probability of transfer. For now, suffice it to say that teachers who choose problem-solving software should do so because they believe the problem-solving strategies taught are useful for their own sake, not because it is hoped the skills will transfer to other domains.

A specific example may be helpful at this point. There is a very popular series of problem-solving software called the Carmen San Diego series (Where in the World Is Carmen San Diego, Where in the U.S.A. Is Carmen San Diego, and others). This software is a simulation of detective work to apprehend a criminal. The user is given a series of clues about the whereabouts and identity of the criminal. In one of these packages, the user must use a world almanac to help solve geography problems to identify and locate the criminal. If such problem-solving skills in geography are deemed important, purchase of this software makes sense. Teachers should not assume that they can purchase this software, turn students loose to interact with it as they choose, and thus achieve improvement in student problem-solving skills in all subject areas.

SUMMARY

In this chapter, we have presented some of the major controversial issues in educational computing. Specifically, we have addressed computer literacy, equity, ethics, labs versus curriculum integration, networking, and teaching problem solving.

In the past, there has been a debate about whether or not computer literacy skills should be taught to all students and whether or not these skills should include programming. We reviewed two frequently heard arguments for teaching literacy: the vocational argument and the national economic imperative argument. Both arguments appear to be flawed.

Although most educators now agree that education should include computer literacy in some form, there is still little agreement about exactly what computer literacy is. Recently, however, the notion has been broadened to include both computer knowledge and computer skills. In addition, there now appears to be more emphasis on teaching tool applications, such as word processing, spreadsheets, and database management, and less on teaching programming.

Computer equity is a concern because of the lack of equal access to educational computing. This has led to fears that computing could actually widen the gap between rich and poor, male and female, nonhandicapped and handicapped, haves and have-nots. Equity problems have arisen because of the way education is funded and because of stereotypic thinking about who should be learning about computers. Real solutions to this problem will await a national reform in educational funding, as well as important changes in national attitudes.

The problem of ethics arises naturally as a result of access to new behaviors through advances in technology. We have discussed ethical problems related to violation of copyright law, invasion of privacy, unethical entrepreneurship by computer educators, and lack of equitable access to computing.

Another problem is the contention by some experts that the time is ripe for curriculum integration. We have concluded that, although integration should be a goal for the future, the time is not yet ripe for such a move. More computers are needed and teachers need more and better computing preservice and inservice education before integration will become feasible.

Networking has become a popular alternative in some schools. The advantages and disadvantages were discussed. Problems are due to increasing the complexity of the computing environment and include restrictions in the number of software packages available, dealing with maintenance and security issues, and the danger that educational decisions will be turned over to noneducators. Advantages include the fact that networks can be highly motivating for both teachers and students and that rural students and others may gain access to experiences not available through traditional educational media. Another problem discussed was instruction in problem solving.

LOOKING AHEAD

This concludes Part One, the introductory portion of this textbook. The first four chapters of the text should have given you an overview of the field of educational computing, including information on (1) how educational change is aided or hampered by events in the culture at large, (2) the current and past roles of computing in education and in the larger culture, (3) the immense importance of software, (4) a classification system for software that provides a conceptual framework for making value judgments about various educational applications, (5) the history of computing, (6) the basics of computer hardware, and (7) issues and trends in computer education.

Part Two of the text begins the more specific material to be learned. This section includes three chapters that will familiarize you with various subcategories of Type I applications. Chapter 5 begins by examining the most common educational computing applications: those involving drill and practice and tutorial uses of computers.

SOME QUESTIONS TO CONSIDER

1. Do you think computer literacy should be taught to all students? Why or why not? Explain what you think should be included.
2. What could be done to encourage more girls to be computer enthusiasts?
3. Do you think it will ever be possible to do away with computer labs in favor of computer integration? Why or why not?

RELATED ACTIVITIES

1. Find a copy of one of the many critical commission reports on education (such as *A Nation at Risk*). Find the recommendations relating to computer education. Do you agree with the rationale for these recommendations or with the recommendations themselves? Why or why not?
2. Interview three people who work with a computer on their desks. Ask them questions designed to determine whether or not other people in their workplace tend to violate their privacy by reading what is displayed on their computer screens.
3. Interview 10 people who are not students in the College of Education. Ask them questions about some of the issues covered in this chapter. (For example, you might ask if they believe that children should be taught how to program computers because they will need such skills in future jobs.)

REFERENCES

Anderson, R. E., Klassen, D. L., & Johnson, D. C. (1981, December). In defense of a comprehensive view of computer literacy: A reply to Luehrmann. *Mathematics Teacher, 74,* 686–688.

Bear, G. G. (1986). Teaching computer ethics: Why, what, who, when, and how. *Computers in the Schools, 3*(2), 113–118.

Bitter, G. (1987). Planning a computer education curriculum. In R. E. Bennett (ed.), *Planning and evaluating computer education programs,* pp. 79–93. Columbus, OH: Merrill.

Bramble, W. J., & Mason, E. J. (1985). *Computers in schools.* New York: McGraw-Hill.

Eltoft, D. (1989). *Specification of computer systems by objectives.* Academic Computing, *3*(6), 20–23, 48–51.

Harris, T. D. (1985). Cautions about copying. *Learning, 13,* 10.

Hoelscher, K. (1986). Computing and information: Steering student learning. In H. F. Olds (ed.), *The computer as an educational tool.* New York: Haworth Press.

Kelman, P. (1984). Computer literacy: A critical reexamination. *Computers in the Schools, 1*(2), 3–18.

Kinzer, C. K., Sherwood, R. D., & Bransford, J. D. (1986). *Computer strategies for education.* Columbus, OH: Merrill.

Lillie, D. L., Wallace, H. H., & Stuck, G. B. (1989). *Computers and effective instruction.* New York: Longman, Inc.

Luehrmann, A. (1981). Computer literacy—What should it be? *Mathematics Teacher, 74*(9), 682–686.

Maddux, C. D., & Cummings, R. W. (1987a, February). Equity for the mildly handicapped. *Computing Teacher,* pp. 16–17, 49.

_____ &_____ . (1987b). Educational computing: A new look at the problem of ethics. *Educational Technology, 27*(11), 31–32.

Mandell, C. J., & Mandell, S. L. (1989). *Computers in education today.* St. Paul, MN: West Publishing.

Molnar, A. R. (1978). The next great crisis in American education: Computer literacy. *AEDS Journal, 12,* 11–20.

Moursand, D. (1983). Computer literacy: Talking and doing. *Computing Teacher, 10*(8), 3–4.

National Commission on Excellence in Education (1983). *A nation at risk: The imperative for educational reform.* Washington, DC: U.S. Government Printing Office.

Office of Technology Assessment (1988). Power on! New tools for teaching and learning (Publication No. 052-003-01125-5). Washington DC: U.S. Government Printing Office.

Riedesel, C. A., & Clements, D. H. (1985). *Coping with computers in the elementary and middle schools.* Englewood Cliffs, NJ: Prentice Hall.

Tinker, R. (1984). What is computer literacy? *Hands On! Newsletter of the Technical Education Research Center, 7*(1), 2.

Turkle, S. (1984). *The second self: Computers and the human spirit.* New York: Simon & Schuster.

Vockell, E., & Schwartz, E. (1988). *The computer in the classroom.* Santa Cruz, CA: Mitchell Publishing.

Watt, D. H. (1981). Computer literacy: What should schools be doing about it. In J. L. Thomas (ed.), *Microcomputers in the Schools.* Phoenix, AZ: Orax Press.

PART TWO

Specific Type I Educational Applications

IN PART TWO WE we discuss the different kinds of Type I educational computing applications. You will recall that Type I applications make it quicker, easier, or otherwise more convenient to use the kinds of teaching methods that we have always used. (Type II applications make available new and better ways of teaching.)

Throughout this book, we have emphasized that there is nothing wrong with using good Type I software. In fact, we have suggested that teachers should acquire and use such software. Even though we obviously rate Type II software as more valuable than Type I software, we believe that both types are worthwhile.

Chapter 5 discusses drill and practice, tutorial and assessment uses. In that chapter, we present some of the research findings about such uses and attempt to differentiate between appropriate and inappropriate implementations.

Chapter 6 includes computer managed instruction (CMI) and tele-communications. We are sometimes asked why we view telecommunications as a Type I application. As you will see, telecommunications has great educational potential, and, like most applications, we believe it could be made into either a Type I or Type II use. However, due to many problems that will be discussed in Chapter 6 (expense, complexity, access to classroom telephone lines, lack of standardization of technical specifications, limited numbers of high-quality data bases), we believe that the potential of telecommunications has gone largely untapped and it is today primarily a Type I application. However, it is quite possible that this application will become one of the most valuable Type II applications in future years. We will class it as a Type II application when and if it makes available new and better teaching methods.

Part Two concludes with Chapter 7, which deals with the administrative uses of computers. Although such uses can be highly productive and may release teachers and others to spend more time and effort on Type II teaching, we class administrative uses as Type I since they deal primarily with mechanical tasks and are not usually involved in direct instructional services.

5

Drill and Practice, Tutorial, and Assessment Uses

GOALS AND OBJECTIVES

Goal: To understand the differences among drill and practice, tutorial, and assessment applications of computers, to be aware of what research says about their use, and to be aware of the advantages and disadvantages of their use in schools.

When you finish studying this chapter, you will be able to:

1. Write a passage discussing some of the reasons why programmed instruction and teaching machines failed to remain popular in education. Include a discussion of how Sputnik I contributed to this failure.
2. Write a paragraph summarizing the research on drill and practice and tutorial computer applications in education.
3. Compare and contrast structured and unstructured problems and explain why expert systems are less successful in solving unstructured problems.

KEY TERMS

affective qualities
artificial intelligence

behaviorism
branching programs

chunking
cognitivism
computerized scoring
drill and practice
electronic spreadsheet
expert system
individual education
program (IEP)
linear programs
meta-analysis
programmed instruction

PLATO Project
reinforcement
Stanford Project
structured
problems
task analysis
teaching machines
tutorial programs
unstructured
problems

This chapter is devoted to some very common and popular educational applications of computers. Drill and practice and tutorial applications have their historical roots in the early work on **teaching machines** and **programmed instruction**. We will, therefore, begin our discussion by presenting a brief history of these innovations. It is hoped that this history will help teachers and other computing advocates to become aware of and avoid the errors made by advocates of this unsuccessful technology. We will also briefly review research investigating the efficacy (efficiency) of drill and practice and tutorial computer programs. We will then consider *assessment applications*. The chapter will first review different ways that computers are currently being used in assessment and then provide our rationale for determining whether current and future applications are appropriate or inappropriate.

A BRIEF HISTORY OF TEACHING MACHINES AND PROGRAMMED INSTRUCTION

The decade of the 1980s has not been the first period of interest in educational computing. During the late 1950s through the early 1970s, a great deal of effort and enthusiasm were devoted to bringing computing and other machine instruction into schools.

This early activity had its roots in the work of Sidney Pressey (1926, 1927). Pressey noted that objective tests were becoming common in schools. He believed that teachers would soon be unable to cope with the logistics of administering and scoring such tests. Therefore, in the 1920s he began experimenting with a machine to administer multiple-choice items (Travers, 1967).

At first, Pressey concentrated on developing the testing and scoring capability of his machine. However, he soon recognized its potential for teaching as well. He then began requiring the user to work through the test a number of times, each time attempting to complete it with fewer errors.

Although Pressey's device generated some interest, it was never widely used. More than 30 years later, however, educators again became interested in the potential of machines. B. F. Skinner, the well-known psychologist, was responsible for this renewed interest. (Skinner is a highly respected Harvard psychologist who extended the work of Edward L. Thorndike. Through his research on the effects of **reinforcement** (usually rewards) on learning, Skinner was instrumental in popularizing a behavioristic approach to teaching and learning. In this approach, actual behaviors are the focus of concern, rather than emotions, thoughts, or other hypothetical constructs.)

Two articles by Skinner stimulated interest in teaching machines (Skinner, 1954, 1958). Unlike Pressey, he required that the machines permit the user to compose an answer, rather than simply choose from a list of alternatives. Also, the machine had to ensure that the learner proceeded through a series of steps in a carefully prescribed order. Each step had to be so small that everyone would be successful, yet each step had to lead closer and closer to the target behavior. (The process of analyzing content and breaking it down into a series of small, discrete steps is called **task analysis**.)

Skinner's machine presented the questions in 30 radial frames on a 12-inch disk. He called the material in the frames the program. Programs that led each user through the same material in the same sequence were referred to as **linear programs**.

Norman Crowder (1959) endorsed Skinner's ideas, but did not agree that every learner should progress through each lesson in the same sequence as every other learner. Crowder's programs varied the sequence of frames, presenting certain frames to some learners while omitting them for others, depending on learner responses. Such programs were called **branching programs**.

Skinner believed that the machine had effects on students similar to the effects of a good private tutor. He believed the machines should (1) stimulate constant interaction between the program and the user, (2) require mastery of each concept or lesson before moving on to the next concept or lesson, (3) present material in small steps, (4) provide prompting, and (5) provide reinforcement (rewards) for each successful step (Skinner, 1958).

It is interesting that these five criteria are still important components in developing modern educational computing programs. However, most experts recommend branching, rather than linear programs, as they do a better job of allowing for individual differences (Rutkaus, 1987).

Although Skinner's work on teaching machines stimulated a great deal of interest and a large body of research, the devices were never widely adopted by educators. However, this work did lead to programmed instruction, an innovation that enjoyed more widespread popularity in education. This term refers to books or workbooks that make use of the principles employed by Skinner in his work with teaching machines (especially task analysis and reinforcement for correct responses).

Many such books and workbooks were published, primarily in the 1960s and 1970s, for use in colleges or public schools. For example, Skinner and a colleague wrote a programmed textbook on analyzing behavior (Holland & Skinner, 1961). Materials for public schools include *The Fitzhugh Plus Program* (Allied Education Council, 1965), the *Sullivan Programmed Materials* (McGraw-Hill, 1965), and *Programmed Reading* (Globe Book Co., 1970).

Osguthorpe and Zhou (1989) have discussed the popularity of this approach during the 1950s and 1960s, but added that programmed instruction "died a rather quick death" (p. 7). Similarly, Gayeski (1989) sums up the history of this technology:

> *Based on aspects of behaviorist psychology, educators embraced programmed instruction enthusiastically during the 1960s. . . . Although this technology too proved itself effective and efficient through both research and field trials, one would be hard-pressed to find a "teaching machine" today. (p. 9)*

There is an important point about teaching machines and programmed textbooks and workbooks. These devices functioned as intended and research showed they were effective (Hilgard & Bower, 1966; Stolurow, 1961; Travers, 1969). Why, then, did they fail to gain wide and lasting acceptance?

Answering this question is important, since the reasons for the failure of this innovation may provide helpful information for those who are working toward the success of educational computing. Certainly, it is vital for educational computing advocates to realize that, historically, the effectiveness of an innovation such as programmed instruction has been no guarantee of acceptance (Slavin, 1989).

Skinner (1986) has recently expressed his opinions about why programmed instruction and/or teaching machines never "caught on":

> *The machines were crude, the programs were untested, and there were no ready standards of comparison. Teaching machines would have cost money that was not budgeted. Teachers misunderstood the role of the machines and were fearful of losing their jobs. (p. 105)*

Criswell (1989) mentions these problems and adds that (1) teachers feared the machines would impart instruction in an undesirable, mechanistic fashion, and (2) a boring, repetitive format was used.

Reiser (1987) suggests that programmed instruction was abandoned because (1) it was shown to be no more effective than traditional teaching, (2) programmed material was boring for students, and (3) educators did not know how to incorporate programmed techniques into their individual teaching styles.

Tillman and Glynn (1987) assert that programmed instruction failed to achieve educational popularity because many programmers adhered too rigidly to the formal behavioral principles outlined by Skinner. This rigidity resulted in overuse of tedious linear programs and neglect of more interesting branching programs. Consequently, most programs were boring and unimaginative and focused on deductive rather than inductive thinking.

In recent years, Skinner (1986) has acknowledged the validity of many of the reasons discussed so far for the failure of teaching machines and programmed learning. In addition, he suggests that the success of the USSR in placing the first satellite in orbit in the late 1950s contributed to that failure by sparking a rejection of behaviorism and a resurgence of cognitivism in American education:

> *Americans were stunned. How could the Russians have beaten us into outer space? Something must be wrong with American education. Congress quickly passed the National Defense Education Act. Students were no longer to be told things; they were to discover things for themselves. They were not to memorize, but to think, grasp concepts, explore, be creative. The cognitive movement that followed Sputnik I seemed to legitimize traditional theories of teaching and learning. (Skinner, 1986, pp. 105–106)*

By the early 1960s, there was a strong and articulate backlash of professional opinion against the use of teaching machines and programmed learning. A widely quoted and highly influential, classic article by Fitzgerald (1970) is illustrative of that backlash. This article began with a list of the advantages claimed for teaching machines. These included (1) saving money for teachers' salaries by making it possible for each teacher to supervise many more students, (2) reducing discipline problems and cheating by having each student work in a separate booth, (3) reducing aversive practices of teachers since machines are patient and nonjudgmental, (4) providing an opportunity for home study, (5) increasing student attention by providing immediate feedback of results, (6) exposing students to the nation's best teachers through written programs, (7) providing uniformity of instruction and grading, and (8) providing a rationale for increasing teaching salaries by increasing teaching productivity.

After listing these claimed advantages, Fitzgerald (1970) went on to assert that most of these claims were not valid. In addition, all advantages were overshadowed by an overriding disadvantage—that of rigidity. A specific problem caused by this rigidity was difficulty in skimming, or browsing through text, or returning briefly to an earlier chapter.

Fitzgerald (1970) also suggested that teaching machines and programmed instruction would lead to authoritarian thinking and dehumanization due to overreliance on machines. His objections did a good job of summing up past objections to teaching machines and programmed instruction, as well as the often heard present objections to computer education:

> *Teaching machines are admittedly based on the theory of reinforcement, of rote learning, of stimulus–response, of a mechanical one question--one answer. This is an intrinsically undemocratic—worse, an anti-intellectual—theory of learning. The next step should be to strengthen "rapid and frequent reinforcement" by, let us say, a mild electric shock. . . . We spend entirely too much time with machines these days. The most prominent example is watching television as a passive substitute for an active, emotional life with real people, but other examples come to mind. . . . I find the thought of millions of children spending hours each day with millions of machines in millions of separate cubicles an appalling prospect. (pp. 486–487)*

Programmed Instruction, Teaching Machines, and Computers

We have devoted considerable space to the history of programmed instruction and teaching machines. We have done this because there are lessons to be learned that are relevant to computer education. This is especially true in the area of drill and practice, tutorial, and assessment applications. As a matter of fact, the same behavioral theory that formed the basis for teaching machines and programmed instruction is now being used as the basis for many drill and practice, tutorial, and assessment applications for microcomputers (Criswell, 1989; Rutkaus, 1987; Tillman and Glynn, 1987). Indeed, Skinner (1986) suggested that the microcomputer is the ideal medium for bringing programmed instruction into the public school! He even suggested that when computers are used in this fashion they should be referred to as teaching machines (Skinner, 1986, p. 110).

Our concern is this: since programmed instruction and teaching machines serve as the underlying models for many drill and practice, tutorial, and assessment computing applications, we must take care to avoid failure that could occur for the same reasons that programmed instruction and teaching machines failed. In looking back over the last few pages and our review of the reasons for the failure of programmed instruction and teaching machines, it is startling how these problems could also be said to apply to computer drill and practice, tutorial, and assessment applications.

After eliminating duplications, the problems identified by the various authorities we have reviewed in this chapter are as follows:

1. Teaching machines were crude.
2. Teaching machines were expensive.
3. Many of the programs they used were untested.
4. Many of the programs were boring and repetitive.
5. Teachers were not sufficiently trained.
6. Research showed that teaching machines and programmed instruction were no more effective than traditional teaching techniques.
7. Teachers feared they would no longer be needed and would lose their jobs.
8. Machines and programmed instruction were viewed as mechanistic and dehumanizing.
9. Fear that the United States was falling behind in science and engineering sparked a resurgence of cognitivism—an educational stance that was not consistent with the behavioral theory underlying teaching machines and programmed instruction.

It is ironic that now, almost 20 years after the programmed instruction movement, all these problems have been cited as problems in computer education:

1. Computers that were state of the art a few years ago are crude by today's standards, and today's machines will undoubtedly appear crude by the standards of the future.
2. Although computers are becoming less expensive, they will continue to require a substantial investment.
3. Most educational software has not been subjected to research, and software houses seem uninterested in testing the efficacy of their products.
4. Software has been criticized because much of it is boring and repetitive. If overused, such software causes students to become as hostile as does overreliance on boring and repetitive worksheets.
5. Nearly every study has revealed that teacher training is a major problem in computer education.
6. Very little quality research has been done, but it appears that, although computers are effective learning tools, they are no more effective in the areas of drill and practice, tutorial, and assessment applications, than are traditional techniques.
7. Some teachers fear replacement by computers, even though most experts emphasize that computers can only supplement and never replace teachers.

8. The charge that computers will dehumanize teaching has been made. Research shows that computers can either stimulate or retard human interaction, depending on how they are implemented by teachers.

9. Finally, the mood in the United States is currently similar to that immediately following Sputnik I. Many Americans are shocked and frightened by the decline of American military, industrial, and economic superiority. A number of national reports condemning education have been published, and many authorities are calling for renewed emphasis on critical and creative thinking.

Again, we have nothing against Type I computer applications such as drill and practice, tutorial, and assessment uses. But we do not believe that these applications can, by themselves, ensure the success of computer education. We must, therefore, resist the temptation to turn computers solely into 1950s-style teaching machines. On the other hand, as long as we provide a number of Type II applications, there is no reason why computers cannot be used sparingly in the areas of drill and practice, tutorials, and assessment.

Drill and Practice and Tutorial Applications

Drill and practice programs are used to provide repetitive exercises over rote skills that have been taught some other way. **Tutorial programs** attempt to teach new material. Hannafin and Peck (1988) describe drill and practice programs as follows:

> *Drill and practice designs provide practice for defined skills, immediate feedback to the student for each response given, and usually some form of correction or remediation for incorrect responses. (p. 144)*

From this description, it is clear that the theoretical base for most drill and practice programs is that of **behaviorism**. This has probably occurred because of the popularity of Skinnerian behaviorism and its application in early teaching machines and programmed textbooks. Then, too, behaviorism, with its focus on observable, measurable behavior, has produced a simple, well- defined, easily verified methodology that enjoys near-universal acceptance among behaviorists. **Cognitivism**, on the other hand, with its emphasis on hypothetical mental processes that are not directly observable, has produced a number of orientations with highly complex, varying methodologies. Empirical verification of the tenets of cognitivism is necessarily more complicated than in the case of behaviorism, which solves the problem of how to observe and measure hypothetical constructs by denying their existence or their scientific relevance.

Actually, there is no reason why drill and practice software based on cognitive psychology could not be written. In fact, Criswell (1989) suggests that either structural (cognitive) or functional (behavioral) principles can underlie drill and practice software. She suggests that software making use of cognitive principles would emphasize mental activities, including pattern recognition, short- and long-term memory, motivation, selective perception, encoding, and retrieval.

Criswell goes on to suggest that memory is the psychological concept most important to cognitivists interested in instructional design. Thus, cognitive software designed to increase memory would emphasize (1) paying attention to input, (2) rehearsal, and (3) **chunking**. Chunking is defined as organizing material to be learned into "coined phrases, acronyms, mental images or mental pictures, invented stories, and rhymes" (Criswell, 1989, p. 35).

A number of other authorities have paid lip service to developing drill and practice and tutorial software that makes use of cognitive principles (for example, Burke, 1982; MacLachlan, 1986; Wilkinson, 1983.) However, most existing drill and practice software relies on behavioral principles.

Early Computer Education Efforts

Although the history of computer-assisted instruction can be traced to Pressey's work on teaching machines, interest in the use of actual computers in education began in the 1960s. A number of experimental projects began at that time. The **PLATO** and **Stanford** projects were two of these especially ambitious and influential efforts.

PLATO stands for Programmed Logic for Automatic Teaching Operations; it was developed during the early 1960s. It has been called "the largest CAI system ever developed" (Burke, 1982, p. 19). The system was installed on a number of university campuses and a few public schools made use of PLATO by installing workstations connected to local university mainframe computers.

The Stanford Project was begun through support by the Carnegie Foundation and targeted the development of computer delivery systems for math and reading (Bullough & Beatty, (1987). The system was intended to employ three levels, including drill and practice, tutorials, and a third, questioning level. The questioning technique was intended to allow students to ask questions of the computer, using their own words. The drill and practice and tutorial levels were quite successful, but the questioning technique was never perfected. Then, as now, it was an elusive goal to program a computer so that it could respond sensibly to children's English language questions that vary widely in spelling, vocabulary, and grammatical structure.

Although these projects generated a great deal of excitement and inspired scores of journal articles, their use never became widespread. Bramble and Mason (1985) sum up the difficulties with these early efforts:

The machines available for CAI were simply too cumbersome, too limited, or too expensive--or all three. Further, educators were just beginning to learn about CAI and often did not make optimal, or even appropriate, use of it. Finally, there was diminishing federal support for educational research and development. The result was a decline in CAI in public education by the mid-1970s. (p. 17)

What Research Says about Computer Learning

The Office of Technology Assessment (1988) has reviewed the literature and concluded that several findings have consistently emerged:

1. Elementary students subjected to brief, daily computer lessons as a supplement to traditional instruction make gains equivalent to 1 to 8 months of instruction over students who are instructed only with traditional, noncomputer methods.
2. Research investigating whether drill and practice and tutorial instruction alone is superior to traditional instruction alone does not consistently favor either one.
3. Computer instruction appears to be best for use with low- achieving students.
4. Drill and practice and tutorial applications seems to result in students completing material faster than with traditional methods.
5. Student attention, motivation, and attention span can be improved by the proper use of computers.
6. Material learned through computing is retained as well as material learned traditionally.
7. The above findings generally hold up at the high school or college level, but achievement gains at those levels are less significant.

Riedesel and Clements (1985) have also reviewed the research on the use of drill and practice and tutorial computer programs and concluded:

1. Such uses are as good or better than traditional instruction.
2. Children at all age levels learn effectively regardless of type of computer or software used.
3. Drill and practice and tutorial programs result in faster learning than traditional teaching.
4. Drill and practice and tutorial programs result in more positive attitudes toward learning than does traditional instruction.
5. Tutorials seem to work better for low-level students than for middle- or high-ability students.
6. If teachers have positive attitudes toward computer learning, the computer applications tend to be more effective.

7. Foreign language and science are particularly well suited for student gains as a result of CAI.
8. Drill and practice is especially good for use as a tool for reviewing material.
9. Computer learning is expensive, but is becoming less so.

One of the most recent and helpful analyses of research is by Roblyer, Castine, & King (1988). These authors analyzed over 80 studies. They used **meta-analysis** to summarize the findings of the studies. (Meta-analysis is a technique in which the reviewer examines the result of a large number of studies focusing on similar questions. Readers who are interested in meta-analysis are encouraged to read a critical Slavin article [1987] as well as supportive material by others such as Glass [1977].) We find this meta-analysis to be particularly persuasive, since the reviewers took pains to avoid the common mistakes of many meta-analyzers.

Roblyer, Castine, and King (1988) concluded:

1. Attitudes toward school and subject matter are improved by the use of computers.
2. Improving student self-image or self-confidence is seldom studied. Only three studies were found, with positive results for the computer groups.
3. Computers are more effective for teaching mathematics than for reading or language skills.
4. Computers are effective in teaching science, especially when science simulations are employed.
5. In math, all types of computer instruction seem equally effective, while tutorial programs are most effective in reading. Drill and practice may be most effective with lower-level skills, while tutorials are most effective with higher-level skills, such as comprehension.
6. Computer applications can be as effective at college and adult levels as at elementary levels.
7. Computers may be most effective for lower-achieving students.
8. There is no gender difference in effectiveness of computer applications.
9. For Spanish-speaking students, computers may not be as effective as other strategies.

Assessment Applications

Whoever coined the phrase "There is no such thing as a free lunch" might have been speaking of educational computing. With advantage comes potential disadvantage. We suspect this is true of education in general; perhaps it is true of life itself.

Although computers hold great potential for improving the assessment process, they also contain the seeds of abuse. We believe that educators have not devoted enough time to the question of what kinds of educational tasks computers ought to be used for (and conversely, what tasks they ought not be used for). In addition, in Chapter 2 we emphasized that streamlining a technique by introducing computers may make the technique faster, more accurate, or more convenient, but does not necessarily otherwise improve the technique.

An example involves astrology. Computer programs exist that can cast horoscopes much more quickly and accurately than can human astrologers. But speeding up the process and improving the accuracy in no way establishes or improves the validity of astrology itself. Weizenbaum (1976) has made the point that "If astrology is nonsense, then computerized astrology is just as surely nonsense" (pp. 34–35).

Unfortunately, there seems to be a tendency to assume that computerizing an activity actually improves the underlying idea on which the activity is based. A businessman who converts his accounting to **electronic spreadsheet** (a computer program for handling numbers or accounting) may assume that he has improved the way he keeps track of money. However, unless he changes the techniques themselves, his accounting system is unchanged (although it may indeed work faster).

In education, we must not assume that assessment is improved merely by moving existing assessment tasks to computer implementation. If the idea of assessing visual closure skills is not a good one, then doing so with the help of computers may merely speed up implementation of a poor idea.

How Computers Are Used in Assessment

Computers can be used in assessment in a number of ways. These include (1) calculation of test scores, (2) storage of assessment results, (3) administration of test items, (4) production of assessment reports, and (5) computerized scoring of tests. Of these five, we believe the first two are appropriate, while the other three are questionable.

Calculation of Test Scores

Items 1 and 5 above differ in that calculation of test scores refers to summing of the number of correct items or performing other arithmetic manipulations, while **computerized scoring** involves the determination of correctness. The calculation of test scores is an ideal task for computers. Such tasks involve rote manipulations that humans find tedious and that are error-prone. Computers are more accurate than human beings when performing tasks such as converting a child's birthdate to a chronological age, locating a score in a table by finding the spot where a given row and column of numbers intersect, calculating the standard error of measurement (the average amount of error in a test), graphing scores, or doing other mechanical transformations of data.

Computers can and should be used to perform these tasks. However, care should be taken to ensure that such computer programs are correctly written so that they produce accurate results. A number of commercial programs of this type contain errors in the formulas used. For this reason, consumers should field test software on simulated data before putting it into the assessment process. Users should be cautioned not to accept results blindly, and to compare the computer-generated figures to their own estimates based on experience and common sense.

Storage of Assessment Results

Another appropriate use of the computer is to store assessment results. Our only concern about this application concerns security and confidentiality. When traditional data are kept, security measures are well established. File cabinets are locked and keys are issued only to authorized users. A record is kept of everyone who sees the data.

In theory, security for computer data is no more difficult to maintain. However, computers are newcomers in education, and security practices are not well understood. Floppy diskettes containing assessment data should be locked away. If the data are stored on a hard disk drive (a nonremovable memory device), care must be taken to ensure that unauthorized users cannot access confidential data.

We do not recommend that assessment data be placed on file servers (external memory devices connected to a number of machines), since it will be difficult to maintain security. (There are commercial security systems for use with hard disk drives and file servers, but no system is foolproof.) If servers or hard disk drives are used, we recommend that names be coded and the key to the code be stored in a different location.

Another security problem is related to popular attitudes about data displayed on a computer screen. Many people behave as if such data are public. Assessment personnel should develop the habit of turning off computer monitors before taking a break or leaving the immediate vicinity. Upon returning, the monitor can be switched back on with no disruption of whatever program is running.

Administration of Test Items

There should be few problems in programming computers to administer objective test items. However, when this is done, tests must be restandardized. Reliability and validity studies must be redone, and previous studies carried out with paper and pencil versions must not be assumed to be representative of computer versions. The effects of variables such as type of keyboard, keyboard skills, and the use of color versus monochrome screens must be investigated. Until such studies are

done, even well-established tests such as the WISC-R must be regarded
as experimental, and the results of computer administration must be
considered suspect. Other problems include how, when, or whether subjects are allowed to change answers, deciding whether a proctor must be
present, and protecting the software from unauthorized use. Other psychometric problems are discussed by Sarvela and Noonan (1988).

Production of Assessment Reports

We believe that computers are appropriate for use in writing reports only
if restricted to mechanical production. For example, word processing can
be a great aid for report writers. Word-processing templates (electronic
blank forms) can be produced in the format a school district prefers, and
the report writer then fills in the blanks, the size of which is controlled by
the user.

The inappropriate use of computers occurs when they are given the
task of interpreting data, because interpretation requires subjectivity,
often called clinical judgment or professional expertise. The development
of expertise seems to emerge from a combination of wide experience;
native intelligence; common sense, intuition, factual knowledge, and
human **affective qualities** such as compassion or empathy. The problem
is that computers are not now, nor are they likely to ever be, capable of
acquiring these characteristics. Human affective qualities (attitudes and
emotions) are unavailable to computers since they require human experiences in their formation. The same is true of human intelligence in
general.

There are those who disagree, however. Some experts believe in the
potential to endow a computer program with human expertise. Hardware
and software intended to accomplish this feat are referred to as an **expert
system**. The goal of producing expert systems is part of a more general
effort known as **artificial intelligence** (AI). Although research into AI
is continuing, AI is far from fulfilling the lofty goals originally set for it.

Dreyfus and Dreyfus (1988), have referred to artificial intelligence
in general, and expert systems in particular, as one of the great commercial
disappointments of our time. They maintain that no one has yet succeeded
in writing a computer program that comes close to emulating the best
and most complex human expertise and that many firms dedicated to
doing so have given up the effort.

The question of why expert systems are unsuccessful is interesting.
Weizenbaum (1976) predicted the failure of artificial intelligence on the
grounds that intelligence is exclusively the product of human experience:

> *I have argued that the individual human being, like any other or-
> ganism, is defined by the problems he confronts. The human is unique
> by virtue of the fact that he must necessarily confront problems that*

arise from his unique biological and emotional needs. . . . No other organism, and certainly no computer, can be made to confront genuine human problems in human terms. (p. 223)

Dreyfus and Dreyfus (1988) focus on the type and complexity of human problems. They assert that the limited successes of expert systems have occurred with only the simplest of problems. They suggest that human expertise is applied to two kinds of problems: (1) **structured**, and (2) **unstructured problems**. Structured problems are least common and call for step by step, sequential, if–then solutions. About these problems, they say, "Here the goal and what information is relevant are clear, the effects of decisions are known, and verifiable solutions can be reasoned out" (p. 20).

There has been some success in developing expert systems for structured problems. Examples include mathematical manipulations, puzzles, delivery truck routing, and petroleum blending. Dreyfus and Dreyfus cite an expert system named AALPS that is used to determine the placement of objects in cargo planes and does this work in minutes, rather than the hours consumed by human experts.

Unfortunately, however, most important human problems are unstructured. Such problems contain "a potentially unlimited number of possibly relevant facts and features, and the ways those elements interrelate and determine other events is unclear" (p. 20). Such professional problem areas include management, nursing, economic forecasting, teaching and all social interactions.

Dreyfus and Dreyfus (1988) go on to present examples of unstructured problems in everyday life, including recognition of a human face or a particular dog's bark, identification of a faint odor, determining socially acceptable behavior, and even walking or riding a bicycle. In other words, all problems are unstructured if it is not feasible to solve them by developing a specific, finite set of if—then rules.

Most assessment problems are clearly unstructured. Therefore, expert systems are not likely to present useful solutions. However, there are currently many commercial programs designed to generate **IEPs (individual educational programs)** for special education students. These programs call for typing in test data and other information. The program then analyzes the data and presents an interpretation. Some of these programs cost thousands of dollars and produce a diagnosis, long-term objectives, short-term objectives, teaching methods, and other IEP requirements. White (1984) has described 10 such programs, and Brown (1986) presented one district's experiences and difficulties in implementing one such system.

We find these programs to be inappropriate. At best, they present a simplistic, if–then solution to unstructured problems. At worst, they undermine the spirit and letter of PL 94-142, the law that mandates that IEPs be produced by a multidisciplinary team (including parents) during a problem-solving meeting.

Computerized Scoring of Tests

So-called objective tests have been scored by computer for many years. Such scoring of multiple choice, true–false, and matching items presents few, if any, difficulties. (One problem is that the complicated computer sheets can be confusing.) Our objection to computerized scoring, however, is when it usurps expert judgment in determining the correctness of responses. Most test manuals give considerable leeway to experienced examiners in judging correctness. Also, human examiners become expert at sensing when a child is too tired or inattentive to continue or when to probe a response. Such determinations are unstructured problems and unsuited for machine solution.

SUMMARY

Current interest in drill and practice, tutorial, and assessment uses can be traced to the work of Pressey in the 1920s and Skinner in the 1950s. These psychologists developed teaching machines and programmed instruction print materials. Although these materials worked well, they never became popular educational tools. They failed because (1) they were complex, (2) they were expensive, (3) teachers lacked expertise in their use, (4) many lessons were boring and repetitive, (5) educators feared they would be replaced by the new devices, (6) many observers suggested that the use of teaching machines and programmed instruction would dehumanize education, and (7) world events led to a movement away from behaviorism and toward cognitivism. Many of these same criticisms are now being leveled at the use of computers in education.

Many research studies have investigated the effects of drill and practice and tutorial computer programs on learning. A meta-analysis of these studies reveals that most research studies have yielded positive results.

Computers have great potential for use in educational assessment. However, they can be greatly abused in this field. One danger is that assessment personnel may assume that computerizing their activities has improved the ideas behind various assessment strategies or techniques, when computers may have merely speeded up or improved the accuracy of assessment procedures.

In assessment, computers can be used to (1) calculate test scores, (2) store assessment results, (3) administer test items, (4) produce assessment reports, and (5) score tests. We suggest that the first two of these are entirely appropriate, while the final three present potential for abuse.

LOOKING AHEAD

This chapter examined drill and practice, tutorial, and assessment uses of computing. These three applications are among the most common of all Type I educational computing uses. Computers can be helpful in carrying out all three of these teaching activities. However, drill and practice and tutorial uses can be overdone quite easily, while assessment applications should be restricted to mechanical aid and should never replace the exercise of human professional judgment.

Chapter 6 will present two other common Type I applications: (1) computer-managed instruction (CMI) and (2) telecommunications. As you will see, we are highly optimistic about the potential of telecommunications as an educational tool, although we do not think this vast potential has yet been tapped by many educators.

SOME QUESTIONS TO CONSIDER

1. What criticisms of teaching machines and programmed instruction have also been leveled at drill and practice and tutorial computer programs?
2. In your opinion, which of the criticisms identified for question 1 are justified, and which are not?

RELATED ACTIVITIES

1. Interview two public school teachers about why they think teaching machines were failures. Then ask them what they think of the potential of educational computing.
2. Do some reading on the history of artificial intelligence. Then interview three college professors, each in a different discipline, about their perceptions of the future of artificial intelligence in their respective fields.

REFERENCES

Bramble, W. J., & Mason, E. J. (1985). *Computers in schools*. New York: McGraw-Hill.

Brown, K. (1986). IEP's and data management: A case in point. *Computers in the schools, 3*(3/4), 85–90.

Bullough, R. V., & Beatty, L. F. (1987). *Classroom applications of microcomputers*. Columbus, OH: Merrill.

Burke, R. L. (1982). *CAI sourcebook*. Englewood Cliffs, NJ: Prentice Hall.

Criswell, E. L. (1989). *The design of computer-based instruction*. New York: Macmillan.

Crowder, N. A. (1959). Automatic tutoring by means of intrinsic programming. In E. H. Galanter (ed.). Automatic teaching: The state of the art. New York: Wiley, pp. 109–116.

Dreyfus, H. L., & Dreyfus, S. E. (1988). *The power of human intuition and expertise in the era of the computer*. New York: Free Press.

Fitzgerald, H. T. (1970). Teaching machines: A demurrer. In H. F. Clarizio, R. C. Craig, & W. A. Mehrens (eds.). *Contemporary issues in educational psychology*. Boston: Allyn and Bacon, 480–487.

The Fitzhugh plus program. (1965). Galien, MI: Allied Education Council. Gayeski, D. (1989). Why information technologies fail. *Educational Technology, 29*(9), 9–17.

Glass, G. V. (1977). Integrating findings: The meta-analysis of research. In L. Shulman (ed.), *Review of research in education*. Itasca, IL: Peacock Press.

Hannafin, M. J., & Peck, K. L. (1988). *The design, development, and evaluation of instructional software*. New York: MacMillan.

Hilgard, E. R., & Bower, G. H. (1966). *Theories of learning* (3rd ed.). New York: Appleton-Century-Crofts.

Holland, J. G., & Skinner, B. F. (1961). *The analysis of behavior: A program for self-instruction*. New York: McGraw-Hill.

MacLachlan, J. (1986). Psychologically based techniques for improving learning within computerized tutorials. *Journal of Computer-based Instruction, 13*, 65–70.

Office of Technology Assessment (1988). *Power on! New tools for teaching and learning* (Publication No. 052-003-01125-5). Washington DC: U.S. Government Printing Office.

Osguthorpe, R. T., & Zhou, L. (1989). Instructional science: What is it and where did it come from? *Educational Technology, 29*(6), 7–17.

Pressey, S. L. (1926). A simple apparatus which gives tests and scores—and teaches. *School and Society, 23*, 373–376.

_____. (1927). A machine for automatic teaching of drill material. School and Society, 25, 549–552.

Programmed reading. (1970). New York: Globe Book Co.

Riedesel, C. A., & Clements, D. H. (1985). *Coping with computers in the elementary and middle schools*. Englewood Cliffs, NJ: Prentice Hall.

Reiser, R. A. (1987). Instructional technology: A history. In R. M. Gagne (ed.), *Instructional technology: Foundations*, pp. 11–48. Hillsdale, NJ: Lawrence Erlbaum.

Roblyer, M. D., Castine, W. H., & King, F. J. (1988). *Assessing the impact of computer-based instruction: A review of recent research*. New York: Haworth Press.

Rutkaus, M. A. (1987). Remember programmed instruction? *Instructional Technology, 27*(10), 46–49.

Sarvela, P. D., & Noonan, J. V. (1988). Testing and computer-based instruction: Psychometric considerations. *Educational Technology*, *28*(5), 17–20.

Skinner, B. F. (1954). The science of learning and the art of teaching. *Harvard Educational Review*, *24*, 86–97.

_____. (1958). Teaching machines. *Science*, *128*, 969–977.

_____. (1986). Programmed instruction revisited. *Phi Delta Kappan*, *68*(2), 103–110.

Slavin, R. E. (1987). Best-evidence synthesis: Why less is more. *Educational Researcher*, *16*(4), 15–16.

_____. (1989, June). PET and the pendulum: Faddism in education and how to stop it. *Phi Delta Kappan*, pp. 752–758.

Stolurow, L. W. (1961). Teaching by machine. *Cooperative Research Monograph No. 6*. Washington DC.: U.S. Department of Health, Education, and Welfare.

Sullivan programmed materials. (1965). New York: McGraw-Hill.

Tillman, M. H., & Glynn, M. (1987). Writing text that teaches: Historical overview. *Educational Technology*, *27*(10), 41–45.

Travers, R. M. (1967). *Essentials of learning* (2nd ed.). New York: Macmillan.

———. (1969). *An introduction to educational research* (3rd ed.). New York: Macmillan.

Weizenbaum, J. (1976). *Computer power and human reason.* San Francisco: W. H. Freeman.

White, G. T. (1984). Micros for the special ed administrator: How to use a computer to keep up with special ed law. *Electronic Learning*, *3*(5), 39–42.

Wilkinson, A. C. (1983). *Classroom computers and cognitive science.* New York: Academic Press.

6

Computer-Managed Instruction and Telecommunications

GOALS AND OBJECTIVES

Goal: To recognize ways that computers are used as tools to help educators manage instruction and exchange information over long distances.

When you finish studying this chapter, you will be able to:

1. Write a paragraph describing what the term CMI means.
2. Draw a continuum to illustrate different types of 'CMI applications and describe the extremes at both ends of the continuum.
3. Write a paragraph describing some of the concerns discussed relating to the ILS approach.
4. List at least three telecommunications applications that have promise for educational use.
5. Write a paragraph describing three reasons that computer telecommunications remains more of a promise than a viable educational application.

KEY TERMS

computer networking
computer-assisted
   instruction

computer-managed
   instruction
demodulation

downloading
electronic bulletin board
Everest syndrome
hype
individualized instruction
information management
information utilities
Integrated Learning
   System

mastery learning
modem
modulation
module
programmed instruction
Systems Operator (SYSOP)
telecommunications

Two diverse, yet related topics are presented in this chapter. While **computer-managed instruction** (CMI) and **telecommunications** represent two distinct computer applications, they share a number of commonalities as educational tools. Both are vaguely defined topics that suggest quite different applications to different people. Both have been plagued with **hype** (unreasonably optimistic claims) concerning their potential impact on education. Both have definite promise as educational tools. Both need to be examined carefully to determine what they can add to present educational practices. Neither should be viewed as panaceas.

We will treat CMI and telecommunications in two major sections of the chapter. In each section, we define the application, describe some situations where the applications are being used by real people in real educational settings to illustrate how they can be profitably used, and point out some problems and cautions.

COMPUTER-MANAGED INSTRUCTION

Students who are registered in a required educational computing course for all pre-service teachers at the University of Nevada find that the computer plays an important role in helping them learn the knowledge and skills taught in the course. The course is self-paced and emphasizes mastery learning. In the first class period, students learn that future class attendance is optional. They are told that there are three reasons they will want to report to the classroom, which is a computer lab, at the scheduled class time. First, that is the time when the instructor will be available for discussion, consultation, and individual help. Second, that is the time when exams can be taken. Third, that is the only time assignments will be accepted by the instructor.

The course is divided into nine distinct modules. Each **module** requires four steps for completion:

1. A text assignment relating to the topic of the module must be read from the course manual.

2. A hands-on computer assignment relating to the topic of the module must be completed. (Specific step by step instructions for completing the module are contained in the course manual.)

3. A 10-item. multiple-choice exam designed to measure the students' understanding of the reading material and mastery of the hands-on computer work must be passed with at least 80 accuracy. The student may take different versions of the test up to five times in order to achieve the 80% criterion.

4. Various written work relating to both the reading material and the hands-on assignment must be completed, properly labeled, and handed in.

A student may use the lab during any open-lab time throughout the week to complete the hands-on assignment and may return to the lab during the scheduled class time to take the tests and hand in completed work. Once all four steps of a module are completed, the student may move on to another module. The student who wants to earn an A in the course must complete nine modules. Students completing less than nine modules receive lower grades. Once a student has completed nine modules, he or she has completed the course and need not return for the rest of the semester. Some students complete the entire course during the first few weeks of the semester, some finish several weeks before the end of the semester, and some finish just as the semester ends.

In this course, the computer plays an important management role. Students take exams on the computer, and the computer scores the exams, displays results, provides study hints for improvement, records passing grades, and prints out reports of individual student standing at any given point in the semester. The computer does not replace the instructor, but is used as a tool to assist the instructor in the clerical work required to make such a course run smoothly.

The preceding example represents one way that computers are used in instructional management. It is also representative of some of the points we think are important in successful CMI. First, there is no attempt to allow the computer to control the curriculum. Second, the computer is viewed as an organizational tool, not a teaching machine. Third, the computer is used to free the instructor from mundane labor-intensive tasks so that he or she can have more one on one contact with students.

Now that you have an idea of what CMI is, let's take a closer look.

The Roots of CMI

The term *computer-managed instruction* was coined to help distinguish certain applications that are management in nature from applications more closely involved in the teaching and learning process. These latter applications are usually referred to as **computer-assisted instruction**

(CAI). In truth, CMI and CAI applications overlap in many ways and neither term serves as a very clear description of what actually goes on in a classroom.

We like the way Bork (1985) has approached CMI. Bork takes a flexible view and recognizes that many variations are possible. He points out that for one school CMI may mean an extensive computerized inventory of curriculum materials. Another school may use the term to refer to using the computer to generate a variety of performance reports. At still another school, teachers may think of CMI as the use of classroom computers to print lists of students who have mastered specific objectives. According to Bork's view, any one or combination of these and other management applications constitutes CMI.

Three main concepts or goals can be identified as catalysts for those applications that fall under the broad umbrella of CMI: (1) **programmed instruction**, (2) **information management**, and (3) **computer networking**.

Programmed Instruction

The idea that learning can be reduced to a series of tightly controlled stimulus and response activities has been a recurring theme in education since the 1930s. By the 1960s, various attempts at mechanizing such a stimulus and response approach to learning had been attempted. Such attempts became known as programmed instruction. Two of the most prominent attempts at designing programmed instructional systems were the teaching machine and the programmed text.

Both teaching machines and programmed texts represented attempts to present small bits of information, require the learner to make a response, provide immediate feedback, and prescribe the next step based on the previous response. Two concepts were central to these mechanized approaches to learning: (1) **mastery learning** and (2) **individualized instruction**.

Mastery learning according to Lockard, Abrams and Many (1990), is based on the belief that all students can achieve at a very high level under the right conditions. One of the most important conditions necessary for students to master a skill or concept is time. The time factor in mastery learning is a key force behind individualized instruction. Very simply put, if each student needs a different amount of time to master the same skill or concept, the instructional system must be individualized.

Time, however, is not the only factor upon which instruction is individualized in programmed learning. Variation in such things as the sequencing of the learning steps and the nature of the learning materials is also important.

The major problem with attempts at programmed instruction during the 1960s and 1970s was how to deal with the massive clerical work required. An obvious solution to this problem was the computer.

The reasoning went like this: With programmed instruction as a teaching strategy and the computer as a delivery device, a technology of education has finely arrived.

Information Management

The second concept or goal that serves as a catalyst for CMI is information management. This concept was borrowed directly from the business world. The idea is that operating an educational program (or a business) requires a great amount of information to be organized and used effectively. Since computers have proved to be effective tools for managing information in business, it was assumed that they would also be effective in education.

The concept of information management is different from the concept of programmed learning in that there is less emphasis on involving the computer in the actual instructional process. The computer is seen simply as a tool to help organize and manipulate the diverse types of information involved in running an educational program. As Bank and Williams (1980) suggest, the computer offers "the potential of providing many types of users with data to serve their decision-making needs" (p. 5).

Computer Networking

The first attempts at using computers in CMI involved mainframe computers with terminals. This proved very ineffective for a number of reasons, and interest in CMI dwindled. When the microcomputer became available, interest in CMI was revived, because the microcomputer was interactive. Beginning with the first generation of microcomputers, networking or linking many computers together began to be advocated.

Today, this idea is alive and well. It often takes the shape of a total package called an *integrated learning system* (ILS). The main idea behind such systems is to provide an electronic classroom.

A loose analogy can be drawn between the networked system and a traditional classroom. Each computer station in the network becomes a student desk containing various learning resources and materials. The central computer containing the software that dispenses, receives, and organizes information is the teacher's desk.

Henderson and Maddux (1988) detailed five advantages commonly proposed by companies who market such networked educational systems. According to these two authors, networking systems are sold on the basis that they will:

1. *Save money on software:* The school only has to purchase one set of software for the file-serving computer rather than one set for each individual computer.

2. *Save money on hardware:* Only the file-serving computer needs to be a full-scale computer; the rest can be stripped down versions.
3. *Simplify instructional management:* The network comes with its own CMI program, allowing the teacher to do all the management with one software package that is designed to complement the system.
4. *Simplify software support, maintenance, and repair:* The same company that sells the networked system updates the software and provides maintenance and repair on the hardware.
5. *Facilitate inservice training:* When a networked system is purchased by a whole district, all teachers who use the system can be trained in one group by a training specialist from the company.

Now that we have examined the three main broad concepts that underpin CMI, we need to look at some of the trends and issues relating to using the computer as an instructional management tool.

Trends and Issues Relating to CMI

After conducting a thorough review of literature relating to CMI, Wyatt (1988) concluded that educational activities carried out under the umbrella of CMI fall on a continuum, as illustrated in Figure 6.1.

As can be seen, at one extreme of this continuum is the classroom computer that is used for simple, straightforward record-keeping chores. In the middle of the continuum are the self-paced classrooms, like the example above, where the computer plays an important role in the classroom organization, but is still used as an information management tool. At the other extreme end of the continuum are the ILS packages—the all-inclusive systems. They include the hardware, the management software, curriculum materials, maintenance, and inservice training.

Glowinski (1984) called attention to one of our main concerns and one of the major controversies in educational computing. According to Glowinski:

> *The microcomputer cannot replace teachers as role models in the classroom, but it can enhance learning by serving as an aide to the teacher, by reducing time spent on clerical duties. (p.231)*

Using a single computer with (ILS) application software as a management tool.	Using a series of computes with managment software independent of the curriculum.	Using an integrated learning system including hardware, software, curriculum, and training
Simple use of CMI	Moderate use of CMI	Extreme use of CMI

FIGURE 6.1   Computer-managed instruction (CMI) continuum.

Maddux, the senior author of this book, has called for caution with regards to the lLS movement. After confronting what he saw as a pendulum swing toward ILS and other networked systems, Maddux (1989) said:

> *I believe many school districts have been led down the primrose path by hardware and software vendors who are taking advantage of this latest swing of the educational pendulum. These entrepreneurs are hawking networking as the panacea for every school in the country. (p. 38)*

The major problem we have with the ILS end of the CMI continuum is that the more comprehensive the system, the more control is taken away from the teacher and given to an unknown group of instructional design and computer programming people. This is moving in the wrong direction. The greatest single advantage of the microcomputer is its interactive nature, making it a very personalized tool. Interactivity means that the student is in control, limited only by the capabilities of one machine and bounded by the capacity of one software package. In its ideal setting, this makes the computer experience completely individualized. The student is in control of rate of progress, selection of options, and format of final product. Each time the student's computer is connected to other computers and each time a decision is made by the software designer, the interactivity and personalization of the computer experience are weakened. To adopt a full ILS system means giving up much of the magic of the personal computer.

In fairness, research needs to be carried out on the use of the ILS approach. It may well be that in some situations this approach will prove to be an efficient and effective way to deliver instruction. Educators, however, need to view this approach with caution and above all, not accept it as the new panacea.

Based on this discussion, it should be obvious where we stand on CMI. We applaud efforts to use the computer in instructional management in ways similar to the classroom described in the first part: of this chapter. We are very nervous about ILS approaches that take more and more of the decision-making power away from the teacher, and urge caution in adopting these systems.

In the article just cited, Maddux (1988) called for research and evaluation to be done on the effectiveness of the extreme networked systems like ILS packages. He did so because he found no such evidence existed at the time. This sentiment makes a proper summary of the CMI topic. Until we have evidence to show otherwise, the best CMI applications are those that clearly place the classroom teacher in control.

COMPUTER TELECOMMUNICATIONS

Three students, John, Mary, and Sue, in Mr. Smith's sixth-grade classroom are excited about a research project. Along with other students their own age, they are interested in investigating the problem of acid rain. The group hopes to offer some suggestions to their fellow students and to their community on ways to solve the problem. The total research group includes students from schools across the United States and around the world.

Their project will be carried out with the following steps:

1. Conduct a search of libraries around the world for reference material on acid rain.
2. Gather data by taking pertinent measurements of air, water, and soil.
3. Compare data with similar data obtained by the other students in their worldwide network.
4. Organize references and data into a concise essay in a group writing process involving fellow researchers from across the United states and in other countries.
5. Share the final version of the report with students around the world and, finally, have it published in the local newspaper.

Four of the five steps in this project will involve computer telecommunications. In step 1, the students will link their classroom computer into libraries and scientific data bases around the world to conduct searches for information on acid rain. Sometimes their searching will only provide them with an abstract to an article, but sometimes the entire article can be obtained.

In step 3, the measurements taken by John, Mary, and Sue will be sent to an **electronic bulletin board** where they can be accessed by other members of this worldwide research team. At the same time, Mr. Smith's students will check the bulletin board each day to review measurements left there by other members of the research group.

In step 4, all the students in the project will participate in a telecommunications conference as they write the final research report. This will involve a small group of students writing the initial draft of the report and sending it to an electronic conference room where it can be reviewed by other members of the group. Each member will then have an opportunity to offer suggestions for editing and revising and these suggestions will be stored in the same electronic conference room.

In the fifth and final step, the finished research report will be stored as an electronic mail document, and project members will be able to save it, print it out, reproduce it for distribution in their school, and offer it for publication in the local newspaper.

The scenario you have just read is based partly on truth and partly on fiction. Some of the activities involved can be done with present technology and some must wait for further development and research. We will discuss both the present technology and the need for further study in the following sections.

The Components of Computer Telecommunications

The word *telecommunications* means communicating across distances. In the broadest sense, it includes media like radio, television, telephone, FAX machine, telegraph, and computer. In this chapter, however, we will focus on using computers for long-distance communications.

The idea of one computer talking to another is almost as old as the computer itself. According to Adams and Bott (1984), "German technicians during the late 1930's used the famous Enigma machine to encode their secret radio messages" (p. 3).

Again, education owes much of what it is able to do with computer telecommunications to the world of business. While business is the major user of telecommunications services, personal and educational applications of telecommunications are growing.

What Is Needed for Commuter Telecommunications?

To send or receive data using your computer, you need a *modem,* communications software, access to a telephone line, and another computer to call. The two computers exchanging information may be of any type or size. For example, you may use an IBM PC to call either an Apple II or a large mainframe computer.

The **modem** is a device that transforms the digital data from the computer into analog tones that can be sent over ordinary telephone lines. The modem of the other computer does the opposite, translating the analog telephone signals back into digital signals for the computer. These two types of conversion are called **modulation** and **demodulation** hence the term modem. A visual representation of the modem's role in the computer telecommunications process is presented in Figure 6.2.

Communications software controls the computer and modem and manages the communications process. Sometimes a communications program is included when you buy a modem. It may also be purchased separately, or it may be included as part of an integrated software package. For example, AppleWorks GS, the version of Appleworks written for the Apple IIGS computer, and Microsoft Works both include a communications program in addition to a word processor, database management program, and spreadsheet.

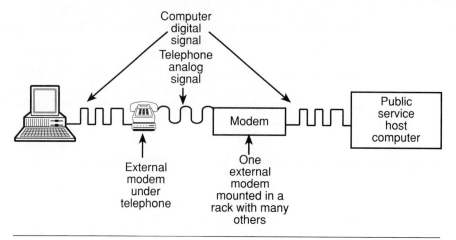

FIGURE 6.2   Illustration of two computers connected for telecommunications.

Where Can You Call?

One of the simplest ways to use a computer to make contact with another computer is to call a local electronic bulletin board service (BBS). A BBS involves a host computer, usually a personal computer that has stored messages, bulletins, and public-domain computer programs. A **system operator (SYSOP)** operates the system. There are many thousands of bulletin board services in the country. Usually, each BBS will have the listing of the other local bulletin boards.

The most advanced computer telecommunications application is the use of **information utilities**. These services include an array of features that may include electronic mail, weather forecasts, stock market quotations, on-line computer games, electronic encyclopedias, research data bases, and electronic conferencing.

There are three common information utilities: CompuServe, The Source, and GEnie. These commercial information services work much like cable television. Subscribers pay a basic fee for use of the system. Most cities have local access telephone numbers for these services so that no long-distance phone charge is involved for calls made from these locations. The main menu of CompuServe is shown in Figure 6.3 to give you an idea what is available from such an information utility.

Sharing Information

The overall purpose of telecommunications is to facilitate the sharing of information. Transferring from a host computer to a user is referred to as **downloading**. Computer programs, text files, and in some cases graphics can be downloaded. After a file is downloaded, it can be saved on a disk or printed.

```
                                    TOP
LOG-ON  SERVICE


1 Subscriber  Assistance
2 Find  a  Topic
3 Community  Bulletin  Boards
4 Electronic  Mail
5 Business  interests
6 Home  and  health


Enter  choice  by  number
Type  F1  for  help
```

FIGURE 6.3   A sample menu from a subscribed public communications service.

Files can also be uploaded. If you have written a program that you wish to share or would like to post a message, you can do so by uploading it to a host computer.

Electronic Research

When you or your students have library research to do, an on-line bibliographic database service may save you considerable time. Such database services usually only contain abstracts of articles or books. The Magazine Index, for example, indexes over 400 popular magazines from 1959 to the present. The ERIC database contains over 400,000 documents and journal articles on all aspects of education.

Some bibliographic databases are available through the information utilities previously discussed. Many others are available through database services such as Bibliographic Retrieval Service (BRS) or Dialog. Some university libraries are now putting their computerized card catalogs on line so that they can be accessed by personal computer.

Some publishers of professional journals are now storing the contents of each issue in electronic data bases. These are then made available through on-line services so that the entire article as well as the abstract can be accessed by personal computer.

One exciting possibility for education is the electronic library, where articles and books can be located, read, and saved by a student: or teacher at home or in the classroom. Such a system, however, is far in the future, and the extent of the materials that will be accessible is unknown at this time.

Like CMI, computer telecommunications holds much promise and at first glance seems to be an educational tool waiting to be used. There are problems and cautions relating to this application, however, and they will be examined in the next section.

Trends and Issues

One the problem with computer telecommunications is that it has been fraught with hype concerning its educational potential. At the same time, we believe that this is an area that does have great potential and needs to be studied carefully with an eye to discovering practical and productive uses. In our opinion, the following three trends have suspended computer telecommunications in the realm of the potential rather than propelling it into a viable educational application.

Labeling by Analogy

Nearly every computer telecommunications application that has been conceived has been named after some common activity in the nonelectronic world. We have, for example, electronic mail, electronic shopping, and electronic bulletin boards. The implication, of course, is that the electronic version is really an improved version of the real thing. The reality is often not so appealing.

Take, for example, the electronic field trip. In 1984, Adams and Bott described this phenomenon in the following way:

> *Imagine a field trip in which a class of fourth graders could visit a site hundreds of miles from their school building and still make it back in time for lunch. With electronic field trips, in fact, students never physically leave the classroom, yet they can be exposed to countless real-life events and people. (p. 13)*

Considering that the above description was written before high-resolution graphics and interactive videodiscs were common, calling a computer telecommunications session a "field trip" was certainly stretching the point. We suggest that realistically naming computer telecommunications applications would help educators develop a more realistic impression of what they actually are.

The Everest Syndrome

In Chapter 2 of this book, we called attention to the fact that educators, in their enthusiasm for change, tend to latch on to new technology simply because "it is there, or the Everest Syndrome. This has certainly been the case with many telecommunications applications. It is as if we are saying, "the fact that we can connect two computers and exchange information long distance is so wonderful, it must have some exotic educational application."

An example of the Everest syndrome is cited by Barron (1989) in a discussion of the merits of distance education. Barron notes an organization called Computer Pals that provides a worldwide communications network for youngsters communicating with pen pals. Is there not a question here that cries out to be asked? "What is the advantage of sending letters to pen pals across the telephone lines via computer?" Such an electronic letter is much more difficult to send and receive than a handwritten letter sent through the mail. In most cases, the cost is more and, in some cases it may be much more. Finally, the electronic letter is far less personal than either a handwritten version or a phone call. Is this simply a contrived application? Are we using it only because it is there?

As with many other computer applications in education, we need to start from a different perspective. We need to ask, "What do we need to do more efficiently or more effectively?" Then ask, "Can the computer help us?"

Type I Applications

We believe the trend in computer telecommunications for education is in the direction of Type I uses. This means that we are using a new tool to do what we have always done, but in a slightly different way. For example, an article in a National Education Association publication (Kurzius, 1989) lauds a program where high school students in Massachusetts write essays and the teacher sends them via an electronic mail service to England where they can be read by students in a sister school. This is a good idea. But how has computer telecommunications helped? Why not just send the essays by air mail? Better yet, if speed is important, why not just send them by FAX?

As we have already pointed out, Type II computer applications, in which the computer does something that we could not do before, have the potential to profoundly improve education. Using computer telecommunications to conduct library research is a good example of a Type II application. As this application becomes more viable and as other Type II applications are developed, computer telecommunications may indeed be a common and valuable educational tool.

At present, John, Mary, and Sue in Mr. Smith's sixth-grade class can exchange information with fellow students around the world. However, their ability to search the libraries of the world from their classroom is only a dream. The scenario we used to introduce the topic of computer telecommunications probably suggests more questions than answers. It calls attention to some of the possibilities computer telecommunications may have for education but, at the same time, points out some trends we think need to be reversed. Like many other educators, we think this exciting capability has great promise. However, it needs to be viewed as something unique and not simply the electronic equivalent of some traditional activity. An objective search for how telecommunications can improve the teaching and learning process needs to begin.

SUMMARY

This chapter discusses two topics relating to educational computing: computer-managed instruction and computer telecommunications. Both topics hold great promise for future ways that computers can be used as tools for improving education. Both, however, have been plagued by hype and have contributed more toward educational promise than educational improvement. After explaining computer-managed instruction and computer telecommunications, we discussed some of the issues relating to the two topics. Our conclusions are that very little evidence can be mustered to show that such applications have found a viable place in educational practice. Much study and research are necessary before we know how best to use computers in these two ways.

LOOKING AHEAD

In this chapter you have seen how telecommunications software allows access to a variety of information systems. However, in our zeal to use this new technology we should be cautious. In the next chapter you will learn of other uses for telecommunications and CMI and how they can be applied to school office management and leadership roles. Even though computers can help automate certain tasks and make administration more time efficient the concerns over technology should be kept in mind.

SOME QUESTIONS TO CONSIDER

1. What problems are associated with turning the entire management of the instructional process over to a computer system like ILS?
2. What role do you think computers should play in instructional management?
3. How do you think computer telecommunications could be used to improve the teaching and learning process?
4. How would you go about setting up a research project to show that allowing students to communicate long distance via computer could be an asset: to their learning a particular subject?

RELATED ACTIVITIES

1. Critique an ILS package presently in use in the school district of your choice. Share your findings with your class.

2. Visit your campus library and ask for a demonstration of an electronic reference search. Discuss with your class how such a search could be valuable in writing a term paper.
3. Using a computer equipped with a modem and telecommunications software, log on to a local electronic bulletin board.

SUGGESTIONS FOR ADDITIONAL READING

Kapisovskey, P. M. (1989/90, Winter). Network science: A new approach to science and math education. *EDU Magazine,* pp. 10–14.

Lynch, C. A. (1989). Library automation and the national research network. *Educom Review, 24*(3), 21–26.

O'Neil, H. F. (1981). *Computer based instruction: A state-of-the-art assessment.* New York: Academic Press.

Phillips, M. G., Santoro, G. M. (1989). Teaching group discussion via computer-mediated communication. *Communication Education, 38*(2), 152–161.

REFERENCES

Adams, D. M., & Bott, D. A. (1984). Tapping into the world: Computer telecommunications networks and schools. *Computers in the Schools, 1*(3), 3–17.

Bank, A., & Williams, R. C. (1980). *Instructional information systems: Dream or nightmare?.* New York: Teachers College Press.

Barron, D. D. (1989, November). Distance education: Removing barriers to knowledge. *School Library Journal,* pp. 28–30.

Bork, A. (1985). *Personal computers for education.* New York: Harper and Row.

Glowinski, D. J. (1984). Computer as an aid, not a classroom teacher. In C.D. Martin and R. S. Heller (eds.), *Capitol-izing on computers in education* (pp. 230–231). Proceedings of the 1984 Association for Educational Data Systems Annual Convention. Rockville, MD: Computer Science Press.

Henderson, A. K., Maddux, C. D. (1988). Problems and pitfalls of computer networking in educational settings. *Educational Technology, 28*(9), 29–32.

Kurzius, A. (1989, May). Networking, transatlantic style. *NEA Today,* p. 12.

Lockard, J., Abrams, P. D., & Many, W. (1990). *Microcomputers for Educators.* Glenview, IL: Scott, Foresman.

Maddux C. D. (1989). Computer networking in education: The need for evaluation studies. *Computers in the Schools, 6*(1/2), 37–43.

Wyatt, A. T. (1988). A comparison of computer and manual instructional management systems in the classroom setting (Doctoral dissertation, Texas Tech University, Lubbock,1988).

_7_

Administrative Uses of Computers

GOALS AND OBJECTIVES

Goal: To understand how computers can be used for administrative applications in schools.

When you finish studying this chapter, you will be able to:

1. Identify computer applications that assist teachers and administrators in dealing with routine management tasks.
2. Describe and give examples of the use of the computer in an automated office.
3. Describe and give examples of the use of the computer to maintain student records.
4. Identify school accounting and business applications for which computer programs exist.
5. Describe potential uses of the computer in areas such as the guidance office, athletic department, and library and media center.
6. Describe ways computer technology can be used to deal with the problems of isolation and lack of up-to-date information.

KEY TERMS

California Technology
  Project
computerized accounting
  programs

computerized scheduling
  programs
desktop publishing
discipline tracking

Electric Pages
electronic information
   utilities
electronic mail
   forums
GC EduNET
gradebook programs
Handicapped Education
   Exchange
inventory management
   programs
Learning Initiatives

modem
on-line catalog
on-line database
PSInet
SchoolLINK
Science Teacher's Network
special interest groups
student information management
   systems
Teacher-Link
telecommunications
teleconferencing

For many prospective teachers the exciting part of a career in education is teaching, working with students to help them develop and learn. That focus on teaching is reinforced in college. The methods courses, the early experiences, and student teaching are all designed to help the future teacher become a competent classroom professional.

There are less glamorous and to many less interesting aspects of any school that are sometimes lumped into one general category—administration. The work of system-level administrators, such as superintendents and supervisors, and the work of building-level administrators, such as principals and department chairs, can be divided into two general categories: *management tasks* and *leadership roles*. Management tasks include routine duties such as maintaining the records of students, keeping track of expenditures in different areas of the school, and overseeing the process of selecting and purchasing new equipment and learning materials. Management tasks are not, however, the sole province of administrators. Classroom teachers today also face the prospect of being overwhelmed by the amount and diversity of the information someone wants them to supply on a daily, weekly, monthly, or yearly basis. Some of the paperwork burden can be handled by secretaries and clerks, but few schools today have enough support staff. Fortunately, computer programs are available that reduce the amount of time and effort required to accomplish many types of management tasks.

The leadership roles of school administrators are a bit more difficult to describe. A school principal, a department chair, and a middle grades supervisor all have responsibilities that relate to the quality of instruction. Their leadership should be a major influence on the quality of instruction provided by a school system. Unfortunately, many administrators rarely function in leadership roles. Management tasks such as completing required reports, updating equipment inventories, and seeing to it that the buses run on schedule often take virtually all an administrator's time. As Raucher (1989), an assistant superintendent for management information systems for Montgomery (Maryland) County Public Schools put it, "If an educator spends too much time doing paperwork, he or she cannot fill the role of instructional leader. With the data reporting requirements we have now, principals could spend all their time behind the closed doors of their offices."

Leadership is a uniquely human task that cannot be turned over to a computer. However, automating management tasks may provide the administrator with more time for leadership responsibilities. In addition, computer resources can be used in ways that support the leadership roles of administrators.

SUPPORTING MANAGEMENT TASKS

The management and operation of today's schools have become increasingly difficult. . . . Rising costs, dwindling enrollments, demands for accountability of staff and programs, and constant requests from regulating agencies for information and reports have compounded administrators' responsibilities. Confronted with the tasks of keeping schools operating within the boundaries of goals and expectations set for them and the financial resources available, administrators have turned to computer technology and computer-based information systems. (Bluhm, 1987, p. 4)

Most of the administrative applications of computers in schools today are Type 1. That is, they do not make new and better teaching methods available. They simply make it easier to perform work that is already being done. Many routine tasks can be performed more efficiently and accurately through the use of computers. However, doing a task more efficiently or better does not necessarily mean the task should be done, with or without computers. Whether the task is worth doing at all is an important question that is rarely asked when computerization is considered. Many routine tasks are useful, and computerizing them can be beneficial. Others, as you will see later in this chapter, should probably not be done at all.

The school office is often a focal point for the performance of routine management tasks. This is where we will start our discussion of computerizing management tasks.

THE AUTOMATED OFFICE

It may sound foolish to talk about automating the school office with sophisticated computer technology and software when, more than 100 years after the invention of the telephone, most teachers still do not have this basic tool of modern society on their office desk. In fact, most teachers do not even have an office, just a desk in a busy classroom. This section will focus on the automation of the school office, but most of the information also applies to the teacher as well. Teachers, like administrators, often find themselves overwhelmed with routine paperwork related to management tasks.

The management tasks of a school office can be divided into several different types. Each type requires a different type of software.

The Computer as Document Processor

Every school office produces hundreds, if not thousands, of documents each year. In many offices all these documents are still produced with typewriters, but a growing number of school offices are using computers and word-processing software such as Word Perfect, Microsoft Word, and Jass.

There are three major advantages of word processing over typewriters:

1. Word processed documents are easily corrected. There is no need to retype the entire document to make a few corrections. Errors must be corrected manually on a typewriter, using correction fluid or tape. With a word processor the error is an electronic image on the screen, rather than ink on paper. The electronic image can be corrected with a few keystrokes. Word processing also allows you to use special programs such as spelling checkers and grammar checkers that spot potential errors you might miss.
2. After creating a template file, form letters can be produced quickly and easily. Many documents produced by school officers are standard form letters.
3. Revisions to existing documents are easier and quicker when the original was word processed rather than typed. For example, changing 20% of the text in a 60-page typewritten student manual probably means the entire manual must be retyped. With word processing, there is no need to retype the 80% of the manual that has not changed. The file containing the manual is loaded back into the computer's memory, material is edited as needed, and the new version is printed. The result is a significant savings in both time and effort over the typewriter.

Most documents produced in a school office can be created with any popular word-processing program. However, some documents need more than can be done with a regular word processor. For example, school newspapers, programs, and announcements are often sent to printshops. **Desktop publishing** programs let you create documents that have a typeset appearance at a much lower cost. Many schools have saved the cost of a desktop publishing system in one year or less, because it allowed the school to produce documents such as programs and school newspapers in house instead of paying a typesetter to create them.

The Computer as Record Keeper

Schools and school systems are constantly creating and updating a seemingly endless list of records. As one North Carolina principal put it,

> *In my seventeen years as a school principal, my teachers and I were constantly frustrated with the seemingly countless hours spent filling out reports and forms of one description or another. Entering and withdrawing students, completing transcripts, scheduling classes, taking daily attendance, filling out health cards, calculating grades and filling out report cards, sending reports to the central office or to Raleigh . . . the list went on and on.*
>
> *The principals and teachers in North Carolina spend less time on all those records today than they did a few years ago because the Department of Public Instruction in North Carolina selected a special computer program for the state and now requires that it be used to produce all the student records created by both elementary and secondary schools. The program, **Student Information Management System** or SIMS, is produced by Columbia Computing Services. SIMS and similar programs are used by many schools all over the nation. SIMS reduces the effort required to produce many of the records a school generates. It keeps track of most types of data needed by operational personnel such as clerical staff, middle administrators such as principals and department chairs, and top administrators such as district and state superintendents (Hussain, 1973).*

The building-level version of SIMS automates the following record keeping procedures.

Daily Attendance

Teachers "bubble in" daily and period (if needed) attendance sheets to indicate students who are absent. These sheets are then scanned by a special optical scanner and placed directly in the SIMS database. The school and the school system thus have an accurate and up-to-date record of attendance, excused and unexcused absences, and standard data such as average daily attendance (ADA). Required reports are automatically generated by the program for submission to the district office. In addition, SIMS can identify students with excessive absence patterns and produce a list of students with potential problems.

Many schools have added an optional computerized telephone system that makes an automated call in the evening to the parents of each student with an unexcused absence for that day. When someone picks up the phone at the student's home, the computer speaks the name of the student and indicates that he or she was absent from school and provides a phone number parents can call the next day.

Students at one high school in Florida call such a system "Big Mouth." It can dial up to 32,000 different numbers and provide any of 99 different messages (Crawford, 1989). The system, which is called PC Truant by the manufacturer, also allows parents to record a message that can then be responded to by school personnel on the following day. Crawford (1989) reports that attendance at the high school increased about 6% after the system was installed. The same system is now used as a voice bulletin board for parents. They can call the system, press a specified number on their Touch-Tone phone, and hear messages on any of up to 10 different topics, such as school closing information, athletic events, awards and honors programs, and PTA meetings.

Academic Progress

The SIMS program is not used to keep track of daily and weekly test grades, project grades, and other criteria for six-week, semester, and yearly grades. Many teachers use programs like Intergrade, which runs on IBM and Apple II computers, or Excelsior, another powerful **gradebook program** and student record program for IBM computers, much as they would standard gradebooks. However, programs like Intergrade and Excelsior can weight and average student marks to arrive at grades. This frees teachers of the tedious task of calculating grades by hand and gives them the opportunity to easily calculate grades with different weights that better represent the importance of a particular test, quiz, or activity.

Once the grade management program has calculated the six-week grades of students, the data can be transferred to SIMS using optical scanning forms. If the teachers use programs like Intergrade, the grades can be transferred from that program to SIMS via a diskette, a procedure that both reduces errors and saves time. SIMS automatically calculates semester and yearly grades and creates a database of academic progress for each student. SIMS will also print school report cards for every student in the school. It can also print standard letters to parents of students whose grades put them in special categories (for example, failing one or more classes or honor roll).

Class Schedules

One of the most onerous tasks in a school where students move from classroom to classroom across the day is scheduling. Before **computerized scheduling programs**, principals, guidance counselors, and department chairs might spend weeks, if not months, producing a schedule or the school might pay a firm thousands of dollars to produce a schedule. With programs like SIMS, even a small school can afford the computer hardware and software needed to bring the scheduling function in house. With a typical scheduling program, about 4% to 8% of the students will have to be hand scheduled because the program cannot find a way to schedule the classes to accommodate these student's needs. That is much easier, however, than hand scheduling 100% of the students.

Although the scheduling abilities of programs like SIMS automate a difficult and frustrating task, there are also opportunities for misuse. For example, programs like SIMS generate data that are transferred to state education agencies. This allows remote, bureaucratic agencies to second guess many of the decisions made by front-line administrators and teachers in a way that was never possible before. For example, suppose a principal knows that, although a particular teacher has not been certified in history, that teacher is the best one available to teach a new honors course in social issues. Without computerized database systems like SIMS, it would be difficult for state department bureaucrats to check such decisions and approve or disapprove. With SIMS it is not difficult for a state official to cross match the list of teachers in the state and their areas of certification with the schedules of employed teachers. The result would be a list of teachers who are covering courses that are "out of field," that is, courses for which they are not certified to teach. From one perspective, this is a great way for state officials to catch local educators who are not following the state's rules. From another perspective, this is an opportunity for a Big Brother administration to inflexibly apply detailed rules that do not always lead to the best decisions. Again, it must be said that computerizing management tasks is no guarantee that the teaching environment will be better. Computerization can actually make things worse in certain situations.

Exceptional Children Database

Several programs are available that automate the process of creating individual educational plans (IEP) for students with special needs. These programs generally provide an electronic form and format for completing IEPs, often with the help of computer data bases of behavioral objectives and instructional methods. The mandated steps in developing IEPs are also built into the procedure.

Discipline Tracking, Health Data, and Basic Student Data

General-purpose student information systems like SIMS also have provisions for information such as immunization records, student address and family data, standardized test data, and discipline tracking. The **discipline tracking** feature records the type of discipline problems a student has had, as well as the way the problem was handled.

Thus far the discussion of SIMS has been limited primarily to the building-level program. SIMS, and other programs like it, also includes a Central Office System that consolidates data from each school in the system and generates system-level reports that can be transmitted to the state education agency. Many types of student, school, and district data can be organized into such reports.

The SIMS program is only one of many student information and management programs available in schools. North Carolina decided to require all of the 2,000 public schools in the state as well as all 140 local school districts to use the same software, because that allows the state to generate an accurate database of information on the state's schools and teachers. The information obtained from SIMS is now used to support funding requests to the state legislature and funding allocations to local school systems.

The system also has the ability to check for compliance with state regulations. This ability was purposely built into the system and was one reason the legislature voted over $20 million to implement the SIMS program statewide. It remains to be seen whether use of the system to check for compliance with regulations is beneficial to the students of the state.

One particularly troubling prospect that is well within the realm of possibility is the use of the system to store achievement test data that will be used to evaluate the success or failure of teachers. Many states currently requires students to complete standardized, multiple-choice achievement tests at the end of many courses. These tests are used in some school systems as virtually the sole criteria for judging the success of teachers. This can certainly be done more efficiently with the help of computer technology. It is not, however, likely to lead to quality educational programs. The dangers of overreliance on multiple-choice tests are so serious that the National Commission on Testing and Public Policy, with funding from the Ford Foundation, has issued a report, "From Gatekeeper to Gateway: Transforming Testing in America" (NCTPP, 1990). It concludes that testing policies and practices in the United States are not sound and that overreliance on multiple-choice tests puts unreasonable barriers in the way of minority students seeking an education and impedes legitimate efforts for school reform. The report concluded that "we must stop pretending that any single standard test can illuminate equally well the talents and help promote the learning of people from dramatically different backgrounds." Schools today administer around 127 million required standardized tests at a cost of almost $1 billion annually. Bernard Gifford, who is chair of the commission as well as a vice-president for education at Apple Computer Corporation, believes excessive testing has transformed many schools into "test-preparation institutions." He recommends the use of a much broader range of educational assessment strategies, including tests with open-ended questions, job performance evaluations, work samples, and biographical data (quoted in Evangelauf, 1990). The report, and many other studies as well, make the point that multiple-choice tests are not widely used because they are the best means of evaluating instruction; they are widely used because they are the easiest means. The scoring and evaluation of multiple-choice tests can easily be computerized, while the automation of other methods of assessment such as essay answers and job performance by computer is still, for the most part, in the future.

The Computer as Accountant and Business Manager

A typical school today has accounts with hundreds of vendors who sell products to the school and expect to be paid for their wares. Some supply the school with only one or two items, while others supply many different items on a daily or weekly basis.

Schools pay for goods from many vendors, and they also receive payments from many different sources. For example, students may pay fees for locker rental, for the use of consumable supplies in the chemistry and physics labs, and for membership in some of the school's organizations. Funds may also come in from federal and state agencies, as well as organizations such as the PTA and local businesses.

The flow of goods and payments into and out of a school creates an accounting environment that is more complex than that of the average medium-sized business. Funds from different sources must be kept in different accounts, and payments for goods and services must be taken from the appropriate account. Often, local, state, and federal regulations must be followed. The complexity of a school's accounts payable and accounts receivable can overwhelm an understaffed school office that uses a manual bookkeeping system. A few schools today use standard accounting programs, but most do not. Schools must follow so many specialized rules that regular accounting programs, designed for use by businesses, cannot deal with all the rules. Most schools and school systems that have automated their bookkeeping tasks are using special **computerized accounting programs** designed specifically for schools. The SIMS program mentioned earlier includes several accounting modules.

Specialized school accounting software often includes **inventory management programs** that help administrators and teachers keep track of what is available in the school system's warehouses and what may need to be ordered. With such powerful software it would be easy for school systems to centralize purchasing decisions and assign that task to one central office administrator. With good computer software, the result might be a very efficient purchasing system. It might also be a system that does not respond to the needs of teachers. The same computer software could also be used to decentralize decision making. For example, when administrators in the Pekin (Illinois) Public Schools evaluated the system's centralized method of purchasing school supplies (Watson & Morgan, 1989), they concluded that the supplies budget was adequate, but teachers often complained because the supplies they needed were not available (or there was an oversupply of one type and an undersupply of another).

The system decided to decentralize the purchase of supplies. As Custer Whiteside, the director of media and technology put it, "We felt the more input local administrators and teachers had in the purchasing of their own supplies, the more ownership they would feel" (quoted in Watson & Morgan, 1989, p. 28). Pekin installed the IBM's CIMS III program (Comprehensive Information Management for Schools). CIMS III requires a medium-sized IBM computer, the System 36, and includes modules for financial management and student records. The financial management component includes a general ledger and modules for purchasing, payroll, and warehouse inventory. Using CIMS III the system changed from having central office staff purchase all supplies at the beginning of the year to one that puts many of the purchasing decisions in the hands of teachers:

> *The district . . . allocates a lump sum (from a combination of federal, state and local funds) to each school every year. Each department and each grade get a budget. A group of teachers works with the principal in each school to decide how to spend the funds. As Whiteside notes, "Instead of us saying: Here is a district-wide blueprint of what you must put your money into," we're giving each school building a lot more flexibility." Purchasing continues throughout the year. If a music teacher wants some harmonicas, he or she goes to the principal. The principal and teacher take a look at the CIMS database to review what is left of the music department's budget. The school secretary keys in a purchase order, which prints out at the district office. The order is approved by one of the four district-level program directors. Then the district office sends the order to the vendor. The harmonicas are delivered directly to the school. (Watson and Morgan, 1989, p. 29)*

The Pekin School System's use of CIMS III empowers teachers. It provides them with much more flexibility and decision-making responsibility than the manual accounting system it replaced. Teacher empowerment is not, however, an inherent aspect of the CIMS III software or any of the other special accounting and inventory software for schools. The empowerment comes from the way the software is used. In another system the same software could have been used to disenfranchise teachers and to centralize purchase decisions.

Computer-Aided Time, Space, Vehicle, and Personnel Management

The use of scheduling programs to assign students to classes has already been mentioned. In many school systems, another annual task can be more difficult than creating student schedules. This is creating a school bus routing plan that efficiently deploys the available vehicles to pick up and deliver all students to the correct schools. This procedure, which has traditionally been performed in some districts through a process that is more akin to alchemy than anything else, has also been computerized. A companion program to SIMS is TIMS—Transportation Information Management System. TIMS requires you to input the addresses of all students who will be attending school. Then a digitized map of the area served by the school transportation system is entered along with details such as one-way streets and intersections. TIMS then creates a bus routing and bus-stop scheme that uses the available buses to transport students in the most cost-effective manner that also minimizes the amount of time children spend riding. TIMS also generates a list of instructions for the bus drivers that details the route and the stops as well as the pickup times for each student. It also produces a student roster list that includes the names and addresses of all students on each bus route.

This all sounds excellent, but programs like TIMS still have some drawbacks. Perhaps the most important drawback is the need to provide the computer with an accurate digitized map. Some school systems discover, for example, that the detailed maps supplied by county or state agencies have many errors and are not up-to-date. After more than a year of work, which included driving over all the roads in the school district at least twice and correcting errors, one school system was even able to sell their digitized map to the county because it was more accurate than any the county had.

Once an accurate map is input, the job is not necessarily over, however. In a growing area a map that is correct at the beginning of the school year may not be accurate by Christmas. Some transportation programs also have trouble dealing with students who have more than one address, but some students may have two or more addresses. Children may spend Monday, Tuesday, and Wednesday with their mother and Thursday and Friday with their father. Some transportation programs do not handle such variations well when developing bus routings.

School systems, like any business, must also keep many different types of data on employees. Maintaining up-to-date personnel records without automation is a major expense. In 1985, W. James Hascott, the personnel director for Orange County Public School District in Orlando, Florida, decided to automate the school district office because his staff was spending hours each week entering the accrued sick leave forms for the district's 500 school bus drives into their computer (Knauth, 1989).

As a result his district has one personnel staff member for every 400 district employees, while the average is about one personnel staff member for every 100 employees. Hascott selected a powerful program, Total Educational Resources Management Systems (TERMS) to keep track of the personnel and financial records of the district. With TERMS the district keeps track of personnel procedures and needs from the moment a prospective employee completes an application for employment until an employee retires. For example, a principal who has a position open can review employment applications on the screen of the school's computer. Should the principal decide to hire an applicant, he or she can put a check mark beside the hire box in the electronic application and enter an anticipated start date. The computer in the district office automatically sends a copy of the information to the human resources department and puts the teacher's name on the school board agenda for the next meeting. If the board approves hiring the teacher, the human resources department sends the information, via the computer, to the payroll department for processing. The entire process is done on line without requiring the applicant or any of the various units in the district to retype information, such as the applicant's name and address.

Once hired, another module in the TERMS program keeps track of every teacher's certification status and provides notification when a certificate is about the expire and must be renewed. Yet another module generates payroll checks and keeps track of tax and retirement deductions.

Some schools also use computers to schedule repair and maintenance work on buildings and vehicles, analyze and control energy usage in school buildings, and keep track of food service operations.

Other Administrative Uses

In schools where computers have been effectively integrated into the day to day activities of the staff, they may also be used in ways that have not been discussed thus far. For example, the athletic department may use programs that analyze the play patterns and performance statistics of opposing basketball and football teams, and the music department may have programs that map band formations and produce printed directions for each member of the band.

Programs are also available that automate many of the standard tasks in a guidance office. For example, students can enter a set of criteria describing their ideal college and the program will identify colleges that meet their criteria. Other programs help students explore career options, and still others provide information on sources of financial aid for college.

A number of school libraries and media centers have already installed computerized circulation systems. When an item is brought to the circulation desk, its bar code is scanned by a bar-code wand. The same wand scans a bar code on the borrower's identification card. When an item is checked out, the circulation program keeps a record of who checked it out and when. Schools are also beginning to add **on-line catalog** software that replaces the rows of card catalogs that have been the stock in trade of libraries for hundreds of years. With an on-line catalog, students can enter topics, titles, or author names and view a list of items in the library that match their search criteria. Many systems will also tell the student whether items are checked out or available.

A related type of program is an **on-line database** of reference information. These programs allow you to type search criteria and see a list of relevant articles and books. The most popular of this type of database in education is ERIC on Disc. All the reference information from the printed ERIC database is on a CD-ROM disk that is attached to a computer. Students can enter search criteria and get a list of articles and papers that appear to match the search criteria. ERIC on Disc also contains abstracts of each paper and article in the database. The ability of CD-ROM disks to store large amounts of data made another type of computer database possible. On-line full-text databases include the entire article, not just abstracts. Several encyclopedia publishers, including Comptons and Grolier, also have electronic versions of their encyclopedias that include both text and graphics. Students can conduct electronic searches of these databases and print out relevant information.

LEADERSHIP SUPPORT FUNCTIONS

Many of the uses discussed thus far support the leadership activities of school administrators and teachers. For example, principals can use the data available in student information systems to project future staffing needs and develop better plans to meet those needs. Exceptional child and discipline tracking information can be analyzed to help determine what types of additional support services are needed in the school, and achievement test data can provide one type of data that is helpful in school improvement efforts. Richards (1989) describes several ways computers can help school leaders make strategic management decisions. For example, an electronic spreadsheet could be used to analyze the cost effectiveness of early childhood programs.

The use of computer-based technology to support leadership functions depends more on the person than on the personal computer. Effective leadership is, and is likely to remain, a human function. The computer can support but will not supplant the person.

However, a few computer applications seem particularly suited to supporting the leadership role. Two of those, **electronic mail** and **tele-conferencing** and accessing remote information databases, will be discussed in this section. They help educators overcome two common problems, isolation and lack of up-to-date information, that limit progress toward more effective instruction.

Electronic Mail and Teleconferencing

> *Schools, by their very nature and organization, tend to isolate professional educators from one another and from sources of information vital to their professional growth. This is sometimes aggravated by geographic factors. . . . Communicating with others who have information and experience vital to the successful completion of one's mission is too often stymied by the lack of funds and time for adequate professional conferencing and other forms of information sharing. (EduNet News, 1989)*

Georgia College, through the **GC EduNet** service, is one of several organizations that has developed electronic methods of overcoming the problem of isolation. With a computer and a **modem**, educators can connect their computer to other computers all across the country and exchange information and ideas with thousands of other educators with similar interests. They do not communicate by voice, however. Instead they type messages on the keyboard of their computer and read messages from other educators on the screen of their computer. This is sometimes referred to a **telecommunications**.

Several major electronic information services, such as GEnie and CompuServe, allow educators with a computer and a special device called a modem to communicate electronically. CompuServe and GEnie have several **special-interest groups** (SIGs). CompuServe's Educators' SIG has hundreds of members and is open to anyone interested in computers and education. This SIG sponsors electronic discussions (called **forums** or teleconferences) on a wide range of topics such as educational administration, computer literacy, special education, and Logo. You can use the Educators' SIG while connected to CompuServe by typing Go HOM-137. Another SIG is the Educational Research Forum on CompuServ. It has 10 sections that deal with topics such as medical education and educational administration. The International Society for Technology in Education (ISTE), which publishes The Computing Teacher, also has a SIG on CompuServe. When you are connected to CompuServe, you can type G EDU18 and press the Enter key on your computer keyboard, and you will be connected to the ISTE SIG. (ISTE has also established a special electronic mail and teleconferencing service through GTE named ISTE.NET.)

The Electric Pages
Most general-purpose information utilities like CompuServe have some

services for educators, but some services cater exclusively to educators. One such service is the **Electric Pages**. It has many services for educators, including electronic mail that allows you to exchange messages with other Electric Pages subscribers. There are ways to send mail to one person or to a large group, such as all the special education teachers in a region.

Several organizations use the Electric Pages for electronic networking. For example, the Texas Association of School Boards has a private network on Electric Pages that is available only to member schools. The network has electronic mail, a legislative update service that keeps members current on relevant national and state legislation, a method of conducting electronic surveys and polls of member systems, and a teleconferencing service for the discussion of topics of interest to administrators and board members. Teleconferencing allows several people to sit at their computers and exchange information with other participants in the teleconference. Some teleconferences are in real time, which means that everyone is on line at the same time. Others teleconferences occur across days or months. When participants sign on to the service and join the conference, they begin reading messages at the point where they stopped in the last session.

The Texas Computer Education Association sponsors a SIG on Electric Pages that includes databases of information such as reviews of educational software and equipment, a calendar of special events of interest to computer-using educators, and bibliographies and articles on educational computing. A number of discussion forums on a variety of topics is available through the Electric Pages. Public conferences are open to any subscriber, and private conferences are open only to members of the organization that sponsors the teleconference (and subscribers who have been given a password by that organization).

Electric Pages is one of the oldest special telecommunications services for educators, but there are several others.

Learning Initiatives and PSInet
In 1989, IBM established **Learning Initiatives**, an organization for educators and administrators who use IBM computers. Learning Initiatives, which is based at the College of Education at Georgia State University in Atlanta, also sponsors a telecommunications service named **PSInet** or People Sharing Information Network. PSInet can be accessed from any computer with a modem. It provides educators with electronic mail services as well as opportunities to participate in teleconferences on a variety of topics and search for information in a number of data bases.

SchoolLink
SchoolLink is sponsored by Tandy/Radio Shack and GTE Education Services. Like PSInet, it provides educators with electronic opportunities

to communicate and share information. For example, the leadership forum on SchoolLink is chaired by Nolan Estes, a professor at the University of Texas and a former school superintendent. SchoolLink also has extensive services that can be used by students to communicate with students in other states or countries. In 1990, for example, one SchoolLink forum contained an electronic letter from a high school student outside Moscow who described his first trip to the new MacDonald's in Moscow.

Regional Systems for Educators

A growing number of telecommunications services are being developed to serve the needs of educators in different regions of the country. Bull and others (1991) describe **Teacher-LINK**, a statewide telecommunications system for Virginia that allows educators throughout the state to communicate with each other. The system provides a communication link for K–12 educators, university-based teacher education faculty, regional education service center staff, and state-level education officials. Teacher-LINK supports electronic mail as well as teleconferencing. Through national and international networks that are interconnected with Teacher-LINK, educators can also communicate with colleagues in other states and countries.

Systems like Teacher-LINK and GC EduNET serve all educators in a particular region. Another service, **the Science Teacher's Network** at the Harvard Graduate School of Education, serves the needs of one type of teacher. It provides science teachers with opportunities for collegial communication with other science teachers (West and others, 1989). In the decade of the 1990s, many more telecommunications services for educators will likely be developed.

Other Systems for Educators

For special education teachers, the **Handicapped Education Exchange** or HEX (11523 Charlton Drive, Silver Springs, MD 20902) maintains an electronic bulletin board that provides up-to-date information on the use of technology in special education. The voice number for HEX is (301) 681-7372 and the computer number is (301) 593-7033. The National Association of State Directors of Special Education (1201 16th Street, NW, Washington, DC 20036) supports SpecialNet, a collection of 17 services that provides many types of services to special education teachers and administrators. HEX is free, but there is a charge for using SpecialNet.

In California the **California Technology Project** (Blurton, 1989) has developed a series of telecommunications services for educators that provides free access to all interested educators. Educators can dial any of 23 services in cities throughout the state. The services, named Technology Resources in Education (TRIE), are "geared for use by K–12 teachers and administrators, district and county office educators and anyone else involved in using technology in California schools" (Dodge and Dodge,

1989). TRIE provides educators with electronic mail services, teleconferencing, and databases that can be searched electronically. See Dodge and Dodge (1989) for a list of the phone numbers that can be used to access TRIE.

Remote Information Databases

Finding, selecting, and using information has become a life's work for many people. Busy educators frequently need information on a particular topic, such as teaching reading through language experience or the benefits and problems of social promotion. However, it can be difficult to locate current information on specialized topics. If you need abstracts of articles on teaching methods for junior high school students with learning disabilities, reviews of educational software for teaching high school physics, or any other type of educational information, you can get it from one of the many **electronic information utilities** that are as near as the keyboard of your computer. With a personal computer you have access to all sorts of electronic information services. GEnie and CompuServe, the best-known general-interest services, have extensive data banks that can be searched electronically from the keyboard of your computer. The information is transmitted to your home or school over the phone line and displayed on the screen of your computer. It can also be saved in a file and printed out by most word processors. Information in electronic information services is organized into databases that contain millions of pieces of information relevant to a particular topic. GEnie and CompuServe as well as specialized services such as the Electric Pages support hundreds of electronic databases of interest to educators. One such database is RICE, Resources in Computer Education. It was developed by the Northwest Regional Educational Laboratory. RICE contains reviews of educational software and related materials, including textbooks and reference books.

SUMMARY

Most routine management tasks associated with operating a school have been computerized. Computerization of management tasks generally saves considerable time and effort, and there are opportunities for more effective use of the information available in computerized files of information. However, the danger of misuse of that information is significant and must always be considered. The leadership roles of administrators and teachers can also be supported by computerization of management tasks. Electronic mail, teleconferencing, and remote databases of educational information are all promising tools for leadership.

LOOKING AHEAD

This chapter has discussed many different types of computer software. The next chapter deals with programming, the process of creating computer software. Chapter 8 introduces you to the concept of programming and to two languages, BASIC and Logo. Chapter 8 also deals with a topic that has been the subject of considerable debate—whether programming should be taught in schools and under what circumstances.

SOME QUESTIONS TO CONSIDER

1. What long-term effects might you expect from an effort to computerize all the routine record keeping of a teacher? How would the time saved be spent? What additional record-keeping demands might be placed on teachers who have access to computing power?
2. What about the dark side of computerized record keeping? Are there types of data that, if collected, might be detrimental to quality education? Do certain types of data lend themselves to misuse by administrators, politicians, or teachers?
3. How do teachers obtain information on educational innovations now? How would access to resources such as electronic databases, electronic mail, and teleconferencing change that process?

REFERENCES

Bluhm, H. (1987). *Administrative Uses of Computers in Schools*. Englewood Cliffs, NJ: Prentice Hall.

Bull, G. L., Sigmon, T. M., Shidisky, C. (1991). Specifications for computer networks for support of cooperative ventures between university and public schools. *Computers in the Schools, 8* (1, 2, 3), 183–186.

Blurton, C. (1989, November/December). California Technology Project Underway. *CUE Newsletter, 12*, 15, 26.

Crawford, C. (1989). Microcomputers for Educational Administrators' Needs. Tallahassee, FL: Chase Crawford.

Dodge, B., and Dodge, J. (1989, November/December). Telecommunications: Free Online Access: California TRIES harder. *CUE Newsletter, 12*, p. 23.

EduNet News, *2*, 1 (Fall, 1989). Published by Georgia College, School of Education, Milledgeville, GA 31061.

Evangelauf, J. (1990, May 30). Reliance on multiple-choice tests said to harm minorities and hinder reform: Panel seeks a new regulatory agency. *Chronicle of Higher Education, 36, 37*, A1, A31.

Hussain, K. (1973). *Development of information systems for education*. Englewood Cliffs, NJ: Prentice Hall.

Knauth, K. (October, 1989). Automating the human perspective. *Electronic Learning Special Supplement: An Administrator's Guide to the Business of Education*, pp. 18–25.

National Commission on Testing and Public Policy (1990). From Gatekeeper to Gateway: Transforming Testing in America. Chesnut Hill, MA: National Commission on Testing and Public Policy (McGuinn 529, Boston College), Chestnut Hill, MA 02167.

Raucher, S. (October, 1989). Quoted in "The Business of Education." *Electronic Learning Special Supplement: An Administrator's Guide to the Business of Education*, p. 1.

Richards, C. (1989). *Microcomputer applications for strategic management in education*. New York: Longman.

Watson, C., & Morgan, B. (1989, October). The Principal as Manager. *Electronic Learning Special Supplement: An Administrator's Guide to the Business of Education*, pp. 26–33.

West, M. and others (1989). *Talking about teaching by writing: The use of computer-based conferencing for collegial exchange amount teachers* (Report TR87-12). Cambridge, MA: Harvard Graduate School of Education, Educational Technology Center (ERIC Document Reproduction Service No. ED303 363).

SOFTWARE PRODUCTS CITED IN TEXT

Total Educational Resource Management Systems (TERMS). Produced by Educational Data Recourses, 2202 Curry Ford Road, Orlando, Florida 32806.

Comprehensive Information Management for Schools (CIMS III). IBM, Applica-

PART THREE

Specific Type II Educational Applications

PART THREE DEALS WITH Type II educational computing applications. As explained in Chapter 3 and elsewhere, these applications make available new and better teaching methods—methods that would not be available without the use of the computer. We believe that it is important that educators encourage the development of more Type II applications, since achieving the objectives of these applications would clearly justify the expense needed to make them available to children in schools.

Part Three includes chapters on programming, simulations, word processing, computers as prosthetic aids for the handicapped, database management and spreadsheets, problem-solving applications, and the teaching of the Logo computer language.

__8__

Fundamental Computer Operations: Programming and Operating Systems

GOALS AND OBJECTIVES

Goal: To understand the nature and purpose of programming languages and operating systems and to become aware of trends and issues relating to teaching programming in schools.

When you finish studying this chapter, you will be able to:

1. Write at least one paragraph contrasting how computers are programmed today with how the first computer was programmed.
2. Write a paragraph contrasting BASIC and Logo in terms of their place in education.
3. Write a short report, at least three paragraphs, on the controversy surrounding teaching programming in schools.
4. Write a paragraph describing what operating systems are and why they are important to computer use.

KEY TERMS

assembly languages
automatic programming
BASIC
booting the system
COBOL
computer languages
degree of control

DOS
ease of use
formatting
FORTRAN
Logo
low- and high-level languages
machine language

mnemonic system   programming
operating systems   RAM
Pascal   ROM
PILOT   spaghetti program

Since the beginning of the computer revolution, radio, television, newspapers, magazines, and books have been filled with claims about what the computer can do. It is important to remember, however, that a computer can do nothing without human instructions.

A set of instructions for a computer is called a *program*. Programs are at the very base of everything any computer does, and a special family of programs called **operating systems** is essential to every computer application. To understand computers, the computer movement, and the use of computers in education, you need an awareness of the functions of programs and operating systems.

In this chapter, we will discuss some important historical developments in the evolution of computer programming. Some issues and trends relating to the role of **programming** in education will also comprise an important part of the chapter. A source of frequent confusion for computer users is the computer operating system. The final section of this chapter, therefore, is devoted to operating systems and their relationship to programming.

PROGRAMMING AND PROGRAMMING LANGUAGES

When the men and women we now think of as programming pioneers stood in front of the first computer, they were faced with the problem of determining the most efficient way to issue instructions. As the art of computer programming evolved, efficiency was always a concern. Efficiency, however, is not easily defined. Central to the question of efficiency is the fact that there is a trade-off between **degree of control** and **ease of use**. To have total control over the machine, the programmer has to work directly with its electronic components. This kind of programming is slow and meticulous. Efforts to make programming easier tend to decrease the programmer's control over the machine.

The trade-off between degree of control and ease of use is at the heart of many controversies in educational computing. But we are getting ahead of the story. We should look briefly at how programming as we know it today developed.

Programming the First Computer

To appreciate the difficulty of programming the first computer, consider the fact that the programmer had to wire the program into the computer

(Stern, 1981). For a simple problem like finding the sum of two numbers, the programmer had to physically change switches and connect wires in several different sequences.

It is the nature of humans to search for easier ways to perform tasks. The problem of programming the first computer stimulated such a search.

Early Programming Languages

The search for easier and more efficient ways to program computers led to the development of **computer languages**. From the beginning of the computer age, there has been a tendency to anthropomorphize computers (to speak of them as if they had human qualities). A case in point is the use of the term *computer languages*. To speak of a computer language improperly implies that computers, like humans, distill meaning from an array of variables that make up the complex systems of human languages.

Although the word *language* is a convenient way of labeling the coding systems we use to program computers, it is far from accurate. While there are surface similarities between human and computer languages, there are also vast differences. Computer languages are extremely simple, austere, and inflexible compared to human languages.

Bearing in mind that computer languages are really only coding systems that allow humans to control computers, we next turn our attention to understanding why there are many different computer languages. We briefly describe some of these.

Machine Language

Using the analogy of human and computer languages, we can say that all computers, including the first electronic computer, the ENIAC, understand only one language and that language is **machine language**. Although it is highly unlikely that you will ever have occasion to program a computer in machine language, the notion of machine language is extremely important in understanding the concept of computer programming.

All computer languages use a set of symbols. Different combinations of these symbols make up the coded instructions used to give instructions to the computer. Machine language uses only two symbols: 1 and 0. There is a certain elegance associated with using 1's and 0's as coding symbols because they are so closely associated with the actual inner workings of the computer.

To appreciate this elegance, picture the first programmer throwing switches on the ENIAC computer. The ENIAC programmer was manually turning the switches on or off. The varying of the on and off settings of the switches enables the computer to manipulate symbols, and through symbol manipulation the computer does its work.

It doesn't take much thought to realize that programming in machine language would be a tedious and laborious process. The pioneer programmers agreed. As they gained experience in programming early computers, they discovered a number of disadvantages to machine language.

The first major breakthrough in overcoming these disadvantages was the creation of a new computer language called assembly language.

Assembly Language

Symbolic assembly language, or as it came to be called, **assembly language**, did not come about in one giant leap. It was the culmination of many small steps taken by the programming pioneers in their quest to make programming easier and more efficient. Calingaert (1979) summarizes the advent of assembly language as follows:

> It was much easier to think of symbolic operation codes, such as "LOAD" and "ADD," rather than of the decimal or even binary numbers used to represent them in machine language. (p. 6)

Assembly language was an improvement over machine language because it used a **mnemonic system** in which instructions have a natural and obvious relationship to what the programmer wants the computer to do. Assembly language uses letters of the alphabet along with numbers and other symbols instead of just numbers. In some cases, English-like words such as MAIN and TRACE are used.

An important concept relating to assembly language, is the concept of translation. Remember, the computer only understands one language. The only way for it to do anything with English words like MAIN and TRACE is to have them translated into binary numbers. One type of translation program is called an assembler. An assembler is a special program written in machine language that recognizes the code used in assembly language. The assembler translates assembly language code into binary numbers so that it can then be turned into actual electronic impulses that will change the switching configuration inside the computer. Any computer language other than machine language has to be translated into machine language, just as assembly language does.

Assembly language, even though it was a great boon for early programmers, was still cumbersome and tedious for humans to use. The next big step in the history of programming was the development of high-level languages.

High-Level Languages

The term **high-level language** has been used in recent years to contrast certain computer languages with machine and assembly language, which are referred to as **low-level languages**. One reason for using the designations high-level and low-level is to indicate how close or how far away the programmer is from the actual logical circuits of the computer.

In machine language, the programmer is very close to actually controlling these circuits directly, so it is a low- level language. The group of languages we will now explore use translating systems that put several layers between the programmer and the logical circuits. The programmer is farther away from the inner workings of the computer when using these languages, and they are therefore called high-level languages.

Hundreds of high-level languages have been developed, most of which have been abandoned. Some high-level languages have had a long life, and new ones are still being developed. Only a few of these languages are relevant to the topic of educational computing and they will be described in this section.

FORTRAN

FORTRAN, named by combining parts of two words, FORmula TRANslation, was the first high-level language and was developed in the early 1950s. During that time period, there was a scramble in the computer world to develop efficient ways to do what was called **automatic programming**. FORTRAN was the first successful result of this effort. Grace Hoppper, in a keynote speech in 1981, said of FORTRAN: "This was a tremendous step. This was the first of the true programming languages" (p. 15).

FORTRAN, still a popular language among scientists and mathematicians, uses a combination of English-like words and mathematical formulas as code. While FORTRAN was an elegant way to direct the computer to solve mathematical problems, it was awkward when dealing with text.

COBOL

In 1959, some computer experts began to hope that computers could serve a wider audience than scientists and mathematicians. A group of such experts from within the industry called a conference of people who shared this hope. The purpose of the conference was to discuss the need for developing a common business language. The end result of the efforts started at this meeting was the development of the COmmon Business Oriented Language or **COBOL**.

COBOL was word oriented rather than number oriented. The people who wanted a language like COBOL were interested in using the computer to manage information such as address lists and inventories. COBOL is important as we follow the development of computer programming because it represents another step forward in making it easier to provide instructions to computers. COBOL became a computer language that favored the maximum use of simple English and avoided mathematical symbols.

The language was considered easy to use and has been given credit for allowing more people to become involved in programming.

By the early 1960s, many different computer languages were being used. However, FORTRAN and COBOL had become the most common languages. At this time, however, some individuals began to wonder if languages like FORTRAN and COBOL weren't still too complicated to encourage wide use.

BASIC

The most popular computer language ever developed is **BASIC**. BASIC is short for *Beginners All-Purpose Symbolic Instruction Code*. In the 1960s, two professors at Dartmouth University, John Kemeny and Thomas Kurtz, developed BASIC. These professors were among the first computer specialists to work toward the goal of making computer programming available to people who were not computer specialists. They believed computers could be tools to improve scholarship in all disciplines, not just the hard sciences and math.

Kemeny and Kurtz wanted to get away from the cold, stern environment they felt surrounded the computer community at the time. They wanted to provide the novice computer user with a more comfortable environment, one where even first experiences could be fun and exciting. Their philosophy was that, if the computer could be made to respond quickly and efficiently to a few simple commands and allow for some degree of error, anyone with minimal training could use the computer as a tool. The language they developed met this goal to a very great extent and, as we have said, became the world's most widely used computer language.

BASIC went further than any other high-level language at that time in making use of English-like words and simple mathematical expressions. A simple test score averaging program written in BASIC can be seen in Figure 8.1.

BASIC has important educational implications because the first microcomputers that appeared in schools were used primarily to teach BASIC programming. BASIC became the language used by nearly all early microcomputer users because the first microcomputers came with BASIC built in. All you had to do was plug the computer in, turn it on, and start programming it in BASIC. That, of course, was about all you could do with such a computer.

Pascal

One of the few computer languages with a name that is not an acronym is **Pascal**. Pascal was named after the French mathematician, Blaise Pascal.

In 1983 (Slesnick, 1983), Pascal, the language not the man, caused a major controversy in educational circles. Suddenly, teachers in high

```
100      DIM  TEST  (3)
110      FOR  I  =  1  TO  3
120           PRINT  "PLEASE  ENTER  TEST  SCORE  ";I;"-";
130           INPUT  TEST(I)
140      NEXT  I
150      TOTAL  =  0
160      FOR  I  =  1  TO  3
170           TOTAL  =  TOTAL  +  TEST  (I)
180      NEXT  I
190      AVG  =  TOTAL  /  3
200      PRINT
210      PRINT  "THE  AVERAGE  OF  YOUR  TEST  SCORES  IS  ";AVG
220      STOP
230      END
```

FIGURE 8.1 Test score averaging program in BASIC.

schools across the country began switching from BASIC, which had been accepted as the language of choice in education, to Pascal. The primary reason for the sudden change was that the Educational Testing Service (ETS) announced that, starting in 1984, their advance placement test in computer science would test for knowledge of Pascal as a measure of computer language proficiency.

The ETS decision was based on the fact that university computer science departments were teaching Pascal as the first computer language. Many computer science programs took the position that Pascal represented the best combination of two factors: ease of learning and sound programming philosophy.

Pascal's attractiveness is largely due to the fact that it is a structured language. This means that it forces the programmer to think through an entire program and organize it into logical pieces, with all the pieces fitting together in the end to make a well-ordered program. The preference for teaching programming with a structured language came about as a reaction to what has been dubbed spaghetti programming. A **spaghetti program** results when the programmer starts with little or no organization and beats out a program that eventually works, but has little order, like a mass of spaghetti on a plate.

Spaghetti programs are difficult for other people to read, and it is frustrating to find and correct errors in them. The question of whether only structured programs should be used exclusively for teaching programming is far from resolved, however. Some people argue that whether a program ends up structured or unstructured is more a result of the programmer than the programming language used. They argue that structured or spaghetti programs can be written in any computer language.

Educational Languages

Two programming languages can be considered specialized languages for education, **Logo** and **PILOT**. While very different, both Logo and PILOT were designed to enhance the teaching and learning process.

Logo

One man, Seymour Papert, is given credit for developing a computer language called Logo. At the same time, he started a minor educational revolution and a major educational controversy. Logo has to be thought of as more than just another computer language. In fact, it could be considered an educational philosophy put into practice through a unique coding system.

The name Logo carries a certain mystique, which is typical of the language and the movement. Logo was developed by Papert and his associates in a Massachusetts Institute of Technology artificial intelligence research laboratory. While the actual development work was carried out during the 1960s and 1970s (Maddux and Johnson, 1988), Logo became known through a book Papert published in 1980. The book's title was *Mind-Storms: Children, Computers, and Powerful Ideas*. Actually, only a single chapter of this book was devoted totally to Logo, while the rest of the book deals with Papert's general educational theories and philosophy. Papert's book was a best seller, and as interest in his ideas for reforming education grew, so did interest in using Logo as an educational tool.

There is little doubt that Logo is a powerful language and that it is easy to learn. Children as young as five can begin writing simple programs that create designs (graphics) by directing the movement of a turtle on the computer screen. However, the idea that Logo represents a new educational tool that can change how children learn is a controversial opinion. Chapter 14 in this book is devoted exclusively to Logo. As you read that chapter, you will gain more of an understanding of Logo and the educational philosophy surrounding it.

In Figure 8.2, you can see how our test score averaging program looks in a version of the Logo language called Logo Writer.

PILOT

John Starkweather developed PILOT while working at the University of California Medical Center. PILOT was developed primarily as a teaching and learning tool, and this goal is reflected in the name itself. PILOT is an acronym for Programmed Inquiry Learning or Teaching (Willis, Johnson, & Dixon, 1983). PILOT was developed because Starkweather felt teachers needed a language that would make it easy to program the interactive dialog necessary for computer-assisted instruction and computer-assisted testing.

```
TO TESTS
                          CT
                          CG
                          HT
                          MAKE "I 0
                          MAKE "TOTAL 0

                          REPEAT 3 [
                               MAKE "I :I + 1
                               (INSERT [PLEASE ENTER TEST SCORE]
                               :I [—] CHAR 32)
                               READLIST]

                          MAKE "AVG :TOTAL / 3
                          PRINT []
                          (PRINT [THE AVERAGE OF YOUR TEST SCORES
                          IS -] :AVG)
END
```

FIGURE 8.2 Test score averaging program in Logo Writer.

In its original form, PILOT had only 8 separate instructions. It was similar to COBOL in that it was a word-oriented language. PILOT looked friendly to people who worked with words and who tended to shy away from anything that looked like algebra.

In spite of its simplicity and the fact that it was designed for teachers, PILOT has not gained great popularity. Still, several software companies do continue to market PILOT for some popular brands of microcomputers.

ISSUES AND TRENDS IN TEACHING PROGRAMMING IN THE SCHOOLS

Teaching programming was one of the first applications of microcomputers in education. Programming is still an important part of most educational computing curricula, but a part that is fraught with controversy. In 1988, your authors wrote, "It is probably safe to say that the issue of whether to program or not to program divides present-day computer educators as sharply as any other issue" (Maddux and Johnson, p. 15).

Since 1988, much has been said on both sides of the issue, some research has been done, and past research evidence has been summarized. As we take another look at the literature on this topic, we conclude that educators are still sharply divided.

Controversies in Teaching Programming

The controversy relating to teaching programming as part of the educational computing curriculum can be divided into five parts. These parts, and the arguments relating to each, follow.

Teaching Programming to Prepare Students for Jobs

One of the first arguments to be made for teaching programming as part of the computer curriculum was that in the future more and more programmers will be needed. This seems like a logical argument at first glance, and this argument accounted for the prominent position given to the teaching of programming when the first microcomputers were placed in schools. As early as 1984, however, Kelman called attention to what should have been obvious. According to Kelman, "There are roughly 40 million students in our schools, and about 20 thousand computer programming jobs" (p. 171).

Today, few would argue with Kelman on this issue. In fact, Reed (1988) wrote:

> The educational computing community has slowly recovered from earlier claims that students need to be taught programming languages to be prepared for the future job market. (p. 55)

Although most writers support Kelman and Reed, many schools still teach programming to all students on the grounds that they are being prepared for the future job market. We believe, however, that as school practice catches up with theory and research the teaching of programming to prepare professional programmers will be left to computer science programs at the college and university level.

Using Programming to Teach Computer Literacy

The idea that experience in programming is an effective way to enhance computer literacy was stated succinctly by Kleiman (1984) when he said that "By learning to program, students acquire a better understanding of the nature of computers" (p. 121). Most computer educators agree with Kleiman. It has been our experience that when students work with a programming language they improve their understanding of how the total computer system works. This understanding is often elusive for students who do not program and who use only one or two application software packages.

Through hands-on experience with a programming language, students become keenly aware of the powers and limitations of computers. They come to appreciate that computers only do what they are instructed to do. They also gain an awareness of the hierarchy of activities that take place between the person sitting at the keyboard and the actual manipulation of symbols in the computer's electronic circuitry.

However, the fact that programming has a side effect of enhancing understanding of what computers can do and how they work does not make a good argument for justifying teaching programming. It may be that the same effects could be obtained with structured lessons designed to complement experience in using applications software.

Computer Programming Is a Tool for Teaching Mathematics

Since their invention, computers have been associated with mathematics. The very first computers were constructed for the purpose of calculating complex mathematical formulas. Perhaps because of these roots, the computer is still viewed by many as a mathematics tool. Additionally, some see it as a tool for teaching mathematics. Shumway (1983) stated, "It seems patently obvious . . . that students who write programs to do mathematics, learn mathematics (p. 2).

McCoy and Burton (1988) echoed this sentiment when they said that mathematics is an area that intuitively seems related to computer programming. McCoy and Burton tested their assumption in a research study from which they concluded:

> *After programming instruction, both Ability to Use Mathematical Variables and Mathematical Problem-SolvingAbility scores were significantly improved. (p. 165)*

While there has been speculation and some research concerning the broad topic of programming and its relationship to mathematics, more specific hypotheses have been set forth and tested concerning the value of using Logo to teach geometry.

An important aspect of the Logo language involves programming a turtle (analogous to the Euclidean point in space) to draw geometric figures on the computer screen. An underlying assumption of the educational philosophy associated with Logo is that skill in solving geometric problems using Logo will transfer to better problem-solving ability in general.

This assumption has been supported by some research results. Lehrer, Guckenburg, and Lee (1988), in summarizing a well-structured study, stated:

> *We attribute children's increased understanding of geometry to knowledge restructuring with turtle geometry rather than to simple participation in this experiment. (p. 551)*

Again, however, the increased understanding of geometry seems to be a side effect of learning and using the Logo language, and the question of whether Logo is a superior method of teaching geometry remains unanswered.

Programming Experience Improves Higher-Order Thinking Skills

The most controversial claim made by the programming advocates is the idea that learning a programming language and gaining experience in programming have a direct, positive effect on higher- order thinking skills. One factor that contributes to the controversial nature of this claim lies in the difficulty of defining higher-order thinking skills. The problem is that when a variable cannot be precisely defined it is difficult to support or refute any claims made regarding it.

A modest body of literature is emerging relating to the topic of using computer programming to develop intellectual development. This literature consists of opinion papers extolling the virtues of using programming to develop intellectual development, as well as research studies attempting to test such claims. Vockell and van Deusen (1989) very successfully summarize the literature on this topic when they state:

> There is no question that effective programmers apply higher-order thinking skills to write efficient, well-designed computer programs. The question is whether already clear and logical thinkers become successful programmers or whether people become clear and logical thinkers by writing computer programs. (p. 53)

Programming Experience Develops Problem-Solving Ability

Closely related, but more specific than the higher-order thinking claim, is the claim that programming experience develops problem-solving ability. While this claim has been set forth and investigated for programming in general, most interest centers around Logo. The reason for such wide interest in Logo as a means of developing problem-solving ability is that Logo enthusiasts, including Papert himself, have made very specific claims for the language.

Maddux (1989) sees the claim for development of problem-solving ability as "less grandiose" (p. 20) than the claim for accelerated intellectual development. Maddux, however, feels that some positive findings are beginning to emerge and that when Logo is used in specified ways it can have a positive effect on children's problem-solving abilities. In a very comprehensive analysis of educational computing research, Roblyer, Castine, and King (1988) concluded:

> Logo shows promise as a method of enhancing cognitive skills of various kinds, and looks especially good in comparison with un-structured, discovery-learning CAI applications. However, more studies need to be done comparing Logo with noncomputer problem-solving programs of instruction. (pp. 106–107)

Conclusions on Teaching Programming

While programming is still an important part of the computer curriculum in the schools, the reasons for its inclusion are changing. Most educators agree that preparing students for future jobs is not a valid reason for including programming at the elementary and secondary levels. While we believe that programming experience can enhance students' understanding of how computers work, we feel this objective might just as effectively be accomplished with short, structured lessons.

Computer programming does have some close relationships with mathematical concepts, and it is possible that lessons involving programming activities geared to teach specific math concepts could prove effective. Certainly, the use of Logo in enhancing the teaching of geometry holds promise. While there is no conclusive evidence to justify teaching programming to accelerate the onset of adult thinking, encouraging evidence is beginning to emerge that suggests programming experience, especially in Logo, can contribute to increased, transferable problem-solving ability.

OPERATING SYSTEMS

We now turn our attention to a different, yet closely related topic, **operating systems**. Operating systems are programs and, like computer languages, they work behind the scenes to make it easier to use a computer. Our experience has convinced us that some understanding of what operating systems are and what they do is an essential part of educational computer training.

Like computer languages, computer operating systems are much too complex to be thoroughly covered in one section of one chapter; there are many different operating systems with books written about each. What will be covered in this section is a practical overview of what operating systems are and what they do.

Computer users are often confused about the difference between the terms *operating system* and *disk operating system*. However, for practical purposes, the two terms mean the same thing. The first microcomputers had a series of programs that were collectively called the operating system. These computers did not have disk drives. Later, as disk drives became part of microcomputer systems, more complex operating systems had to be developed to coordinate the activities of the disk drives with the rest of the computer system. Since the disk drives, from the user's standpoint, are central to the operations of the total system, these new programs were called disk operating systems. The acronym **DOS** has become a common way of referring to the operating system of microcomputer systems. We prefer the more generic term *operating sys-*

tem because it communicates a more comprehensive view of what these specialized programs are.

We will present some of the essential concepts relating to computer operating systems by answering a series of often asked questions.

What Is a Computer Operating System?

According to DeVoney (1987) "An operating system is a collection of programs that gives control of a computer's resources to the computer's user" (p. 7). The resources of the computer are the many elements that make up the total computer system. Some of these elements are the keyboard, disk drives, memory, monitor, and printer.

The operating system gives control to the user by carrying out two basic functions: it coordinates all the activities of the total computer system, and, like a high-level language, it allows the user to give English-like word commands. The end result of both these functions is to make using a computer infinitely easier than it would be without the operating system.

To get just a glimpse of what the operating system does, let's look at a typical computer session where Mrs. Jones uses a computer as an electronic grade book. Mrs. Jones sits down at her computer to update her grade book for English class. She puts a floppy diskette in the disk drive and presses the ON switch. After a brief pause, Mrs. Jones exchanges the first floppy disk with a second and types the word GRADES. The computer tells her that her grade book program is now loaded into its internal memory and awaits further instructions. Mrs. Jones types EN-GLISH 3 and the computer displays the names and grades of her third period English class. After doing the necessary updating of grades, Mrs. Jones types PRINT and a copy of the updated grade book is printed. Finally, Mrs. Jones types SAVE and her work is saved on a floppy disk so that it can be recalled and updated later.

The updating of the grade book by Mrs. Jones seems very easy, and it was. But more was happening than meets the eye. While Mrs. Jones was directing the computer with English-like words, the computer was performing many complex operations. Let's go through the grade book update again, this time considering what the computer is doing.

The steps below are intended to make you aware of some of the things a typical operating system does during a short computing session like updating a grade book.

1. When the first disk is placed in the disk drive and Mrs. Jones presses the power button, a program goes into action that is part of the operating system. This program is stored in a **ROM** (read only memory) chip inside the computer. The program begins printing messages on the screen that identifies for Mrs. Jones some of the elements that make up the computer system she is using.

FIGURE 8.3   Computers are not a replacement for a teacher or textbook. However, a computer as shown here can be a very effective and relaxing tool for updating management and lecture materials.

2. Next, this program tests the elements of the computer system to see if they are connected and operational. This test is called the power-on self-test. One important part of this test is performed on the computer's **RAM** (random-access memory). If there is a problem with the RAM, it could cause serious complications in running software, storing data, and retrieving data.

3. Next, the program sends a signal to the disk drive where Mrs. Jones has placed the first disk. The computer then checks to see if there is a disk in the disk drive and if the disk has a program that the computer can read. If there is a disk with the right program, the computer proceeds. If not, it puts a message on the screen warning that the appropriate disk is not in the disk drive.

4. In our example, the disk that Mrs. Jones has placed in the disk drive is labeled DOS (disk operating system). The DOS disk contains programs that are essential parts of the total operating system.

5. Some of the programs on the DOS disk need to be on "red alert" so they can be used at any time. These programs are read off the DOS disk and stored in RAM. Other programs merely need to be on "stand by" and can be read from the disk each time they are needed.

6. Next, the operating system sends messages to the screen asking

Mrs. Jones for the date and time. The fact that Mrs. Jones can press the keys on the keyboard and have the computer understand the signals sent by the keys is all part of the service provided by the operating system.

7. Finally, all the tests have been run and the total operating system is ready to do its work. In Mrs. Jone's case, a prompt is on the screen that tells her the computer awaits further instructions.

8. Mrs. Jones now places her grade book software, which is called GRADES, in the disk drive and types GRADES. The operating system translates this English word into computer code and sends a signal out to the disk drive to find a program called GRADES. When it finds the program it reads it off the disk and stores it in RAM. The operating system then signals Mrs. Jones that her program is ready for use.

9. When Mrs. Jones has updated her grade book for the English class, she types the word PRINT. The operating system then becomes involved in selecting the right information from RAM and sending it to the printer. If the printer is not ready to print, the operating system discovers this and let Mrs. Jones know. Otherwise, the updated grade book information is sent to the printer and is printed.

10. Finally, Mrs. Jones tells the computer to SAVE the updated grade book information and the operating system checks to see where Mrs. Jones wants the information saved. The GRADES program has already been set to save the information on a disk drive labeled B, and the operating system complies. The information is then sent to the B drive and stored on the disk.

Why Do We Need Operating Systems?

To gain an appreciation of why an operating system is important to the modern computer, we need to look briefly back to the first computers. Not only were the first computer programmers forced to program these machines using very cumbersome coding systems, they also had to program each specific thing the computer did. A modern-day computer operation as complex as finding information on a floppy disk and moving it into RAM would have been a lengthy programming task.

Fortunately, early programmers quickly saw that it was foolish to repeat a set of instructions in machine language each time an operation was carried out. So, along with developing high-level computer languages, they developed operating systems. This involved storing a program that caused complicated things to happen and that provided the user with one simple command to set that program in motion. For example, something as simple as typing the word PRINT can set in motion a program that finds information, sends it to the printer, and causes the printer to print it out in a specified format and style. The real work of directing and carrying out these tasks is being done by the operating system.

An old iceberg analogy can help us understand why we need an operating system. When we use a computer, we deal with only a small part of what is actually going on. The rest is invisible and is handled by the operating system.

What Is Essential to Teach about Operating Systems?

Although operating systems differ in many ways, they do perform common functions. Some of the most common functions that all students need to be familiar with are summarized in the next sections.

Booting the System

The common computer term **booting the system** stems from the phrase "pulling oneself up by the bootstraps," implying the ability or determination to take the initiative and get things going. One of the first things every student should know is how to boot the system. To understand the boot function, the student needs to know what an operating system is, to be aware that he or she is working with the operating system, and to be able to distinguish between the operating system and other types of software.

Formatting Diskettes

It is likely that the most common frustration among new computer users results from a lack of understanding about **formatting** diskettes. The confusion on this matter seems to stem from the fact that some diskettes can be placed in a disk drive and the computer can both read and store information on that diskette, while in other cases the computer treats the disk as if it were a piece of cardboard. The reason for this is that when the operating system checks the disk drive it is looking for a tiny program that will tell it what information is already on the disk and how that information is organized. Unless a disk has been properly formatted, the computer cannot find such a program and has no way of determining what is in the disk drive.

One important thing an operating system can do is to format your new disks or reformat used disks. When the operating system receives the format command, it checks to see if anything recognizable is on the disk, checks the disk for flaws, erases the existing information, and then writes the necessary organizational program on the disk so that it can be recognized in the future. The specific commands for formatting vary, but each student should know how to do this with the computer he or she is using.

Organizing and Locating Files

The computer is sometimes characterized as a great aid in helping people get organized. The truth is that people can be just as disorganized using a computer as with any other system. This fact is often verified by computer users who don't understand how to use their operating system to keep their files organized. In many cases, people have saved hundreds of files, ranging from manuscripts to lesson plans, with no organization. In such cases it is just as difficult to find a particular file as it is to find a piece of information in an unorganized filing cabinet.

All operating systems have a way to organize and locate files. Some systems are more elaborate than others, but in some cases the ease of locating a file is directly related to how well files are organized. It is important that students know how the filing system works for the computer that they are using and understand why it is important to use the organizational power of operating system.

Moving and Copying Files

Besides being careful about the initial organization of files, the wise computer user knows how to move files from one storage device to another and knows the importance of backing up (duplicating) files. The user who knows how to use the computer's operating system can quickly and easily make second or third copies of files that will help insure against lost work.

Using the operating system of the computer they are working with, students need to know how to copy single files to other disks and how to make backup copies of complete disks. Computer users seem to encounter the greatest difficulty in this area when using systems that have hard disk drives. Moving and copying files back and forth between the hard disks and floppy disks is an essential skill for anyone using a hard disk drive system.

We have really only touched on the topic of operating systems in this section. We have done so to impress on you the importance of gaining for yourself and providing for your students the foundation knowledge and skills related to operating systems. We strongly recommend that you become familiar with the operating system of any computer you use and that you make it an important part of your curriculum should you become involved in any type of computer training.

SUMMARY

This chapter is divided into three main sections. First, we presented you with a perspective of what it means to program a computer, and we described a variety of computer languages. Next, we discussed some of the issues and trends in teaching computer programming as part of the school curriculum. Finally, we defined computer operating systems and tried to provide an appreciation for what an operating system is and what it does.

LOOKING AHEAD

In this chapter we emphasized the fact that progress made in programming languages and operating systems has been driven by an attempt to give humans more power with less effort over the computer. A potential result of such power is the ability for humans to program computers to simulate complex real-world events. Such programs are called computer simulations. Computer simulations are already widely used in such fields as aviation training and medicine. In the next chapter, you will discover what is happening with regard to using computer simulations in education.

RELATED ACTIVITIES

1. Interview two public school teachers who use Logo or **Pilot**. Describe in a report how these programs are used and offer suggestions on how they could be used more efficiently.
2. Interview several instructors or students in the computer science department at your school and identify which computer language they prefer and why. Write a brief summary of your findings.
3. Describe what you think the computer languages of the twenty-first century will be.

REFERENCES

Calingaert, P. (1979). *Assemblers, compilers, and program translation*. Chapel Hill, NC: Computer Science Press

DeVoney, C. (1987). *Using PC DOS*. Carmel, IN: QUE Corporation.

Kelman, P. (1984). Computer literacy: A critical reexamination. *Computers in the schools, 1*(2), 3–18.

Kleiman, G. M. (1984). Learning with computers: Potentials and limitations. *Compute, 6*(2), 120–121.

Lehrer, R., Guckenburg, T., & Lee, O. (1988). Comparative study of the cognitive consequences of inquiry-based Logo instruction. *Journal of Educational Psychology, 80*(4), 543-553.

Maddux, C. D. (1989). Logo: Scientific dedication or religious fanaticism in the 1990's. *Educational Technology*, February 1989.

_____, & Johnson, D. L. (1988). *LOGO methods and curriculum for teachers*. New York: Haworth Press.

McCoy, L. P., & Burton, J. K. (1988). The relationship of computer programming and mathematics in secondary schools. *Computers in the Schools, 4*(3/4), 159–169.

Papert, S. (1980). *Mind-Storms*. New York: Basic Books.

Reed, W. M. (1988). A philosophical case for teaching programming languages. *Computers in the Schools, 4*(3/4) 55.

Roblyer, M. D., Castine, W. H., & King, F. J. (1988). *Assessing the impact of computer-based instruction*. New York: Haworth Press.

Shumway, R. J. (1983). One point of view: let kids write programs. *Arithmetic Teacher, 30*(6), 2, 56.

Slesnick, T. (1983). Who's Pascal and why is he messing up my curriculum? *Classroom Computer Learning, 4*(4), 54–60.

Stern, N. (1981). *From ENIAC to UNIVAC: An appraisal of the Eckert–Mauchly Computers*. Bedford, MA: Digital Press.

Vockell, E., & van Deusen, R. M. (1989). *The computer and higher-order thinking skills*. Watsonville, CA: Mitchell Publishing.

Willis, J. W., Johnson, D. L., & Dixon, P. N. (1983). *Computers, teaching & learning: A guide to using computers in schools*. Beaverton, OR: Dilithium Press.

9

Educational Simulations

GOALS AND OBJECTIVES

Goal: To understand the nature of computer simulations and their use for instruction, to become aware of the different ways computers can be used and their advantages and potential weaknesses, and to understand the procedures for selecting and using simulations in the classroom.

When you finish studying this chapter, you will be able to:

1. Write a brief overview of the history of simulations before and after the advent of microcomputers.
2. Describe the barriers to wider use of simulations in schools versus the use of drill and practice and simulation software.
3. Relate theories of play to the use of simulations in schools.
4. List and explain Malone's three factors that make computer games fun and relate them to instructional simulations.
5. Discuss the potential advantages of instructional simulations.
6. Discuss the potential problems and limitations of instructional simulations.
7. List and explain the steps involved in integrating a computer simulation into the curriculum.
8. Write a brief lesson plan describing how a particular simulation could be integrated into the curriculum the student plans to teach.

KEY TERMS

concrete and abstract
   environments
instructional simulation
Kriegspiel
play

real and fantasy environments
Sell Bicycles
Sell Lemonade
Top Management Decision
   Simulation

173

When a teenager drops a quarter into an arcade game and takes control of an interstellar fighter with laser guns and force-field shields, the teenager is spending money on a computer adventure game—or, more precisely, a computer-generated simulation. Many of the more successful arcade games are, in fact, adventure games or simulations that allow you to take a role in a computer-simulated environment.

Simulations are models or descriptions of events and conditions. Players take a role in the simulation and help determine what happens next by the decisions they make. Computer-generated simulations have three major functions today: recreation, decision support, and instruction. The first function, recreation, was very popular in the early 1980s.

While video games are not as popular as they once were, many individuals of all ages still spend their quarters on arcade games that simulate everything from galactic warfare to the Los Angeles freeway. In addition, millions of homes also have video game systems made by Nintendo and its competitors, and many of the game cartridges used in those systems are simulations.

At the same time that your younger brother or sister is playing the latest video game, thousands of specialists in multinational corporations, intelligence agencies, and the military are also putting computer simulations to work. Many aspects of the popular movie "War Games" were inaccurate, but it is true that computers are used to simulate different world and national conditions in an effort to make better decisions.

On a less grandiose level, a corporation can simulate the effects of marketing a product under several different advertising strategies (for example, up-scale ads that emphasize snob appeal to justify a higher price versus "its for everybody" ads that aim for high volume and emphasize a lower price). Simulations of this sort are often called *models*. Essentially, models are aids to making important decisions.

While both recreational and decision support simulations are fascinating in their own right, this chapter will concentrate on **instructional simulations**. Simulations designed primarily for instructional purposes are called *games* in some of the literature. The terms *game* and *simulation* sometimes refer to programs that re-create aspects of a **real** or semireal **environment**. The terms *adventure simulation* or *adventure game* often refer to re-creations of imaginary or **fantasy environments**. However, the way the four terms are used is very inconsistent in the research and professional literature. In this chapter the general term simulation will be used to refer to games and simulations.

A BIT OF HISTORY

Although computer simulations are relatively new and educational applications are even more recent, the method has a long history.

Military Uses

Current applications of simulations can be traced back at least to the seventeenth century, when war games were used to simulate battles between opposing forces. Chess, in fact, is a somewhat abstract extension of a war game that is hundreds of years old. The modern war game derives from a simulation developed by Von Reisswitz for the Prussian army. Called **Kriegspiel**, it used maps and wooden blocks that represented troops, and officers in charge of opposing armies positioned their troops. Each side took a turn until a victory was declared by the supervisors. By World War I, versions of Kriegspiel were played by officers in virtually every modern army in the world. Today, many computerized versions simulate everything from a major nuclear war to the logistics of operating a supply depot in peacetime.

Business Uses

Although business applications do not date back quite as far as military uses, there has been a great deal of interest in business simulations since the mid-1950s. If the game Monopoly is disqualified because it is primarily recreational, the first business simulation or game was probably the **Top Management Decision Simulation**, which was published by the American Management Association in 1956. It was a computerized simulation that divided participants into teams that ran two competing one-product companies. Teams were required to review information on current market conditions and then make decisions that would be in effect for three months. At the end of each quarter, information on the market and company performance was given each team. The teams then made decisions for the following quarter.

Today, hundreds of business-oriented simulations deal with virtually every aspect of enterprise. Today most colleges of business include some simulation experiences in their graduate and undergraduate programs. These simulations may be relatively simple activities that allow players to make only a few decisions in a relatively uncomplicated simulation. Others require hours or even days to play, and require players to make hundreds or even thousands of decisions. Some business schools require students to complete a capstone course that is really a semester-long simulation.

Two popular simulations, **Sell Bicycles** and **Sell Lemonade**, are examples of business-oriented simulations that run on Apple II computers. Both were developed by the Minnesota Educational Computing Consortium for use in elementary schools. Both teach the concepts of supply and demand. Players make decisions about production, retail costs, price structure, and advertising. In Sell Bicycles, two teams start with $5,000 in their accounts and 200 bicycles worth $20 each in their warehouses. The objectives of the lemonade simulation are similar to those of Sell Bicycles. Students run a simulated lemonade stand and must make decisions about the amount of lemonade to make each day, the price of a glass, and how much to spend on advertising.

Educational Uses

With the exception of their use in business, educationalsimulations, especially those using a computer, received little attention until the 1960s when several were developed for use in medicine, law, and teaching. The typical teacher education simulation described a classroom situation, presented an incident that called for action on the part of the teacher, and then let the player decide what to do. The sequence presented after the decision depended on how the player choose to handle the situation. Although these early teacher education simulations received a great deal of attention, they were not widely used even in the larger colleges of education. Many of the early simulations required more computing power than was available to teacher education programs.

During the 1970s, the cost of computer power decreased, and the possibility of using simulations for instruction became a reality in many institutions. Computer simulations were developed and used in many fields. Schools of medicine began training medical students to diagnose illnesses by playing a simulation of a patient with a set of symptoms. Psychologists learned to administer tests with simulations that presented the responses of an imaginary client. Simulations also began to be used more frequently in elementary and secondary schools. In the 1970s, many of these simulations did not require a computer. Some, however, were computer based, often running on large computers that were accessed through terminals placed in classrooms. Simulations were particularly popular in science education and in training programs for special education teachers.

In the 1980s, simulations became an important method of using computers in the classroom. Simulations were important, but they were not the primary way computers were used. Even today computers are far more likely to teach basic factual information through drill and practice or tutorial programs. A high percentage of the commercial instructional software available today and most of the software developed by educators for local use are based on either a simple drill and practice model or a linear tutorial model that is similar to programmed instruction (Merrill, 1987). Simulations are not even the third most common use of computers in schools. The technology is used to teach general computer literacy skills and computer programming skills much more often than it is used to provide students with simulated experiences.

WHY ARE SIMULATIONS USED SO INFREQUENTLY?

There are numerous reasons for the limited use of instructional simulations. First, at all levels of education, from kindergarten to graduate school, it is easier and more convenient to teach declarative information (that is, facts, information that answers "what" questions) than procedural (how to do something), intellectual skills, or problem solving. Second, at all levels of education, from kindergarten to graduate school, teachers have had more training and more experience teaching declarative information than any other type. It is therefore not surprising that the focus at virtually all levels of education is on teaching this type of information.

Given this context, it is not difficult to see why a great deal of drill and practice and tutorial software is available and widely used. It is relatively easy to develop (in comparison to simulations), and it fits the teaching pattern of many educators. Incorporating drill and practice or tutorial software into the curriculum is relatively easy for many teachers. Computer-based tutorials would simply be an extension of an established pattern. Simulations would require a rethinking of the course objectives, the way the teacher interacts with students, the way students interact with each other, and the method of evaluating students and assigning grades.

Simulations call for adjustments, but those adjustments have been made by many educators. For example, McMinn (1988), a professor at George Fox College, developed Ethics Case Study Simulation. McMinn's computer simulations require students to make decisions at crucial points in a series of simulated situations, such as practicing psychology in a small town. At several points in the simulation, students must make decisions, such as whether to report child abuse. After each decision the simulation continues and reports the consequence. After the last choice the simulation reports the outcome.

The Ethics Case Study Simulation does not attempt to teach the principles of ethical practice. McMinn recommends having students complete the simulation before combining the simulation with other instructional methods, such as discussions, reading assignments, and lectures. After students have worked through the simulation and made their own decisions, the topics covered in lectures or discussions may have much more relevance for them. McMinn's simulation, which is written in the BASIC computer language, is available from the author. The accompanying manual includes instructions for creating case study simulations in your own field of study.

The requirement that teachers change their teaching style is a barrier to wider use of simulations, but many teachers are willing to make the extra effort. Another reason for the relatively rare use of computer simulations in schools is availability. "The scarcity of good simulations is probably due to the fact that developers must be expert in programming, in the experience to be simulated, and in child psychology and learning principles. Such people are scarce" (Maddux and Cummings, 1986). Thus the creation of simulations is more difficult than other types of educational software, and the decision to use simulations in the classroom is also more complex and more difficult. It is not surprising, therefore, that simulations are relatively rare in classrooms at all levels. It is also unfortunate because computer simulations have a great deal to offer.

Maddux and Cummings (1986) have argued that educational computing "is at risk of failure, due to the manner in which it is being used." Maddux and Cummings are concerned that educational computing may become a passing fad, like many other instructional technologies of the past, if it continues to concentrate on Type I uses. The increased use of Type II applications such as simulations would benefit the cause of educational computing. It would also benefit students and education.

WHY DO STUDENTS FIND SIMULATIONS APPEALING?

A simulation is not the same thing as on the job training,but it is one of several types of instructional strategies that comes close. Simulations put the student in an active role in an environment that has a set of rules. The environment may be real or fictional. For example, GAS is one of eight programs in the third volume of MODERN PHYSICS, a series of physics simulations developed by Blas Cabera and his colleagues at Stanford University. GAS simulates the thermal motion of gas molecules in a box. Students can adjust several variables, such as pressure, temperature, and the ratio of spectral to diffuse wall reflections. Students then observe what effect changes have on the behavior of the molecules. Although the environment simulated in GAS is real, it does not take into consideration all factors that influence the behavior of real gas atoms in an enclosed space. Although GAS is not a complete re-creation of reality, it does simulate real events and relationships.

GAS deals with aspects of the real world, but many simulations do not. For example, Winnie the Pooh and the Hundred Acre Wood, a simulation for young children distributed by Sierra On Line, takes place in British author A. A. Milne's Hundred Acre Wood where Christopher Robin's friend, Pooh Bear, lives. The skills learned playing this simulation, map coordinate skills and logical thinking skills, can be used in the real world, but the environment of the simulation is fantasy.

The **environment** simulated may also be **concrete** or **abstract**. Santa Fe Trail, from Educational Activities, is a concrete simulation. Set in the period between 1820 and 1829, players try to freight goods from Franklin, Missouri, on the Mississippi River through desolate and dangerous territory to Santa Fe, a trip of about 800 miles. Santa Fe Trail helps students understand an interesting and important aspect of U.S. history. Another program, The Would-Be Gentleman, also simulates a concrete environment. The Would-Be Gentleman, a Macintosh program developed by Garolyn Lougee at Stanford University, is a simulation of social mobility during the reign of Louis XIV of France. The model underlying the simulation reflects the economic and social conditions of the time, and players find it difficult to succeed if they do not have considerable knowledge of the period. The Would-Be Gentleman begins in 1638 and ends in 1715. The simulation comes with a short manual, but the program is intended for use in classes where students learn about this period of French history through readings or lectures. The simulation allows students to take a role in that society and use their knowledge to succeed.

The context of The Would-Be Gentleman is complex but it is still concrete. Tarski's World, on the other hand, simulates an abstract environment. A Macintosh program, Tarski's World was developed by Jon Barwise and John Etchemedy, philosophy professors at Stanford University. It is named after a famous Polish-American logician, Alfred Tarski. Tarski's World is an introduction to first-order logic, a subject many students have difficulty grasping. Tarski's World allows students to learn about first-order logic in abstract, artificial worlds populated by geometric figures (cubes, tetrahedrons, and dodecahedrons of varying sizes). Students can write sentences in first-order logic using a set of symbols that have very specific meanings and then test their sentences to see whether they are logically correct for the world displayed on the computer's screen. Tarski's World then checks them for semantic and syntactic correctness to determine if they are true in the world currently displayed on the screen. The program also allows students to create their own worlds.

Tarski's World does not simulate a real world and it is not, like many simulations, a program you use once and then move on. It is much like a test bench where you take a newly manufactured product or a succession of products and test it to see if it works correctly. The product in this case is a sentence that must meet the semantic and syntactical rules of first-order logic.

Regardless of whether the environment simulated is real orfantasy, concrete or abstract, all simulations are active. They call for the student to become involved in the simulation, and that is a major factor contributing to their effectiveness. It is difficult to passively experience a simulation. You must process input, make decisions, monitor progress, and coordinate your efforts to accomplish the goal. This participatory element in training has been championed by many different theoretical perspectives. John Dewey, Jean Piaget, and Jerome Bruner have all argued that involvement in the learning process is crucial to success. Sociologists use the terms *formal education* and *informal education* to distinguish between the type of learning that goes on in a typical U.S. high school history class (formal) and the way a child on an undeveloped Pacific island learns to fish by going out in a boat with an experienced fisherman (informal learning). Simulations are a way of bringing some aspects of informal learning into the classroom.

Why is an algebra class taught through lectures and assignments drudgery for some students while a video game is just the opposite? One answer to the question may come from the field of ethology. Ethologists have studied the behavior of many different species of animals in their natural habitat. One type of behavior that seems to be natural and crucial in the development of many animals is **play**. Play is more than recreation and fun. For many species, including humans, play serves important learning functions. Puppies, as they do mock battle, growl, attack, and retreat, but it is not difficult to see that this is play and not serious combat. In many species play is not a break from learning; it is one of the most effective learning strategies. Computer programs sold for entertainment seem to take advantage of an inherent human tendency—we enjoy play.

Simulations are also play. They are games in which we can take roles that we know are not real. The play in simulations may be a primary reason for their appeal. Through simulations, computers can become electronic playgrounds as well as tools for learning.

> *Some researchers believe play may well have been an important factor in the development of our species: Skills for producing workable adjustments may well have propelled manlike primates over the evolutionary threshold to "Homo sapiens." Anthropologists have hypothesized that mans' great evolutionary leaps began in play with tools, with language, or with social roles. To recreate the physical and social features of one's world by wrestling with, chasing around, leaping on, and otherwise physically interacting with them is a biological core of play. Even humans seem to make these sallies. . . . When current-day adolescents chase and fight imaginary intergalactic foes in the electronic playground of a computer arcade, we may speculate that they are following genetic imperatives to experience and to create. (Fagen, 1983)*

Chris Crawford, a well-known programmer who has created a number of educational simulations, including an international relations program called Balance of Power, also has strong views on the importance of play:

> *A teenager stands transfixed before a video machine. His pockets bulge with quarters, and his dinner—a room-temperature slice of pizza—sits forgotten on a paper plate. Asked what he is doing, he responds "Nothing, just playing." His mother feels differently: "He's wasting his time," she says. "That's what he's doing."*

*They're both wrong. The teenager is learning—and learning well.
Games are one of the most ancient and time-honored methods of
educating. They are the ideal learning technology, for they have
received the seal of approval of natural selection. (Crawford, 1983)*

Crawford and other proponents of simulations and games aslearning
mediums offer many reasons why they are powerful learning tools.
Simulations and games are play. For Crawford, play thus becomes the
"original means of educating children, and formal education, with classrooms, certified teachers, curricula, and all the other trappings, are 'the
newfangled notion, the untested fad, the violators of tradition.'"

Another scientist interested in both play and learning is psychologist
Thomas Malone (1980) who worked for several years at the Xerox Palo
Alto Research Center, where many innovative approaches to making the
human—computer interface more efficient and enjoyable were developed.
His dissertation at Stanford University was a study of what makes
computer games fun. One of his major conclusions was that the three
factors that make games fun would also make educational programs
more fun for students:

1. *Challenge*: A challenging activity must have a goal whose outcome
   is uncertain. Kids don't like games they can beat every time and
   they don't like games that are impossible to beat. Games with several difficulty levels have wider and more long-lasting appeal because
   a player can adjust the uncertainty level.
2. *Fantasy*: Children seem to enjoy and prefer activities that involve
   fantasy. For example, learning Boolean logic in a computer simulation that involves working with a fantasy character named Rocky
   who has magic boots is much preferred by most children to lectures
   on Boolean logic followed by work sheets and an end of the week
   test.
3. *Curiosity*: In Malone's words, learning situations "should be neither
   too complicated nor too simple with respect to the learner's existing
   knowledge." The optimal learning environment is one where "the
   learner knows enough to have expectations about what will happen,
   but where these expectations are sometimes unmet."

Many of the best educational simulations are excellent examples of
how Malone's three elements can be expressed in educational software.
Crawford (1983) hopes someday, with technology fully integrated into
the educational system, that "students may frolic through multiplication
tables and algebra, through adverbs and prepositions, as gaily as lion
cubs wrestling with each other on the plains of the Serengeti."

All three of Malone's factors are found in Scotland 100 Years Ago, a
simulation-database package of software designed for use with a class of
9 to 13 year olds who are divided into several groups (Martin, 1984).

Each group takes on the identity of a fictional but realistic character in Scotland 100 years ago. The task of each character is to complete a journey across Scotland, making many decisions as well as overcoming obstacles encountered along the way. Students access the computer database as they play the simulation. It provides some data on the sections the character is passing through and describes other sources of information the group can consult, such as books and maps.

The computer manages the journey and can even provide printed copies of maps and section descriptions. Much of the work and the learning occurs away from the computer as students gather information and work in groups to decide what to do next. In a typical classroom application, students may engage in a variety of activities, such as map interpretation, writing diaries about the character's journey, presentations of progress reports, and problem solving. Simulations like Scotland 100 Years Ago become the center of a wide range of learning activities.

ADVANTAGES OF SIMULATIONS

That students find good simulations inherently appealing makesthem potentially useful as instructional strategies. Do they have other advantages over alternative instructional strategies? There are nine potential advantages of simulations. These are potential advantages because all simulations do not exhibit those advantages. There are poorly designed educational simulations just as there are poorly designed drill and practice and tutorial programs.

Fun
It is probably easier to make simulations attractive and interesting than most other instructional procedures.

Inexpensive
Simulations are almost always less expensive than allowing students to learning in the real world. As Balajthy (1984) put it, "Simulations are an inexpensive way to provide background experience. An actual visit to a forest lake to observe the food chain may be optimal but not feasible." Simulations like Odell Lake, which is distributed by Minnesota Educational Computing Consortium, let students explore the food chain of a freshwater lake from the keyboard of their classroom computer.

Safe
Simulations can provide training in areas where it would be dangerous to allow students to freely experiment. Many simulations allow students

to perform experiments or practice skills in ways that would not be possible in the real world because of safety issues. As Roman (1986) put it:

> *When learning by doing isn't possible, the next best thing is learning by "almost doing." That is the main benefit offered by computer-generated simulations—realistic representations of work conditions or situations that expose employees to the problems they might encounter—before they arrive at the firing line.*

Realism

Simulations are one way of representing aspects of the real world in the classroom. Useful simulations need not, however, exactly re-create the real world. In commenting on the use of simulations to train business executives, Judy Censor, manager of a company that creates business simulations, commented, "As long as a simulation asks users to make the same kinds of decisions they'd make in real life, it doesn't have to exactly match a corporation's business" (cited in Roman, 1986).

Better Transfer

Students who learn a skill by playing some simulations may find it easier to transfer the skill to the real world. Pilots, for example, spend hours in flight simulators instead of in lecture halls because the skills they learn in the flight simulator are more easily transferred to the cockpit of a real plane than lectures on the same topic from an experienced pilot. As Huntington (1984) put it, "I think it is more important for a child to use multiplication in a practical application than to memorize the times tables. What good is it if children know the times tables but then cannot apply them?"

Less Threat and Anxiety

Some simulations permit students to experiment, to try out alternatives they might avoid in other situations. Students tend to view simulations as play and to respond to them with more motivation and less anxiety.

Teach Critical Thinking as Well as Content

> *As a teacher, I would ask students "What-if" questions. Then we would sit around and talk about what would happen if an event were to occur. These days a student can type a what-if question into a simulation game and receive an answer almost immediately. Many simulation games available today stimulate a student's thinking and help him or her become a more critical thinker. . . . Critical thinking is not taught by lecture. Children learn to think critically*

by doing. If a child puts all of his or her money into advertising and sells lemonade cheaply [in the simulation Sell Lemonade], then he or she soon learns about the economics of pricing and advertising. A lecture on good business strategies is not as effective as having the child actually practice them. (Huntington, 1984)

Encourage Socialization and Collaboration

Some instructional simulations require competition or collaboration between players. Many business simulations, for example, divide the class into two or more groups that compete against each other. Other simulations require groups of players to collaborate on the decisions that will determine the outcome. These aspects of simulations may provide students with experiences that help them develop social and leadership skills as well as skills in working in groups.

Maximum Use of Learning Time

Simulations need not exactly duplicate the real world. This is, in fact, often an advantage. In many learning situations, the real event occurs very quickly or very slowly. Fast-paced events may be unsuitable for training because novices cannot process the information quickly enough to learn what to do. Slow-paced events may waste time because the student spends most of the time waiting. Simulations can slow down fast changing events in the beginning of the simulation and speed them up as the student learns the correct procedures for handling them. Simulations can also condense the essential elements of a slow process, such as the ecology of a tropical island, so that students more effectively use the time available for instruction. Simulations may also make better use of learning time when the real environment provides learning opportunities only under certain, unpredictable circumstances. For example, the responses of simulated students in a simulation to teach administration of an informal reading inventory (Willis and Willis, 1991) and a simulation to teach classroom management skills (Strang, Landrum, and Ulmer, 1991) provide students with far more effective practice than they might receive in a real, uncontrolled, situation.

POTENTIAL PROBLEMS OF SIMULATIONS

Although some simulations do exhibit many of the advantagesdiscussed in the previous section, virtually all simulations can be subject to the limitations and problems described in this section.

Reality Is More Than the Simulation

Students who become experts at working through a simulation may not realize there are substantial differences between the simulation and the real world. Teachers must be particularly attentive to the task of pointing out the differences between simulations and the real-world processes or procedures that they simulate.

The Time Demands of Simulations
Another major problem most educators face when they use simulations in the classroom is that most simulations do not fit neatly into a standard class period, and students would prefer more, not less, simulation time. A major task is creating a lesson plan that will make maximum use of the time available for the simulation.

More Threat and Anxiety
Less threat and anxiety were discussed earlier as an advantage of simulations, but the opposite can also be true, because simulations call for intensive interaction among participants, and the results of decisions and suggestions a student may make are immediately apparent to participants. Simulations can be more threatening and more anxiety provoking than traditional lecture methods.

Objectives Mismatch
It is an unfortunate fact that many types of educational software, including simulations, do not always accomplish the learning objectives they purport to achieve. When determining whether a particular simulation is appropriate for your setting, do not rely on the advertising blurb, or the documentation. Work through it yourself and form your own opinion.

Competitive Focus
Reality is in some situations naturally competitive, and it is to be expected that simulations of those situations are competitive. Competitive learning environments are not necessarily all bad, but students should also learn collaborative and cooperative skills. Too few simulations are available today that require collaboration and cooperation between participants. In addition, the way the teacher structures the use of the simulation can also add to or decrease the competitive nature of the program.

Lack of Research Support
To this point the discussion has relied on professional experience and a large body of professional practice literature without reference to the research literature. For example, books by Greenblat (1988), Jones (1988), and Horn and Cleaves (1980) are all rich sources of advice and suggestions on the use of simulations in education. Several journals, including *Simulation & Games* and *Simulation/Games for Learning*, regularly publish articles written by educators who use simulations.

Although there is also a growing body of research on simulations, it is more often discussed than conducted. The status of instructional simulations was examined by Butler, Markulis, and Strang (1988). They reviewed articles published in the journal *Simulation & Games* and the annual proceedings of the Association for Business Simulations and Experiental Learning. Although many of the articles reported positive results, the reviewers concluded that "researchers in this area may have underutilized the techniques of randomization, . . . control groups . . . , and control of the treatment variable." That is a polite way of saying the quality of the available research is not high enough to allow us to conclude anything.

There is definitely a need for both more and better research on the effectiveness of instructional simulations. Currently, decisions to use an instructional simulation are generally made on a basis other than strong research support for the simulation's effectiveness. There are, however, several positive reviews of the available research. For example, Wolfe (1985) reviewed 39 studies on the effectiveness of simulations and games used in schools of business. Wolfe concluded that sufficient positive evidence exists to establish the effectiveness of business simulation games. Two recent reviews of simulations in teacher education (Cruickshank, 1988; Smith, 1987) also concluded that the data support the effectiveness of computer simulations, while one (Willis, 1989) concluded there was not enough high-quality research to make that conclusion.

Poor Execution

The final potential problem with simulations is poor execution. Because students enjoy many instructional simulations, some teachers simply give students the program disk and tell them to go play at the computer. The instructional objectives of the simulation are rarely achieved using this approach. Think of simulations as instruments, such as a piano. You would not roll a piano into a classroom and then set aside 30 minutes to 1 hour each day for students to bang the keys. Simulations are a tool a skilled teacher can use for instruction, but they require planning, supervision, and follow-up for maximum benefit. The final section of this chapter provides an overview of a six-stage model for using simulations.

USING SIMULATIONS IN THE CLASSROOM

Using a simulation in the classroom involvesmore than simply plugging in the computer and providing the software. Horn and Cleaves (1980) divided the use of instructional simulations into three phases: preparation, supervision, and debriefing. Willis, Hovey, and Hovey (1987) added three additional phases: selection, adaptation, and evaluation. The role of the teacher in each of these phases is crucial to the success of the simulation. The precise role of the teacher will vary with the type of simulation used, but the overview provided here is a broad outline of teacher responsibilities. Suppose, for example, that a fifth-grade teacher named Jan wants to use a simulation that is relevant to several social studies objectives on migration. The process of using a particular simulation might proceed as follows.

Selection

The process begins with the selection of a simulation. Local sources such as the school media center or the district software library may be explored. Where no local source is available, a number of sources such as software catalogs and journals may be consulted. Printed databases of information on educational software such as TESS: The Educational Software Selector are available in many college libraries as well as media centers. Electronic databases such as RICE (Resources in Computer Education) are also very useful. RICE can be accessed through several electronic information services. Both TESS and RICE contain reviews written by teachers who have actually used the software in question.

Jan, our hypothetical fifth grade teacher, checks the databases for reviews and discovers a program named Oregon Trail. This program is distributed by Minnesota Educational Computing Consortium, and Jan's school district has a site license for MECC software. Thus the district can make as many copies of the software and documentation as needed as long as they are used in one of the district's schools.

Adaptation

Virtually any simulation you select will require some adaptation to fit local needs and conditions. Issues such as the time available and the resources needed may force you to make changes in the directions for using the simulation. Adaptations may also have to be made because your objectives are somewhat different from those of the pioneers on the trail in 1847. The trip begins in Independence, Missouri, and ends in Oregon City, Oregon. Players must make many decisions on the 2,000-mile trip. The prices and probabilities of different events are based on books about the period and historical records such as diaries.

The objectives listed in the documentation coincide with several of Jan's for the semester, and, after looking over the recommended lesson plan for the simulation, Jan decides to use most of the suggestions.

Preparation

Educational simulations must be integrated into the overall instructional plan if they are to be maximally effective. The manual for Oregon Trail includes a five-day lesson plan that begins with a discussion of the Westward Movement and ends with follow-up activities that include a comparison of the student's results on the simulation with the actual results of wagon trains to Oregon. Because Jan's objectives are broader than just an understanding of the Westward Movement, Jan omits some activities in the standard lesson plan and adds others. To prepare students for Oregon Trail, Jan makes reading assignments on migration from the fifth grade social studies text. Students also spend some time in the school library reading about the Westward Movement and other migrations. Jan also leads a discussion on the meaning and reasons of migrations and reads a few passages from the diary of a pioneer that was referenced in documentation for Oregon Trail.

Supervision

When students play the simulation, the role of the teacher depends on the objectives of the simulation, the type of simulation used, the maturity of the students, and the educational setting. The teacher's role can range from that of a war games style referee to helper and guide or hardware and software troubleshooter.

There may also be important windows of learning opportunitiesor teachable moments while students are playing a simulation. With careful encouragement and leadership, the simulation can become the hub for a wide range of learning activities.

After two days of preparatory activities, Jan introduces Oregon Trail. Handouts from the manual are duplicated and passed out. The mechanics of running the simulation are explained, as well as the types of decisions that must be made. Then the class is divided into groups of four. Decisions are to be made by the group after discussion, but students in each group are assigned tasks, such as treasurer, diary keeper, and map recorder. The students will run Oregon Trail on an IBM-PC in the classroom (Apple II versions are also available).

Each group runs the simulation once and keeps a record of its problems. Because Jan is also interested in developing group problem-solving skills, each group is instructed to analyze the reasons why their wagon train did not make it to Oregon City (few do on the first try). Jan leads a class discussion on the reasons for lack of success and models some general problem-solving procedures. Then each group formulates strategies for a second and third try. Most groups are successful by the third try. As groups run the simulation, Jan takes a supportive but nonintrusive role.

Debriefing

An important, though often overlooked, aspect of any instructional procedure is the postactivity debriefing, or closure (Pearson and Smith, 1986). Debriefing is especially important with simulations. During the debriefing phase a discussion of the issues students dealt with in the simulation often helps them consolidate the concepts and procedures they learned. Debriefing also helps students identify misconceptions or inaccurate assumptions about the simulation and provides an opportunity for students to discuss the differences between the simulation and reality.

Jan's follow-up activities for Oregon Trail are somewhat different from those in the program's manual because Jan's objectives are somewhat different. Some of the recommended activities are used, such as having a group write a letter to relatives "back East" telling them of the hardships of the trip. Most of Jan's other debriefing activities are not in the manual. They include a discussion of the reasons for migration. Each of the groups then selects another migration (for example, from Vietnam after the fall of South Vietnam, or from Ireland to America during the potato famine). The group studies and reports on the reasons for the migration and the perils immigrants faced.

Evaluation

The final phase in using a simulation is an evaluation of its effectiveness. This does not necessarily mean students take a 40-item multiple-choice test on the simulation. The evaluation can take many forms. It is important, however, to ask yourself a number of questions. Did the simulation accomplish the desired cognitive and/or affective objectives? When it is used again, would it be more effective if some adjustments or changes were made? In many cases, students can provide excellent suggestions for improving the way the simulation is used.

Most of Jan's methods of evaluation were informal. The reports and analyses of the groups were examined, and during the debriefing phase students were asked for suggestions. Jan concluded that Oregon Trail was a very effective focal activity for the study of migration. However, two changes are planned for next year. Students suggested that additional simulations be added to the lesson. Jan plans to check the databases and select one or two more simulations to support Oregon Trail next year. Jan also plans to use Oregon Trail as part of the instruction on a math topic, probability. The Oregon Trail manual includes a list of the probabilities for events such as getting lost in the mountains (10% at each two-week turn) and illness (25% if eating poorly, 19% if eating moderately, and 13% if eating well). After the first two turns, Jan will provide students with information on the probabilities of different events and help groups interpret the probabilities and use them to adjust their decisions to maximize the likelihood of success. Adding this aspect to the work on Oregon Trail will take a bit more time, but playing the simulation seems to create a teachable moment when students can learn and apply the concepts of probability.

SUMMARY

Simulations have been used for centuries, but until the advent of personal computers the use of computer-based simulations for instruction was not widespread. In the 1960s, fields such as business, teacher education, and medicine began using computer-based simulations on large mainframe computers. With the spread of relatively inexpensive computers, instructional simulations are moving into elementary and secondary classrooms as well as higher education. Simulations are still not used as frequently as other forms of computer-based instruction, such as drill and practice and tutorials. There are many reasons for this pattern, but two of the most important are the small number of good simulations available and the fact that significant adjustments in teaching style may be required to use them. The increased use of simulations is warranted, however, because they have a number of potential advantages. On the other hand, simulations also have a number of significant problems and potential weaknesses that teachers must be aware of. Using a simulation for instruction is a six-stage process that begins with selection of the simulation and proceeds through the steps of adapting the simulation, preparing students to use the simulation, supervising student use, debriefing, and evaluation.

SOME QUESTIONS TO CONSIDER

1. Describe a teacher training program and a school environment that would encourage and facilitate the use of simulations.
2. Identify several difficult concepts or principles in your field of study that could be effectively taught with simulations.

LOOKING AHEAD

Simulations represent a different way of deliveringinstruction to students. In the next chapter, you will learn about a popular use of computers, word processing, that represents a new way of accomplishing tasks that have traditionally been a part of education.

REFERENCES

Balajthy, E. (1984, March). Computer simulations and reading. *Reading Teacher*, pp. 590–593.

Borko, H. (1962). *Computer applications in the behavioral sciences*. Englewood Cliffs, NJ: Prentice Hall.

Butler, R. J., Markulis, P. M., & Strang, D. R. (1988). Where are we? An analysis of the methods and focus of the research on simulation gaming. *Simulation & Games, 19*(1), 3–26.

Crawford, C. (1983, December). Programmed to play. *Science Digest*, pp. 78–79.

Cruickshank, D. R. (1988). The uses of simulations in teacher preparation: Past, present and future. *Simulation & Games, 19*(2), 133–156.

Fagen, R. (1983, December). Horseplay and Monkeyshines. *Science, 83*, pp. 71–76.

Greenblat, C. (1988). Designing games and simulations: An illustrated handbook. Beverly Hills, CA: Sage Publications.

Horn, R., & Cleaves, A. (eds.) (1980). *Guide to simulations/games for education and training*. Beverly Hills, CA: Sage Publications.

Huntington, F. (1984, October). *Thinking is an Adventure*. InCider, pp. 33–36.

Jones, K. (1988). *Simulations: A Handbook for Teachers*. London: Logan Page.

Maddux, C., & Cummings, R. (1986, July). Educational computing at the crossroads: Type I or Type II uses to predominate? *Educational Technology*, pp. 34–38.

Malone, T. W. (1980). *What makes things fun to learn?*
A study of intrinsically motivating computer games. Unpublished doctoral dissertation, Stanford University, Stanford, CA

Martin, A. (1984). Microworld for the classroom.
Interactive Learning International, *1*, 7–8.

McMinn, G. (1988). *Ethics case study simulation manual.*
Newberg, OR: George Fox College.

Merrill, M. D. (1987). The new component design theory: Instructional design for courseware authoring. *Instructional Science*, *16*, 19–34.

Pearson, M., & Smith, D. (1986). Debriefing in experience-based learning. Simulations/Games for Learning, 16(4), 155-171.

Roman, D. (1986, February). Realism without risk, *Computer Decisions*, pp. 62–64.

Smith, P. E. (1987). Simulating the classroom with media and computers: Past efforts, future possibilities. *Simulation & Games*, *18*, 395–413.

Strang, H., Landrum, M., & Ulmer, C. (1991). A self-administered simulation for training basic classroom skills. *Computers in the Schools, 8*(1, 2, 3), 229–243.

Willis, D. (1989). *Development and evaluation of IRIS: A computer simulation to teach preservice teachers to administer an informal reading inventory*. Unpublished doctoral dissertation. Texas Tech University, Lubbock.

————, & Willis, J. (1991). IRIS: A training
simulation for the informal reading inventory. *Computers in the Schools, 8*(1, 2, 3), 245–250.

Willis, J., Hovey, L., & Hovey, K. (1987). *Computer simulations: A source book to learning in an electronic environment*. New York: Girlond Publishing.

10

Word Processing in Education

GOALS AND OBJECTIVES

Goal: To understand what word processing is and why and how it could be useful in education.

When you finish studying this chapter, you will be able to:

1. Write a paragraph explaining at least three ways in which word processing is superior to handwriting or typewriting.
2. Tell why ease of production and revision is sometimes cited as a reason to use word processing in writing classes.
3. Compose a paragraph explaining how word processing might relate to research on academic learning time.
4. Some writing experts believe that the real value of word processing in writing instruction is to facilitate establishment of "a new social organization for writing." Explain this.
5. Tell how computers might be used in schools to promote a sense of audience for what is written.

KEY TERMS

academic learning time
classroom communication
environments
collaboration

command driven
cursor
full screen editing
functional learning

icon driven   sense of audience
import/export capability   spelling checker program
menu driven   thesaurus
metacognition   windows
print formatting   word processing
search and replace   word wraparound

This chapter will provide an overview of one of the most useful and popular Type II educational applications for computers, **word processing**. We begin by providing an explanation of what word processing is and why it has been so widely accepted in both business and education. We then provide guidelines concerning the proper age to begin keyboarding instruction as well as what to look for in computer programs designed to teach these skills. We provide a review of research on word processing in education, followed by sections on idea processors and other, related computer-writing aids. We conclude with a review of four popular word-processing packages available for popular microcomputers.

WORD PROCESSING: A USEFUL AND POPULAR TOOL

Many computer users believe that word processing is the most useful of all microcomputer applications. Lillie, Hannum, and Stuck (1989) suggest that "If there were a vote taken on the most useful application of computers in today's society, word processing would no doubt win" (p. 138).

Be that as it may, word processing is certainly the most widely used form of computing in our country (Flake, McClintock, and Turner, 1990). In fact, Collis (1988) suggests that more than 60% of all personal computer use is for word processing.

Although teachers have been slower than business or home users in adopting word processing, they are beginning to make extensive use of this application (Flake, McClintock, and Turner, 1990). Bullough and Beatty (1987) have observed:

> *To date, the greatest impact has been in the business sector, but the technology is rapidly gaining favor in many other areas where people work with the written language. Because one of the more important functions of the school is teaching students to express themselves through writing, we would expect that they would be well along in the implementation of word processing practices. After a slow start, this now appears to be the case. (p. 158)*

The idea that word processing has had a beneficial impact on business is rarely disputed. Its success there was due partly to its great power and partly to the fact that in the 1980s business was uniquely in need of a new productivity tool. This latter condition came about because, in the seventies, office productivity had increased by only 5% while factory productivity increased by almost 100% (Fuori and Aufiero, 1986). In light of the fact that studies have shown that word processing increases typing productivity by approximately 100 percent, and in some cases 400% (Fuori and Aufiero, 1986), it is easy to see why word processing was eagerly adopted by business. It is gradually becoming common in education.

WHAT IS WORD PROCESSING?

Flake, McClintock, and Turner (1990) define a word processor as "A computer program that allows for writing, inserting, deleting, changing and formatting the written word" (pp. 382–383). Long (1988) defines word processing as "Using the computer to enter, store, manipulate, and print text in letters, reports, and books" (p. 256). Roberts and coauthors (1988) suggest that all word processors allow three related activities: "The ability to create and edit text; the ability to format and print text; and the ability to store and retrieve files or works in progress" (p. 77). Mandell and Mandell (1989) say that word processing is "A computer application that enables you to write, edit, format, print, store, and retrieve text" (p. 64).

After reading these definitions, it should be clear that word processing is a computer writing tool that replaces traditional writing tools, such as paper and pencil or typewriters.

THE ADVANTAGES OF WORD PROCESSING

The major advantage of word processing over other writing tools is that the word processor imparts to the user great power and ease of revision. This power is so important that we believe that moving from typewriting to word processing is even more beneficial than moving from handwriting to typewriting.

Although the typewriter is a wonderful writing tool, its major advantage over handwriting is speed. However, typewriting does not make it easier to make revisions. In fact, it could be argued that typewritten text is even more difficult to revise than is handwritten text. After all, text that is handwritten in pencil can be easily erased, while the same cannot be said for typewritten text. Word processing, on the other hand, brings the advantage of speed, while making even major revisions possible with only a keystroke or two.

To give you some idea of what word processing is like, we will contrast using typewriting and using word processing to write an essay for an English course.

An Imaginary Typewriting Session

To begin, you will roll a piece of typing paper into your typewriter and begin typing. As you approach the end of each line, you will listen for a bell. When you hear the bell, you will try to finish the word you are typing and then you will push a button that will cause the typewriter to space down to the next line and move the carriage to the beginning of that line. Minor typing errors can be corrected fairly easily if you catch them as you make them. If not, correction will be much more difficult.

Many major revisions will be impossible without a great deal of retyping. For example, if you complete your rough draft and then decide that you should have added a paragraph in the middle of page seven, you will have to retype the entire document from page 7 to the end of the text.

An Imaginary Word-Processing Session

When word processing, you will begin by turning on your computer system and loading your word-processing software into computer memory. You then begin typing. As you reach the end of each line, the computer keeps track of how much space is left, and automatically moves to the next line when appropriate, taking any partial words to that line (This is called **word wraparound**).

Minor typing errors are simple to correct. If you misspell a word, you use the arrow keys to move the **cursor** (usually a flashing line or block indicating your place in the document) onto the word and type the correct word over the incorrect one. The computer substitutes the new spelling for the old one. You can delete an extra space with a single keystroke. Such corrections can be made as soon as errors are made or at any later time with no difference in ease.

Even major revisions can be made easily. To add a paragraph to the middle of page 7, you simply place the cursor at the point where you wish the paragraph to begin. Then you type the paragraph. As you type, the computer automatically moves to the right all of the following text on that line to make room for the new text. The computer also adjusts the rest of the document all the way to the end of the text, making each page end at the new, appropriate spot without any retyping whatsoever. You can print out any number of clean copies at any time.

When you are satisfied with the text, you may elect to use a **spelling checker program** that will show you any words not found in a 50,000-word (or larger) electronic dictionary. The spelling checker may

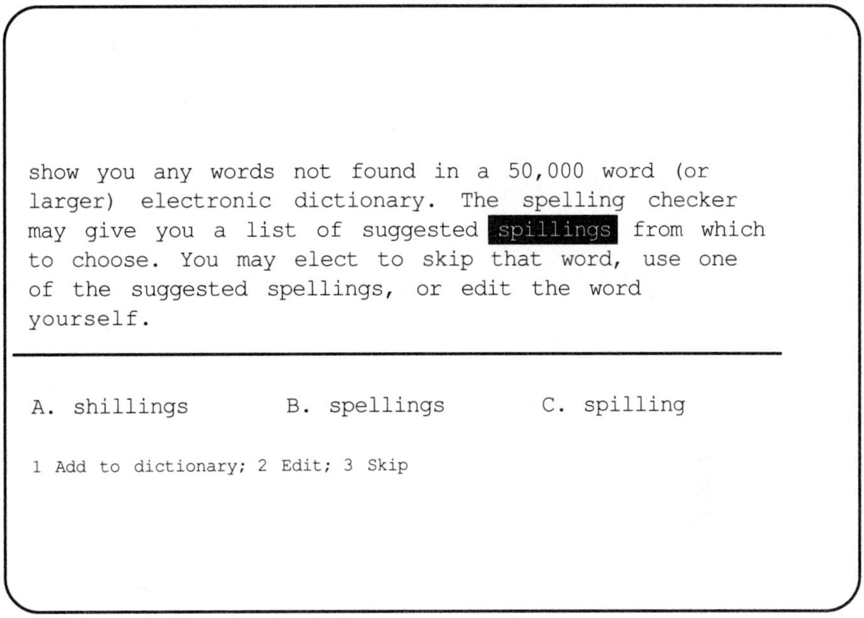

show you any words not found in a 50,000 word (or
larger) electronic dictionary. The spelling checker
may give you a list of suggested `spillings` from which
to choose. You may elect to skip that word, use one
of the suggested spellings, or edit the word
yourself.

A. shillings   B. spellings   C. spilling

1 Add to dictionary; 2 Edit; 3 Skip

FIGURE 10.1   Using a spelling checker.

give you a list of suggested spellings from which to choose. You may elect
to skip that word, use one of the suggested spellings, or edit the word
yourself.

You may then choose to use a grammar checker that will look for
certain common errors and make suggestions for revision.

When you are finished with the document, you can print out a final
draft. You may also decide to save a copy of the document on a floppy disk
and send it through the mail to a friend. Your instructor may even allow
you to turn the essay in on diskette. The instructor may use a computer
to write suggestions on the diskette and then return it to you for revision.
If you decide to print out a copy on paper, you can specify top and bottom
as well as right and left margins, order automatic page numbering, place
a header or footer on every page, change the size of type, or make other
formatting changes. The chances are good that when you are finished
with the essay you will be satisfied that it is as good as you are capable of
making it.

After reading the above description, you will probably agree that
word processing is a good example of a Type II computer application.
Like many other Type II applications, word processing gives the user a
blank screen and an extremely powerful way to fill that screen with
whatever the user desires. Empowerment of the user is always a strong
clue that an application falls into the category of Type II.

SELECTING A WORD PROCESSOR

In the past, most educational computing books included long lists of desirable word-processing features. Such discussions are no longer as important as they once were, because almost all word processors now include most of these features. For those readers who may not be familiar with word processing, we will provide a short description of important word-processing features.

Word processors are often characterized as either **command driven** or **menu** or **icon driven**. Command-driven word processors require the user to memorize which keystrokes will accomplish given ends. (For example, an "S" followed by a name may cause the document to be "SAVED" on a diskette.) A menu-driven word processor presents the user with a list of choices. Icon-driven programs also present menus, but these menus include symbols or pictures to help in making choices. In general, menu- and icon-driven word processors are easier for beginners to learn (although you must still learn which keystrokes will access given menus). On the other hand, expert users sometimes say they are irritated (and delayed) by being forced to look at menus or icons.

Quality word processors include the following:

1. *Word wraparound*: If text is typed to the end of a line, the computer automatically brings additional text, including partial words, to the next line.

2. *Full screen editing***:** This feature enables the use of cursor keys or mouse to move the cursor anywhere on the screen and make changes.

3. *Flexible **print formatting** commands*: It should be possible to quickly set margins, spacing, page breaks (where a page should end), page length, page numbers, headers or footers (text placed at the top or bottom of every page), justification (making the text line up at the right margin), italics, boldfacing, underlining, style of type, and other print variables. The word processor should also be capable of working with a variety of popular printers.

4. *Import/export capability*: It should be possible to save portions of text as a separate file or to import portions of text from another document into the current document.

5. *Search and replace* **commands**: Good word processors allow the user to search a document for any word or words and to replace this "string" with another.

6. *File management capabilities*: It should be possible to format a diskette and issue other system commands from within the word processor.

7. *Spelling checker and **thesaurus***: There should be a resident spelling checker and thesaurus. This eliminates the necessity of leaving the word-processing program to use speller or thesaurus.

8. *Other capabilities*: These include the ability to create windows, generate outlines automatically, perform mathematics, create a form letter that will insert names and addresses from a previously prepared list, automatically create tables of contents or indexes, import graphics (pictures) into the document, or perform any one of many other tasks.

WORD PROCESSING IN SCHOOLS

Many teachers sense the potential of word processing in education. Although research is just beginning (MacArthur, 1988), the literature of the past 10 years or so is full of endorsements of word processing as a tool in the teaching of writing. Most of these endorsements are based on (1) logic, (2) personal experiences of the author with word processing as an aid to professional writing, or (3) personal experiences in teaching writing using word processing.

We have surveyed this literature and found that the endorsements of word processing as a tool for teaching writing fall into four categories: (1) ease of production and revision, (2) cognitive advantages, (3) social advantages, and (4) attitudinal advantages.

Ease of Production and Revision of Text

Ease of production and revision is the most obvious advantage of word processing, whether it is used by professional writers, teachers, students, or anyone else. Roblyer, Castine, and King (1988) have suggested that teachers have found word processing attractive primarily because it takes the drudgery out of composition. Dudley-Marling (1985) agrees and attempts to explain why some students are reluctant to write and why word processing helps them:

> *Probably because good writing requires editing and editing requires recopying, which is tedious and may even be viewed as punishment. . . . Word processing makes editing easy. Text can be inserted, deleted, or moved about with the touch of a key. Once satisfied with what they have written, students can obtain nicely typed, perfectly formatted texts by performing a few additional operations. (p. 390)*

The U.S. Office of Technology Assessment (1988) says of word processing:

> *While these tools do not, in and of themselves, create better writers, they have demonstrated their importance in easing the physical requirements of writing and revising. (p. 44)*

Rosegrant (1985) is another advocate whose arguments fall into this category:

> *Young writers appreciate the lack of finality to text they put on the screen. Errors caused by inexperience or motor difficulties can be corrected without recopying every word. (p. 114)*

Those who argue for word processing because it makes writing easier frequently point to research on **academic learning time**. Academic learning time is the amount of time that a student spends paying attention to relevant academic tasks while performing those tasks with a high rate of success (Vockell and Schwartz, 1988). Another way of saying this with respect to writing is that the more time a student spends writing successfully, the better he or she will become at writing.

Research has shown that the typical high school student spends less than 3% of the school day writing anything longer than a paragraph (Branan, 1984). Since word processing makes it possible for students to spend less time recopying drafts and more time composing and revising, word processing should be a beneficial tool in the writing classroom.

Vockell and Schwartz (1988) describe the advantages of word processing as follows:

> *Students without computers who have an hour to revise their compositions tend to spend as little as ten minutes thinking about their ideas, since they need to spend most of the hour recopying their text. Frequently, they revise while recopying and do not make changes that would call for more effort. This may be an effective use of time in a penmanship or typing course, but merely recopying one's work is hardly an efficient way to develop the ability to express one's ideas more clearly. . . . Using computers to teach writing skills was effective, therefore, precisely because it enabled the learners to increase the amount of time they were actively involved in the learning process. (p. 17)*

Word Processing and Cognitive Advantages

Some educators base their word-processing advocacy on cognitive advantages. Kinzer, Sherwood, and Bransford (1986), for example, suggest that word processing facilitates efficient use of memory and provides more immediate reinforcement:

> *The word processor enables student writers to free short-term memory by concentrating on large-scale revision of ideas, while holding con-*

cerns with spelling and punctuation for later. In addition, having several neatly revised drafts quickly available allows the writer instant feedback on global revisions without the burden of reading through messy corrections and deletions. Having the capability to receive clean copy immediately after revising provides strong, immediate reinforcement. (p. 239)

Similarly, writing expert Donald Graves is enthusiastic because he thinks there is a match between the capabilities bestowed by the word processor and the thought processes of the writer:

In word processing the computer no longer merely "computes"; it manipulates symbols in the form of letters and words. The way it can move ideas, fragments and finished segments here, there and back again at the flick of a key or two makes it a near ideal companion for the writer's finicky thought processes. As far as writers are concerned, if the computer did nothing else besides word processing it would still be the invention of the century. (Green, 1984, p. 21)

Another cognitive advantage for word processing is the potential for specialized word processing tools designed to teach or facilitate the cognitive processes known to be involved in writing. Montague (1990) suggests that such programs "facilitate and prompt cognitive activity during the composing process" (p; 51).

Even nonspecialized, popular word-processing packages sometimes have features that can be used in this way. For example, many popular packages have a feature that permits creation of **windows**. In its simplest form, a window is *a portion of the computer screen that can be reserved for creation, display, and editing of a secondary document while the rest of the screen is used for creation, display, and editing of the primary document.* Thus, those writers who work from an outline or from notes can display them in the window while working on the document itself in the primary portion of the screen.

Other applications focusing on cognition include specially designed word processors that have an interactive component. The programs contain prompts to stimulate self-questioning and self-instruction. Such programs attempt to make use of metacognitive principles. (**Metacognition** refers to the knowledge we have about our own thought processes,in this case thought processes related to writing.)

Other programs making use of knowledge of cognition may contain hints or cues to help writers revise their work. Some of these programs focus on prewriting or planning activities, while others focus on evaluating or revising what has already been written.

Word Processing and Social Advantages

Some word-processing advocates highlight the social advantages or side effects of using word processing in writing instruction in the school. Collis (1988) suggests that students are more likely to work together when writing with a word processor. Bruce, Michaels, and Watson-Gegeo (1985) also refer to social changes as a result of work processing.

Cannings and Brown (1986) believe that word processing can facilitate the creation of **functional learning environments**. They define these environments as "Those in which reading and writing are organized for communicative purposes rather than just as an exercise for teachers to evaluate" (p. 149). They go on to discuss the primary value of the microcomputer:

> *While we have found that the microcomputer itself cannot transform unskilled writers into skilled ones, it does present a medium that makes a new social organization for reading and writing possible. It is this social organization and not the computer alone that has positive effects on the reading and writing process. (p. 149)*

Bruce, Michaels, and Watson-Gegeo (1985) note that word processors make it possible to set up "**classroom communication environments**" (p. 143). In such environments, the social life of the students involves reading and criticizing the work of peers and using writing to communicate with each other for valid purposes. They note that students spend time milling around the computer while waiting to use it, and that during this time, they read and discuss each other's work. This reading and interacting makes writing relevant and tends to improve writing skills. They go on to state:

> *Similarly, peer interactions during writing on the computer, student access to other students' work stored in the computer, and programs like "mailbag" in which students send messages to each other, can affect students' understanding of purpose in writing, and their sense of audience. (p. 147)*

Many other word-processing advocates mention the potential of the computer in helping to cultivate a sense of audience. (Branan, 1984; MacArthur, 1988; Montague, in press) Graves makes this point in a recent interview in *Classroom Computer Learning*, and suggests that a sense of audience can best be established by publishing students' work:

> *One of the questions that kids have, any writer has, is, Who will read this—other than the teacher? We did a study last spring that showed*

that the kid who has the greatest difficulty in writing—no suprise—
doesn't think anyone will read his work but the teacher. (Green,
1984, p. 21)

Graves goes on to point out that word processing greatly increases the capacity of the teacher to publish students' work or for students to publish their own work. There are even specialized programs such as *Newsroom* (Springboard Software, Inc., 7808 Creekridge Circle, Minneapolis, MN 55435) that are designed to assist in producing a class newspaper using a computer.

A related social advantage is the opportunity for **collaboration** (teaming up with others) in writing classes using word processing (Heap, 1986; Dickinson, 1986). Collaboration is seen as desirable for its own sake and has been shown to have a beneficial effect on writing.

Word Processing and Attitudinal Advantages

Many educators value word processing because of its potential to change students' attitudes about writing. Reidesel and Clements (1985) take the position that the computer is ideal for helping students become more positive about writing. Rosegrant (1985) suggests that a more favorable attitude toward writing is a function of ease of revision. Flake, McClintock, and Turner (1990) also emphasize that word processing can change students' attitudes about revision by helping them realize that their work is part of a drafting process instead of finished copy. Similarly, MacArthur (1988) emphasizes the importance of using word processing to help foster the attitude that writing is a process involving cycles of planning, writing, and revising.

What about Keyboarding Skills?

We are often asked a variety of questions about keyboarding. Teachers are sometimes concerned that young children will not be able to master keyboarding well enough to benefit from word processing. As Collis (1988) points out, most studies have shown that young children can learn to handle the keyboarding required to profit from word processing. This was true even for those grade 1 children included in the IBM Writing to Read evaluation study (Murphy and Appel, 1984).

Sometimes teachers ask how early to begin touch typewriting instruction. We feel that third or fourth grade is about the earliest for such instruction. Even then, research shows that frequent practice is needed to avoid losing typing skills.

A variety of software is available to help children improve keyboarding skills. Yacht (1985) includes a helpful list of features that good programs of this type should contain. She suggests that the methods used in the program should be based on five stages of instruction: (1) keyboard presentation, (2) straight-copy drills, (3) timed writings, (4) production typing, and (5) related knowledge. She goes on to say that good programs should (1) start immediately and easily with a minimum of menus and waiting, (2) incorporate practice in typing real words, (3) reward correct keystrokes immediately, (4) teach the alphanumeric keyboard and the 10-key number pad, (5) require use of only one diskette, (6) allow continuation to the next exercise or review of the previous one, (7) provide periodic speed testing, (8) provide for teacher customizing of lessons, (9) be inexpensive, and (10) be self-explanatory to the extent that documentation is largely unneeded.

RESEARCH ON WORD PROCESSING IN EDUCATION

Research on word processing is just beginning (Montague, in press). It is far easier to find endorsements of word processing than empirical studies of effectiveness. However, Roblyer, Castine, and King (1988) make the interesting point that since word processing clearly takes the drudgery out of writing, it is not necessary to prove that it is better than other writing methods—its use will be justified if it is merely equivalent. We agree. Encouraging results are beginning to emerge from studies on the effects of word processing on writing. The U.S. Office of Technology Assessment (1988) reviewed this research and concluded that both normal and learning disabled students who used the word processor as a supplement to writing instruction made significant gains in writing ability, compared to control groups that did not receive the computer- assisted intervention.

The claims concerning word processing are that it improves "quality of writing, length of compositions, number and kind of revisions, and students' attitudes toward writing" (Roblyer, Castine, and King, 1988, p. 100).

Quality of Writing

Roblyer, Castine, and King (1988) reviewed eight studies on the effect of word processing on quality of writing and concluded that there was clear evidence that writing was improved. Collis (1988) agrees that most studies have reported improvements, although she points out that there have been mixed results. Barker (1987) suggests that the mixed results in this area may be due to factors such as the type of word-processing system used (for example, non-user-friendly systems may frustrate users and slow them down) or the adaptability of the user. Barker goes on to hypothesize that writers do better on systems that genuinely make writing easier.

Length of Compositions

Although there are a few exceptions, most researchers agree that word processing results in more writing than handwriting or typewriting (Loheyde, 1984; Montague, 1990). More research is needed, and teaching methods and classroom environments must be described and held steady.

Revisions

Many word processing advocates have been disappointed in the results of studies on revision. Surprisingly, research shows that the increased revisions made when word processing tend to be surface revisions such as spelling and mechanical changes, while pencil and paper tends to foster content-level changes (Barker, 1987; Daiute, 1986; MacArthur, 1988; Montague, 1990).

Barker (1987) reviewed this research and pointed out that there are many problems in trying to interpret the findings:

> *These studies were beset with the lack of control over the same kind of variables that skewed the results of composition studies we looked at previously: variables in machine and program design, in the amount of word-processing instruction subjects have, and in the overall instructional context of the study. (p. 116)*

Many improvements need to made in research strategies on revision. Nevertheless, we agree with Barker's conclusions about this topic:

> *The truly positive applications of word processing it now seems may lie in the areas of composing and student attitudes. (Barker, 1987, p. 119)*

Attitudes

Encouraging results have been obtained from studies on effects of computer use on student attitudes. Roblyer, Castine, and King (1988) suggest that this is the most promising result of word processing. A similar conclusion is reached by Barker (1987), who suggests that this finding is so universal that there is little need to continue research on the topic.

Collis (1988) reviewed a number of studies that reported positive attitude changes as a result of word processing. Only one study found a decline in positive attitudes toward writing, and this study also reported problems such as poor typing skills, insufficient equipment, hardware and software problems, and poor writing assignments.

Interpreting Research on Word Processing

Word-processing research is flawed, probably because it is so new. However, we can tentatively conclude that word processing leads to better attitudes toward writing, and to longer manuscripts with more surface revisions than text written with paper and pen. These advantages may be available by merely introducing word processing into the writing curriculum with no changes in teaching methods.

Improved quality of writing and increased content or deeper revisions do not seem to take place automatically, and will depend on improved teaching methods, rather than mere computer use. We do not find this surprising, since we have always maintained that it is unrealistic to expect good things to happen in schools merely by exposing children to computers. With word processing, as with any learning tool, efficacy depends on how it is used, rather than on its mere presence or absence.

IDEA PROCESSORS

A relatively new development has been the marketing and use of *idea processors*. Sometimes called *thought processors* or *outline generators* (Willis, 1987), these tools are used in the planning stages of writing. They make it very easy to create and edit an outline of a paper. Then, later, when the user is ready to write, he or she can choose to view only main ideas and hide all subordinate items. The user may also choose to zoom in on subheadings in a variety of ways.

Another writing tool related to idea processors are interactive programs such as QUILL, developed by D. C. Heath (Rubin and Bruce, 1985). QUILL includes a planning aid called Planner, that quizzes students to help them generate ideas. The questions can be changed by the teacher to make them appropriate for different kinds of writing. QUILL also contains an aid called Library, which allows users to store their manuscripts under key words. Another QUILL aid, called Mailbag, permits students to write messages to groups or individuals, thereby stimulating collaboration and informal writing for communication.

OTHER COMPUTER WRITING AIDS

Word processors, idea processors, and the newer interactive programs are not the only computer writing aids. Supplementary aids are sometimes added to word processors and sometimes produced as separate tools.

Grammar Checkers

Grammar checkers are not named well. They do not check for all kinds of grammar errors, and they check for other errors as well. They also call the writer's attention to commonly misused words such as affect/effect, or principal/principle. Many will check for trite phrases such as at this point in time, or in order to. Some will flag sexist language. Improper punctuation is also highlighted.

Properly used, grammar checkers can be useful writing aids. Willis (1987) evaluated all term papers written in a university graduate class and concluded that over 70% could have been substantially improved had the students used a grammar checker. Users should remember, however, that suggestions made are only suggestions, and the final judgment concerning a change should be made by the human writer who is aware of the entire context.

Spelling Checkers

Spelling checkers scan a document and list, in context, any words not found on a diskette containing a dictionary. The user then decides whether the word is spelled wrong and whether he or she wants to make a change in the manuscript. Some spelling checkers display a list of suggested spellings. Most spelling checkers permit the user to add words. This latter feature permits users to add names, professional jargon, or other unusual words.

Some teachers do not like spelling checkers. They think the checker may be a crutch that will prevent the student from learning to spell. However, most experts believe that the use of spelling checkers improves spelling (Collis, 1988; Willis, 1987). The improvement may be due to frequent exposure to correct spelling or to immediate reinforcement, long known to aid learning of any kind.

Electronic Thesaurus

An electronic thesaurus gives the user the option of viewing a list of synonyms for any word on the word-processing screen. The user may choose one of the suggested words to be substituted into the text or the original word may be retained. Again, little research has been conducted on the use of electronic thesauri. It is possible, however, that their use may result in user vocabulary growth and the production of manuscripts with more varied vocabularies.

SPECIFIC WORD PROCESSING SYSTEMS

As Willis (1987) notes, recommending specific word-processing systems is hazardous. Products come and go so swiftly that a book that relied heavily on such recommendations would quickly become obsolete. For that reason, we will not attempt an exhaustive review of specific packages. The best place for such reviews are the various computer periodicals and journals intended for writing teachers. We will, however, provide brief descriptions of a few packages that are so popular that they are likely to continue to be available for years to come.

AppleWorks

The most popular word-processing program for the Apple II line of computers is AppleWorks, originally available from Apple Computer Company, and now marketed by Claris (440 Clyde Avenue, Mountain View, California 94043). AppleWorks is an integrated package, meaning that it contains more than one program. AppleWorks includes a word processor, a spreadsheet, and database management software. Documents made in any one of these applications can be loaded into either of the other two.

The word-processing portion of AppleWorks is menu driven, which makes it easy for beginners to learn. The program is powerful and contains most advanced word-processing features. The most cumbersome part of AppleWorks is specifying what the printout should look like. To do so, the user must enter a complex options screen that many beginners find confusing. At the time of this writing, AppleWorks was the best choice for Apple II users.

The Bank Street Writer III

The Bank Street Writer was developed by personnel at the Bank Street College of Education in New York and by Broderbund Software and is currently available from Scholastic Software (730 Broadway, New York, NY 10003). This software is available for use with a variety of popular microcomputers, including MS-DOS machines and Apple II Computers. It was designed specifically for use by children and contains elaborate safeguards to minimize the chances of accidentally erasing data. It is menu-driven. The newest implementation of the program is much improved and includes integrated spelling checker and thesaurus. The spelling checker is outstanding. Weaknesses include the fact that in some instances the screen cannot be made to display exactly what will be printed (centered or indented text cannot be displayed, for example). This is a very simple but limited word processor that will not be appreciated by older or more expert users.

WordPerfect

The story of WordPerfect is one of the many Cinderella stories in computing. The company began in 1979 as a two-man operation selling one or two copies of WordPerfect per month. By 1989, the company, now called WordPerfect Corporation (1555 North Technology Way, Orem, UT 84057), employed more than 1,300 people and sales topped $275 million. In 1989, there were more than 3 million WordPerfect users, making it the most popular word processor ever, with more than 60% of the word-processing market worldwide.

By 1989, WordPerfect was available for MS-DOS, Apple II, VAX, Amiga, Atari, Macintosh, UNIX, IBM 370 VM, and OS/2; and the program was available in over 15 different languages. It is one of the most powerful word-processing programs available. It includes a resident spelling checker and thesaurus and many other sophisticated features.

The company employs more than 500 people to answer customers' questions over 14 different toll-free lines. Such excellent customer support is a valuable selling feature to teachers who may need assistance with the software. At the time of this writing, WordPerfect was quite clearly the finest word-processing program available.

FrEdWriter

FrEdWriter (Free Educational Writer) is a public-domain word processor for Apple II computers (CUE SoftSwap, P.O. Box 271704, Concord CA 95527). For a small fee to cover diskettes and mailing, teachers are given the software and the right to make as many copies as they wish. Although certainly not a high-end word processor, FrEdWriter is surprisingly good for public-domain software. A unique feature is the ability of the teacher to create files of prompts that cannot be erased by students. The students load the prompts and then follow the teacher directions found there to complete an assignment.

SUMMARY

Word processing is the most popular, the most rapidly growing, and perhaps the most useful computer application yet devised. Word processing is beginning to receive wide usage in schools. The major advantage of word processing is that it imparts to the user great power and ease of revision. It is a Type II application.

The advantages often cited for using word processing in schools fall into one of the following categories: (1) ease of production and revision, (2) cognitive advantages, (3) social advantages, (4) attitudinal advantages.

Those who argue for adoption of word processing because it eases production and revision maintain that word processing takes the drudgery out of composing and editing, thus making good writing more practical. Cognitive advantages that are sometimes mentioned include the freeing of short-term memory by allowing the concentration on large-scale revision of ideas; provision of immediate reinforcement by being able to print clean, neat copies at any time; the match between word processing capabilities and thought processes of writers; and the existence of specialized word processors containing interactive sections or questions aimed at metacognitive principles. Social advantages include the stimulation of collaborative writing and the establishment of a new social structure incorporating peer criticism, a sense of audience, and a consequent increase in the relevance of writing ability. Many educators believe that word processing helps improve children's attitudes toward writing and leads to the conception of writing as a process.

Research on word processing in education is just beginning. Most authorities agree, however, that there are promising indications. Word processing seems to lead to better attitudes toward writing and to longer manuscripts with more surface revisions than text written with paper and pen. We can be less confident about whether word processing improves the quality of writing or encourages content revisions. The most informed conclusion we can come to is that word processing, combined with excellent teaching methods, can result in improved teaching and learning of writing skills.

Idea processors are specialized word processors that make it easy to create and access outlines and are intended to be used in the planning stages of writing. Other aids include grammar checkers, spelling checkers, and thesauri. Although little research has been done on these aids, they probably improve, rather than impede, mechanical skills.

Specific word-processing packages come and go. Three popular packages are AppleWorks for Apple II computers, the Bank Street Writer for several microcomputers, and WordPerfect for use on a variety of machines.

LOOKING AHEAD

Word processing is a Type II application because it makes it possible to use new and better methods for teaching writing. The next chapter will examine another Type II application, the use of the computer as a prosthetic aid for the handicapped.

Type II applications such as the ones dealt with in Part Three represent the most exciting potential for computer education. As you read about these applications, be thinking about how they contrast with the useful, but less innovative Type I applications described in Part Two.

SOME QUESTIONS TO CONSIDER

1. The business community was quick to adopt word processing. Do you think it is easier to the assess success or failure of a business innovation than an educational innovation? Explain.

2. A few people have suggested that word processing may have some disadvantages. What might these be?
3. Good research on educational computing in general and on word processing in education in particular is scarce. Can you think of any special problems in doing such research?

RELATED ACTIVITIES

1. Visit an office on your campus in which the secretarial staff uses word processing. Interview a secretary and record her impressions of the advantages and disadvantages of word processing.
2. Visit an office on your campus or elsewhere in which the secretarial staff do not use word processing. Ask why they do not use this tool. Record their responses.
3. Locate a public school teacher who uses word processing to help teach children writing skills. (Ask one of your education professors to recommend such a teacher.) Interview that teacher about how she uses word processing. If possible, visit her class and observe.

REFERENCES

Barker, T. T. (1987). Studies in word processing and writing. *Computers in the Schools, 4*(1), 109–121.

Branan, K. (1984, October). Moving the writing process along. *Learning*, pp. 22–26.

Bruce, B., Michaels, S., & Watson-Gegeo, K. (1985). How computers can change the writing process. *Language Arts, 62*(2), 143–149.

Bullough, R. V., & Beatty, L. F. (1987). *Classroom applications of microcomputers*. Columbus, OH: Merrill.

Cannings, T. R., & Brown, S. W. (1986). *The information age classroom: Using the computer as a tool*. Irvine, CA: Franklin, Beedle & Associates.

Collis, B. (1988). *Computers, curriculum, and whole- class instruction: Issues and ideas*. Belmont, CA: Wadsworth.

Daiute, C. (1986). Physical and cognitive factors in revision: Insights from studies with computers. *Research in the Teaching of English, 20*, 141–159.

Dickinson, D. (1986). Cooperation, collaboration, and a computer: Integrating a computer into a first- second grade writing program. *Research in the Teaching of English, 20*, 357–378.

Dudley-Marling, C. C. (1985, January). Microcomputers, reading, and writing: Alternatives to drill and practice. *Reading Teacher*, pp. 388–391.

Flake, J. L, McClintock, C. E., & Turner, S. (1990). *Fundamentals of computer education*. Belmont, CA: Wadsworth.

Fuori, W. M, & Aufiero, L. J. (1986). *Computers and information processing*. Englewood Cliffs, NJ: Prentice Hall.

Green, J. O. (1984). An interview with Donald Graves. *Classroom Computer Learning, 4*(8), 21-22, 28.

Heap, J. (1986, April). *Collaborative practices during computer writing in a first grade classroom*. Paper presented at the American Educational Research Association, San Francisco, CA.

Kinzer, C. K., Sherwood, R. D., & Bransford, J. D. (1986). *Computer strategies for education: Foundations and content-area applications*. Columbus, OH: Merrill.

Lillie, D. L., Hannum, W. H., & Stuck, G. B. (1989). *Computers and effective instruction: Using computers and software in the classroom*. New York: Longman.

Loheyde, K. M. (1984). Computer use in the teaching of composition: Considerations for teachers of writing. *Computers in the Schools, 1*, 81–85.

Long, L. (1988). *Introduction to computers and information processing* (2nd ed.). Englewood Cliffs, NJ: Prentice Hall.

MacArthur, C. A. (1988, Winter). Computers and writing instruction. *Teaching Exceptional Children*, pp. 37–39.

Mandell, C. J., & Mandell, S. L. (1989). *Computers in education today*. St. Paul, MN: West Publishing.

Montague, M. M. (In press). *Computers, cognition, and writing instruction*. New York: State University of New York Press.

Murphy, R. T., & Appel, L. R. (1984). *Evaluation of the Writing to Read instructional system, 1982–1984*. Princeton, NJ: Educational Testing Service.

Office of Technology Assessment (1988). *Power on! New tools for teaching and learning* (Publication No. 052-003-01125-5). Washington, DC: U.S. Government Printing Office.

Reidesel, C. A., & Clements, D. H. (1985). *Coping with computers in the elementary and middle schools*. Englewood Cliffs, NJ: Prentice Hall.

Roberts, N.,and others. (1988). *Integrating computers into the elementary and middle school*. Englewood Cliffs, NJ: Prentice Hall.

Roblyer, M. D., Castine, W. H., & King, F. J. (1988). *Assessing the impact of computer-based instruction: A review of recent research*. New York: Haworth Press.

Rosegrant, T. (1985). Using the microcomputer as a tool for learning to read and write. *Journal of Learning Disabilities, 18*(2), 113–115.

Rubin, A., & Bruce, B. (1985). *Learning with QUILL: Lessons for students, teachers and software designers*. Reading Report No. 60. Washington, DC: National Institute of Education.

Vockell, E., & Schwartz, E. (1988). The computer in the classroom. Santa Cruz, CA: Mitchell Publishing.

Willis, J. W. (1987). *Educational computing: A guide to practical applications*. Scottsdale, AZ: Gorsuch, Scarisbrick, Publishers.

Yacht, C. (1985, November). Microcomputer keyboarding: Software suggestions and curriculum guidelines. *Business Education Forum*, 18–19.

__11__

Computers as Prosthetic Aids

GOALS AND OBJECTIVES

Goal: To recognize ways that computers and other modern technology can be used as prosthetic devices for helping handicapped people achieve their full potential.

When you finish studying this chapter, you will be able to:

1. List at least three ways that computers are being used as prosthetic devices.
2. Write a paragraph explaining how computers can help a person with severe motor impairments.
3. Write a paragraph explaining how computers can help a person who is blind.
4. List at least three sources that a teacher could use to find information on how to help a handicapped student get appropriate assistance from a computer as a prosthetic device.
5. Write a paragraph explaining how the problems relating to using the computer as a prosthetic device are similar to problems faced in all aspects of educational computing.

KEY TERMS

Adaptive Firmware Card
computer operating
  systems
decoded

diphones
electronic signals
encoded
information utility

light pen
macro
motor impairment
on-line services
peripheral devices
prosthesis
scanning device

serial port
special input device
switches
synthesized speech
touch screen
vibrations
voice-control keyboard

The word **prosthesis** originated as a medical term for an artificial limb. As science and medicine advanced, prosthetic devices were developed to help people compensate for handicaps that extended beyond just the loss of an arm or a leg. Today, engineers, computer scientists, medical personnel, and educators are working together to find ways that computers and related technology can be used to assist people with a wide array of handicapping conditions. This chapter is devoted to the role of the computer as an aid to students who have diminished capacity in various human functions.

We will first share some examples to illustrate the legitimacy of the computer as a prosthetic aid. We then describe some of the common ways computers are being used as prostheses. Next, some sample hardware and software products are described along with some resources for obtaining information and assistance. The final section of the chapter is devoted to a discussion of some of the issues and concerns relating to adopting the computer as a prosthetic device.

THE CASE FOR THE COMPUTER AS A PROSTHETIC DEVICE

Tyre (1988) suggests that computers are important in special education because students "are able to learn more, thus achieving a greater amount of their natural potential" (p. 14). Testimonials to the value of the computer in helping students develop their full potential abound. Hale (1983) reported that a group of vocational trainers and their students claimed that the microcomputer was "the best thing that ever happened to anyone in a wheelchair" (pp. 7–8). Hannaford and Sloane (1981), in describing how a computer could be used by handicapped students, stated, "Microcomputers, if used appropriately with proper software programs, are powerful learning tools" (p. 132).

Your authors are acquainted with one of the many success stories in which the computer freed the potential of a student whose intellectual abilities lay dormant due to limited communication. On August 15, 1983, this young high school student, Scott Tooke, spoke to an audience of educators attending a computer inservice day. In his speech, Scott said:

> *Until two and a half years ago, an independent future was in the dark for me. I had to have an aide around all day to write out assignments and to do many other things. I had many friends, but I could not verbalize my personality. (Tooke, 1983, p. 1)*

Scott suffers from cerebral palsy and has beenseverely physically disabled since birth. Scott's mind was filled with ideas, stories, and jokes, but, like many people with this handicapping condition, his lack of motor control made it almost impossible to communicate. Scott could neither speak nor write. Through the help of the community, Scott was provided with a computerized communication system that attached to his wheel-chair. With this communication system, Scott was able to share his thoughts and ideas.

The significance of this story lies in the discovery and development of Scott's hidden talents. As Scott became more adept at using the new technology, his teachers and fellow students were surprised to discover his high level of cognition. Scott graduated magna cum laude from his high school and went on to study accounting at the local university.

A similar success story was reported by Divoky (1987). Divoky tells of a young lady named Shoshana Brand who, like Scott, was severely handicapped by cerebral palsy. Shoshana had **motor impairments** and very limited vision. Her parents improvised a computer system that would free Shoshana's potential. Shoshana's computer was equipped with a speech synthesizer that substituted for her own, uncontrollable voice. Also part of the system were a voice activator that could turn words on the computer screen into spoken words and a special keyboard with oversized letters.

The success achieved by Shoshana with this special computer con-figuration motivated her mother, Jacqueline Brand, to begin work in cooperation with other parents, the local school district, and Apple Computer, Inc., to start a Disabled Children's Computer Group. This group later evolved into a national organization called the Foundation for Technology Access. This organization has become a model program for helping parents and teachers across America to adapt computer technology to free the potential of handicapped children.

Shoshana meanwhile finished middle school with high marks and in the spring of 1990 was looking forward to the start of school when she would be attending a regular high school.

Now that you have a general impression of how computers can work as prosthetic devices to enhance human potential, we turn our attention to describing some of the ways this can be accomplished.

GENERAL TYPES OF COMPUTER PROSTHETIC DEVICES

Four types of computer prosthetic devices will be described to help you gain a sense of how people with various handicaps are developing their potential through the aid of technology. While the devices discussed here are not exhaustive, they are representative of the major ways that computers are being using as prosthetic aids.

Speech Synthesis

Computer users (along with science fictionwriters) have long been fascinated with **synthesized speech**. The idea of a machine that could listen, understand, process, and talk like Darth Vader makes for fascinating speculation. While such machines exist only in the realm of science fiction, machines that can simulate human speech are very real and serve as valuable aids to handicapped people, especially those with visual and motor handicaps. Bronson (1987) has stated that "for the blind, speech synthesis is becoming a preferred method for getting information into and out of computers" (p. 140).

While speech synthesis is certainly a boon to handicapped individuals, it still has a long way to go. Most speech synthesis, while intelligible, is of fairly low quality. It still sounds far too much like Darth Vadar. The tremendous potential of speech synthesis, however, is driving advanced research projects that have as their goal the development of speech synthesis that can truly become a substitute voice for those who cannot speak.

Handicapped individuals like Scott Tooke, who cannot control their own voices to speak, are able to point to words or letters for spelling words that are then spoken through the speech synthesizer. Blind people can operate computers by having the contents of the screen read to them by a speech synthesizer.

An example of research to improve the quality of speech synthesis is a project being carried out at Tufts University, where scientists are working to solve one of the key obstacles to making computer speech sound like human speech. Bronson (1987) explains that a major obstacle lies in the fact that human speech contains **diphones**, which are the slight variations in sound produced by a letter or combination of letters depending on word context. For example, the sound the letter b makes at the beginning of the word bulb is quite different from the sound the b makes at the end of that word. Current synthesized speech is not able to keep track of and render such nuances accurately. Researchers at Tufts hope to teach the computer to handle these subtleties and become a better substitute voice.

Special Input Devices

One type of prosthetic aid that has done much torelease human potential is the **special input device**. We use the term to describe a variety of adaptations to traditional computer input. These adaptations allow people with motor impairments to communicate with a computer. This is essential, since the computer can only enhance a person's intellectual potential if that person is able to control the machine. For people like Scott Tooke, getting information into the computer with a keyboard, a mouse, a **light pen**, or even a **touch screen** is impossible. Such devices require more motor control than is possible for many people. Figure 11.1 shows the use of a special light pen that is attached to the computer user's head so that the head can be used to point the light pen.

The central idea associated with a special input device is to provide a mechanism the allows the handicapped person to use what degree of motor control he or she has to send signals to the computer. In some cases this might be a special keyboard with very large keys. Or it might be a keyboardlike structure where characters and words are pointed to

FIGURE 11.1   Light pens can be attached to a hat to run a menu program. As the light remains on a letter or a number for a few seconds the character is entered into the program

with some object. In other cases, the computer user can control the computer by simply selecting menu items by touching the computer screen.

For some handicapped individuals, however, even such devices as special keyboards and touch-sensitive screens still demand too much motor control. For these individuals, the computer has to be controlled by the slightest movement of only one body part.

At first glance, it might seem preposterous to suggest that a person could control the power of a computer by a simple movement of a finger or by puffing and sipping on something resembling a drinking straw. A group of devices that allow this to happen are called **switches**. To the individual whose motor movement is limited to something as tiny as an eye blink or a finger tap, such a switch becomes the gateway to a whole new world of freedom and access.

Switches are very simple devices and can be tailored to almost any movement of the human body. The type of switch we are talking about here is similar to a simple light switch. A light switch has only two positions: it is either on or off. All the various switching devices used by handicapped individuals to control computers do the same thing. They send two signals to the computer, on and off. What allows the handicapped person to use the computer is a special kind of program that is controlled by the on—off signals sent to it through the switch. An example of a switch used by a handicapped person is shown in Figure 11.2.

An example of the type of program that can be controlled by a switch is a *special word processor*. When using such a word processor, the writer sees letters and numbers clustered in groups on the screen. A cursor slowly scans across the clusters until it arrives at the desired cluster. At this point, the writer activates the switch and the cursor pauses. It then scans the characters within the cluster, and the writer again actuates the switch when the cursor points to the desired character. The selected character is then placed in a text area of the screen. In this way letters, numbers, and punctuation marks are linked together just as they would be by a writer using a standard keyboard.

Obviously, this is a slow and tedious process when compared to fluent typing. A typical person with a severe motor handicap produces only about five words per minute using such a device. However, this process may open a new world to the person whose only previous form of communication has been a nod or a blink.

Aids for the Blind

Julia Anderson (1989), writing about computers andthe handicapped in *Harvard Business Review*, said "This technology revolution has forced corporations to rethink notions of the physical limitations on job performance in information processing" (p. 36). This is particularly true for individuals who are blind or visually impaired. Depending on the sever-

FIGURE 11.2   Different types of computer switches.

ity of the handicap and the personal preference of the individual, the visually handicapped person has a variety of electronic options to choose from. Once information has been **encoded** into **electronic signals**, it can be **decoded** into speech, Braille, or enlarged print on paper or computer monitor. The signals can even be turned into **vibrations** that can be interpreted by some blind people.

IBM has developed a computer mouse that allows a blind person to read the computer screen (Bronson, 1987). Words and numbers on the screen are translated into electronic signals and sent back to the mouse. These signals are then translated into vibrations that can be felt and interpreted by the blind person.

Helps for the blind are not limited to output devices. Prab Command has developed a voice command system they call a **voice-control keyboard** (Rash, 1989). This device can recognize and carry out 160 spoken commands. This, of course, is a small vocabulary compared to conversational speech, but it must be kept in mind that any or all of these commands can be **macros**. (A macro is a series of commands that is preprogrammed into the computer system so that the entire series can then be actuated with just a single command.) An example of a macro in word processing would be a series of preprogrammed commands that access a blank memorandum form, place the current date on the form, allow the user to insert a message, and print out the completed memo. This whole process

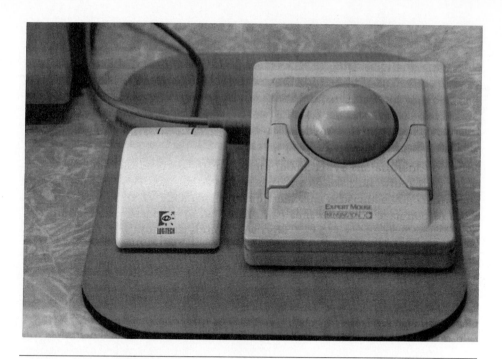

FIGURE 11.3   IBM's computer mouse.

FIGURE 11.4   Compton, a blind staff member from Nevada's Technology Center, uses scan readers to enlarge types of print and the Dectalk to communicate with computer programs

could be activated by issuing a single command such as "memo." With a voice-controlled keyboard and a vibrating mouse, a totally blind person could become very proficient at working with such programs as databases and spreadsheets

HARDWARE AND SOFTWARE FOR THE HANDICAPPED

Rapid advances are being made in hardware andsoftware designed to turn computers into prosthetic aids for handicapped individuals. Many educators may not even be aware of such computer uses, and even those who work exclusively with handicapped students will probably find it difficult to stay abreast of the latest developments. Both commercial and public organizations are available, however, that can provide quick and easy assistance in matching hardware and software to specific handicapping conditions. In this section, we describe some of the hardware and software products that have become established as standards in the area of prosthetic devices and discuss some resources educators can use in planning technology assistance for handicapped students.

Some Established Standards

One of the first efforts to market hardware andsoftware for handicapped individuals involved the **Adaptive Firmware Card**. This was a card (circuit board) that could be installed in the Apple II line of computers (Figure 11.5). It provided both the hardware and the software to give handicapped individuals access to the computer.

With the Adaptive Firmware Card, some off the shelf software packages can be used by a person whose motor control is limited to special keyboards or to switching devices like the ones described earlier in this chapter. The card will accommodate any switching device, a variety of special keyboards, and other input devices. The software built into the card can turn the computer screen into a **scanning device** like the one described earlier, in which a cursor scans across the screen and the computer user can select screen options by any movement that can send a signal to the computer. The card also has built-in speech synthesis, making voice-controlled keyboarding possible for visually handicapped individuals and providing a substitute voice for those who cannot speak.

The Adaptive Firmware Card was originally marketed by Adaptive Peripheral, but was later acquired by Don Johnston Developmental Equipment, 1000 N. Rand Road, Wauconda, IL. This device can be installed in either the Apple IIe or Apple IIGS computer.

The Adaptive Firmware Card has become a standard in special education classrooms for two reasons. First, the card was designed for the Apple computer series, which has been and still is the most common school computer. Second, it was developed shortly after the first micro-

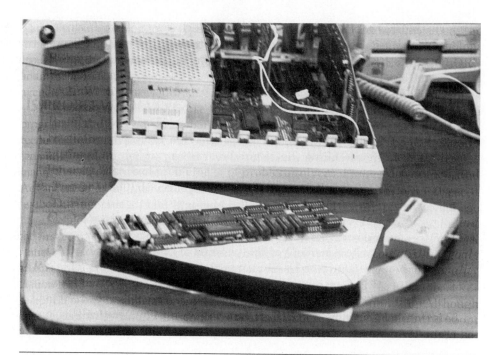

FIGURE 11.5   Adaptive Firmware Card.

computers came along and has gone through a steady evolution of improvements.

A system that is similar in function to the Adaptive Firmware Card, but compatible with MS-DOS computers, is PC Serial A.I.D. This is a small box that plugs into a **serial port** in the back of most MS-DOS computers. It is distributed by TASH, Inc., 70 Gibson Dr., Unit 12, Markham, Ontario, Canada, L3R4C2.

Many adaptive devices that allow handicapped individuals access to computers are so specialized that they need to be custom constructed. The one company that has become the standard in developing and marketing such adaptive devices is the Prentke-Romich Company, 1022 Hey Road, Wooster, OH 44691. We would recommend this company as a good starting point for anyone looking for special keyboards, switches, or other adaptive devices.

In the area of speech synthesis, prices and quality vary widely. As might be expected, the better the quality is, the higher the price. The standard in speech synthesis for school use is the Echo II, marketed by Street Electronics, 1140 Mark Ave., Carpenteria, CA 93013. Again, we use this as a standard because it has grown up alongside the microcomputer industry and is compatible with the Apple IIe and IIGS computers. Street Electronics also markets a speech synthesizer for MS-DOS com-

FIGURE 11.6   Echo II.

puters called the Echo PC Plus. At less than $200, these speech synthesizers are at the low end of the cost continuum. However, until synthesized speech takes a giant leap forward in terms of quality, this level of product is appropriate for school use.

In 1988, a new standard was set for turning printed material into Braille for the blind. A combination of special hardware and software can translate either printed or typeset materials to braille at a rate of 9,000 characters per minute with 99.9% accuracy. The hardware includes either an MS-DOS or Macintosh computer, a desktop scanner, and a Braille printer. The key software for the system is ReadStar II Plus, which is billed as intelligent optical character recognition software. ReadStar II Plus is distributed by Inovatic of Arlington, Virginia.

While these are only a few of the products available, they represent some of the companies that have made a significant commitment to developing and improving computer prosthetic devices for the handicapped. We next turn our attention to some sources that provide information and assistance in using computers as prosthetic devices.

Where to Go for Help

One of the first places you should look for help for handicapped students is your state's Vocational Rehabilitation Commission. In most states, this agency has become very active in providing technical assistance and job support to handicapped individuals. Most states have highly skilled specialists who can recommend hardware and software for use by people with special needs. Often, these agencies also offer training on how to use such hardware and software and may even loan certain products on a short-term basis.

Another organization that can often provide advice on appropriate hardware and software for handicapped students is the Alliance for Technology Access. This organization was originally begun with help from the Office of Special Education of Apple Computer, Inc. The primary supporter of the Alliance is now The Foundation for Technology Access.

Jacqueline Brand, executive director of this alliance, is the mother of Shoshana Brand, the young lady we mentioned at the beginning of this chapter. The alliance has 44 centers spread across 23 states. Their goal is to offer advice and training in using computer technology as prosthetic devices to teachers and parents of handicapped students. Contact can be made with this important resource by calling 415-528-0747 or writing to the Alliance for Technology Access, 1307 Soano Avenue, Albany, CA 94706.

What would be more logical than to use the computer itself to provide information on how to use computers to help handicapped students? Both IBM and Apple Computer, Inc., support on-line information services dedicated to exchanging information on using computers for individuals with special needs. These **on-line services** can be accessed over telephone lines with any personal computer and a modem. Like most services, however, this one is not free. You must pay to subscribe to these services.

The IBM-supported information service is IBM Special Needs Forum and is part of CompuServe, a large **information utility** that makes a wide array of information available to microcomputer users. By logging onto this information system, you can obtain information for teachers, students, and parents on hardware and software for individuals with special needs.

This service also provides an opportunity for interested subscribers to share ideas and information. Users can exchange messages or can interact in a long-distance conference session via computer.

IBM Special Needs Forum is available to anyone who has a subscription to CompuServe. For information on CompuServe, see Chapter 6.

AppleLink is Apple's information service. This on- line service has as one of its features a comprehensive special education database called Special Education Solutions. This data base provides a comprehensive list of hardware devices and software packages applicable to disabled individuals. It also contains a directory of software packages and a list of various support organizations and publications pertinent to the disabled population.

For information on how to take advantage of Special Education Solutions, contact your local Apple Computer dealer, or write to Apple Computer, Inc., 20525 Marian Avenue, Cupertino, CA 95014.

A major on-line service totally dedicated to sharing ideas and information relating to special education is Special Net. This service is supported by Council for Exceptional Children and is housed in Washington, D.C. It is a repository of a wide range of information relating to special education. By logging on to the service, you can obtain information on resources as well as teaching strategies.

ISSUES AND CONCERNS

While there have been many encouragingbreakthroughs in using computers as prosthetic devices, there are still some serious issues and concerns to be addressed. These issues and concerns are much the same as those that apply to computer applications for the nonhandicapped. Appropriate computer systems are still too expensive to provide adequate access, software development lags far behind hardware development, training and motivating students to use the technology that is available are difficult, and there is little research being done.

Success stories like those of Scott Tooke and Shoshana Brand, for whom computer systems helped make dreams come true, are showcase situations and are not typical of the experiences of most handicapped students. Cost represents a major hurdle.

Sokoloff, in 1985, cautioned educators with the following statement:

> *The new technologies and materials can be used to release unknown capabilities in young people who have disabling conditions. But we must not fool ourselves into thinking that those capabilities will be released simply by turning on a switch. The link up with the appropriate technology is not an easy one. While many devices can be put into action with a minimum cost, expense is definitely a big factor.* (p. 45)

Unlike many other computer applications, astechnology for handicapped has advanced, the cost has continued to increase. The reason for this is that the technology is highly specialized, and the potential market is small. When a company spends money on research and development for a better prosthetic device, it is nearly impossible to recapture that investment through sales. When such a device is sold to only a few hundred or even a few thousand people, it must be sold with a high price tag.

Equipping a seriously handicapped student with the appropriate prosthetic system, teaching that student to use the system effectively, maintaining the system, and keeping the system current are still expensive tasks. Often, funds are made available only through an unusually intense effort by a community or an agency. In an era where educational resources are scarce, funding will continue to be one of the major barriers preventing handicapped students from obtaining and using computer prosthetic devices.

The slow progress being made in developing appropriate software is also related to financial difficulties. Starting with the first microcomputer, our inability to develop software to maximize the capabilities of available hardware has been a frustration. This problem is accentuated for the handicapped person who relies on a computer system to function on a day to day basis.

The software dilemma for the handicapped is highlighted in a statement by Arditi and Gillman (1986) who, after describing a "best possible" system for the blind computer user, said, "Perhaps the major disadvantage of our example system is that it is not possible for us to run any applications programs that are not specifically designed for the blind user" (p. 206).

What these two writers were referring to is the fact that **computer operating systems** (the programs that coordinate all of the parts of a computer system) are not designed with the handicapped user in mind. A handicapped student may have all the appropriate hardware, including special **peripheral devices**, but still may not be able to use many software packages because they are not specifically designed for his or her system.

Two things need to be done in the area of software development to improve computer access for the handicapped. First, more software geared to the needs of persons with handicaps must be developed. Second, computer operating systems need to be made general enough that they can accommodate a wide variety of different specialized peripheral devices.

Funding and software development are problems that can be overcome with relative ease compared to the problem of persuading handicapped individuals to learn the use of the technology that is available. While much excellent technology is available, the handicapped student must be highly motivated and must work hard to master its use. June Holmstrom (1988) and her colleagues in the Poudre School District in Fort Collins, Colorado, learned this through a program designed to use technology to establish communication skills among a group of nonverbal students with severe motor disabilities. According to Holmstrom:

Most students resisted change and were very resistant to giving up the communication methods (eye gaze and twenty questions) that were comfortable for them, even though these methods were severely limited. It was comfortable to be a spectator. (p. 7)

As with many other uses of computers in education,the use of computers as prosthetic devices is not a well-researched topic. Most of what could be classed as research in this area has been and is now being directed toward the development of improved devices and software. This is appropriate, because as hardware and software advance, the prosthetic value of the computer will increase. As Holmstrom and her associates discovered, however, larger and more difficult issues wait to be studied, such as how to motivate and train handicapped students to use the new technology to maximize their own human potential.

In conclusion, we can say that using the computer as a prosthetic device that will allow the handicapped to enjoy a richer and fuller life is an exciting proposition, but is not without problems. The challenge to education is to tackle these problems with serious research efforts. Engineers and business leaders will continue to provide us with improved technology. Educators must take the lead in discovering how to harness this technology for maximum enhancement of human potential.

SUMMARY

Our goal in this chapter was to alert you to thecapabilities of the computer and related technology in opening new windows of opportunity for people with handicaps. The computer has become a valuable prosthetic device for students with varying handicapping conditions, ranging from blindness and limited vision to lack of motor control. In cases like Scott Tooke and Shoshana Brand, the computer has opened up a world of opportunity that would have otherwise remained closed. In the limited space of this chapter, we have described only a few of the more common uses of computers as prosthetic devices, along with some specific products that have become standards. In keeping with the spirit and intent of this book, we have concluded by pointing out some cautions and concerns and by offering a challenge to educators.

LOOKING AHEAD

The examples in this chapter have drawn attention to the advantages of and concerns over the use of the computer as a prosthetic device for the handicapped. We hope you have a better understanding of the impact computers can have on individuals with limited lifestyles. The future possibilities of the computer are endless.

Among the computer tools that can help handicapped individuals are spreadsheets and data bases. In the next chapter we will specify how database and spreadsheet software is being applied to businesses and education and how such software packages can turn computers into powerful educational tools.

SOME QUESTIONS TO CONSIDER

1. How are the problems associated with using the computer as a prosthetic device for students similar to the problems associated with the educational computing discipline in general?
2. What do you think some of the computer prosthetic devices of the future might be like?
3. What is a possible solution to the problem of providing access to appropriate prosthetic devices for all handicapped students?
4. What kind of training programs might be developed to motivate handicapped students to make use of available computer prosthetic devices?

RELATED ACTIVITIES

1. Contact a community service agency such as Services for the Blind or Easter Seals and find out what is currently being done with computers for the handicapped. Prepare a 5-minute oral presentation of your findings.
2. Obtain 5 articles on future directions of the computer as a prosthetic device.
3. Interview a handicapped individual who uses the computer and summarize in a written report how the computer has changed his or her lifestyle.
4. Using a computer system designed for a handicapped individual, role play a person with that particular handicap and write a brief report on your feelings as you tried to use the computer to compensate for the assumed handicap.

SUGGESTIONS FOR ADDITIONAL READING

Bowe, F. G. *Personal computers & special needs*. Berkeley, CA: Sybex.
Lindsey, J. (1987). *Computers and exceptional Individuals*. Columbus, OH: Merrill.
Hagen, D. (1984) *Microcomputer resource book for special education*. Reston, VA: Reston.

Johnson, D. L., Maddux, C. D., & Candler, A. C. (1987). *Computers in special education*. New York: Haworth Press.

REFERENCES

Anderson, J. (1989). How technology brings blind people into the workplace. *Harvard Business Review*, *67*(2), 36–40.

Arditi, A., & Gillman, A. E. (1986, March). Computing for the blind user. *Byte*, pp. 199–208.

Bronson, G. (1987, March 23). In the blink of an eye. *Forbes*, pp. 140–141.

Divoky, D. (1983). Apple sponsors a new alliance for disabled computer users. *Classroom Computer Learning*, *8*(Oct.), 46–49.

Hale, M. (1983). The best thing that ever happened to anyone in a wheelchair. *Apple Education News*, *4*(2), 7–8.

Hannaford, A., & Sloane, E. (1981). Microcomputers: Powerful learning tools with proper programming. *Teaching Exceptional Children*, *14*(2), 54–57.

Holmstrom, J. (1988). Perseverance in teaching children with CP helps them communicate through computers. *OT Week*, *2*(21), 6–7, 18.

Rash, W. (1989). A helping hand. *Byte*, *14*(13), 129–130. Sokoloff, M. (1985, March–April). Linking the new technologies with special education. *Media + Methods*, pp. 12–14, 16.

Tooke, S. (1983, August 15). *The computer in-service*. Paper presented at Coronado High School, Lubbock, Texas.

Tyre, T. (1988). Technology gives kids with special needs the power to learn. *T.H.E. Journal*, *15*(10), 14, 16.

12

Database Management and Spreadsheets

GOALS AND OBJECTIVES

Goal: To understand what electronic databases and spreadsheets are and to appreciate their value as educational tools that can enhance the teaching and learning process.

When you finish studying this chapter, you will be able to:

1. Write an explanation of what an electronic database is.
2. Draw and label a diagram showing how data are organized and subdivided in a typical electronic database.
3. Write a paragraph explaining what an electronic spreadsheet is.
4. Create an example of how an electronic spreadsheet could be used to enhance the teaching of a concept.

KEY TERMS

analogy	file
comment category feature	forecasting
compatible	free-form style
electronic database	grid
electronic memory	integrated software spreadsheet
field	cells

menu options	spreadsheet formulas
records	symbol manipulation
sorting information	template
spreadsheet	user friendly

Everyone knows that large gray filing cabinets stuffed with papers belong in musty offices, not in classrooms. And thick ledgers with rows and columns of numbers beside high-powered calculators normally belong on the desks of accountants and bookkeepers. Yet the ability to store and manipulate such information electronically has caused some educators to start thinking about electronic databases and spreadsheets as teaching and learning tools.

In Chapter 1, we made the point that most computer applications were developed and adopted by business, with education adopting them later. This is certainly true when it comes to the electronic database and the electronic spreadsheet. Business looked for a way to automate the filing cabinet, and the end result was database management software. Business looked for a way to automate the ledger book and the end result was electronic spreadsheet software. As the use of these tools grew in business, educators began to discover that they were not merely business tools, but natural educational tools as well.

In this chapter, we describe the electronic database and the electronic spreadsheet. We explore the concept of using the database and the spreadsheet as educational tools and examine some database and spreadsheet software being used in education. Finally, we explore integrating the computer into the curriculum using these new educational tools.

ELECTRONIC DATABASES AND DATABASE MANAGEMENT SOFTWARE

The simplest definition of the term **electronic database** is: An organized collection of information that is stored electronically. Database management software turns a computer into a machine that can be used to create electronic databases and to manipulate the information stored in such databases.

The term *database* may be used to describe collections of information that range from a simple set of note cards in a shoe box to a large library. Even the library at your school can be thought of as a giant database. When such information is organized and stored electronically, it is an electronic database. Because modern technology is constantly expanding our ability to store information electronically, the collection of information we call a library today may one day be an electronic database to be accessed by a microcomputer.

Managing Data with a Computer

Organizing and holding information are natural applications for a computer. As we move further into the information age, more and more information will be organized into electronic storage media. Newer generations of small computers will be able to store the vast amounts of information that are only possible to store on the very largest of today's computers.

The filing cabinet used to be a common **analogy** for describing an electronic database, because the first electronic databases were little more than electronic storage bins. Information stored in these electronic data bases could be retrieved and examined in much the same way that information in a filing cabinet could be retrieved and examined. Today, however, data base management software is available that does much more than just store information. Current software allows for powerful manipulation of data as well.

The power of the computer as a tool lies in the fact that it has two unique qualities. First, it can **manipulate symbols** much faster than the human brian. Second, it can manipulate symbols much more accurately than the human brain. As advances are made in database software, more of the power of the computer is used. Easy to use database management systems are now available that can organize, sort, rearrange, and exchange information at very rapid speeds.

The Electronic Database as a Type II Application

A database management program that can organize, sort, rearrange, and exchange information at very rapid speeds is a Type II computer application (see Chapter 2). This is true since, with such software, the computer user is in control of a machine and can do something that is impossible to do without that machine.

Imagine, for example, that you work in a very large school district where records of 10,000 students are kept. A measles epidemic breaks out in the community and the school district needs to know which children have been vaccinated for measles within the past four years. What do you think a secretary is going to say when told to search through every file in every drawer of every filing cabinet and record the name, address, and phone number of every student who has not been vaccinated in the past four years? This task would take one person approximately 20 days. By the time the task was accomplished, its purpose would, of course, be obsolete. If this same school district were using a typical database management system with a typical microcomputer for record-keeping purposes, such a task could be accomplished in seconds.

Imagine further that a new records manager is hired for this school district with 10,000 children. This individual decides that it is more efficient to organize all records according to social security number, rather than according to name. How long would it take someone to go through all 10,000 files and reorganize them? Again, such a task could be accomplished in minutes or even seconds with an electronic database.

As you will see as you read further in this chapter, the electronic database is not just an efficient administrative tool, but a powerful teaching and learning tool as well.

Database Management Software

Although, as you would expect, there are differences in database management software, all packages allow you to do the following five things:

1. Create a database
2. Add information to and delete information from the database
3. Sort or rearrange the information in the database
4. Search for specific information in the database
5. Print out reports containing information selected from the database

We next present a brief description of these five database functions.

Creating a Database

Creating a database from scratch using database management software is similar to setting up a traditional filing system. As a teacher, if you were going to set up a filing system for use in your classroom, you would first gather the physical materials you need to work with. Perhaps you would want to have a filing cabinet, file folders, some indexing materials, and paper or cards upon which you could record specific information. When creating an electronic database, the database management software you choose provides you with the electronic equivalents of all these physical materials.

Using the materials you gathered for creating a traditional database, it is crucial that you think about the information you want in your database and decide just how to organize it so that it will work most efficiently for you. The same is true of an electronic database. The database management software merely provides you with the tools. How you organize the information requires careful thought to assure that the database will serve you well. One advantage of the electronic database over the traditional database is that the electronic version can be changed easily when the information needs to be organized differently.

Although the terminology used in database management software packages differs slightly, most packages use terms that draw an analogy between the electronic database and the traditional database. The word **file** in database management software usually refers to a whole collection of information that has some common elements.

For example, information about each student in your classroom, when collected and organized together, could be a file. Likewise, information about each of the 50 states in the United States could be a file.

Electronic database files are usually broken down into **records**. A record is a standardized set of information for one logical subunit of the file. The information on each student in your classroom or the information on each state in the United States could be a single record.

The terms **field** and category are used by different database management systems to denote the next smaller unit in a file. A field or a category contains one specific piece of information relating to one record. In your student file, for example, a student's name could be one field or category, while a student's math grade could be another. In the file on states, size and population could be two different fields or categories for each record.

Often, an electronic database consists of just one file. In this case, the terms *database* and *file* are used interchangeably. With very large and sophisticated databases, however, a single database may contain more than one file. In such a case, a database is subdivided into files, which are subdivided into records, which are subdivided into fields or categories.

Adding and Deleting Information to and from the Database

Developing a good database is an evolutionary process. Once the database format has been decided on and an initial body of information is organized, new information will need to be added constantly. Sometimes existing information will need to be deleted. Good database management software will allow you to add and delete a whole record in a file or a field or category from each record. The power of the computer comes into play at this point by automatically inserting new information into its proper

FILE—COLLECTION OF INFORMATION
Example: Information on all students in a school
LOGICAL   RECORD—~~LOGICAL~~ SUBUNIT OF A FILE
Example: information on each student in the school
FIELD OR CATEGORY—SPECIFIC ITEM OF INFORMATION
Example: Name of a single student

FIGURE 12.1   How information is organized in a database.

place in the file or automatically reorganizing the file so that deleted information is not missed.

Sorting the Information in the Database

When it comes to **sorting information** in a database, computer power really goes to work. Sorting means to rearrange the information. Some database management software packages use the term *arrange* instead of sort to indicate the reorganization of the database contents.

The most common way to organize a database is alphabetically. When setting up your student database, for example, you would probably organize it alphabetically according to last name. Likewise, when setting up a database on the states, it would be logical to organize the records alphabetically by state name. Either of these databases could then be quickly rearranged by using the sort or arrange feature of your database management software. For example, the student database could be reorganized according to birth date or according to math grade. The states database could be reorganized according to size or according to date of entry into the union.

Searching for Specific Information in the Database

The major purpose for setting up any kind of database or filing system is to make it possible to find information quickly. Using appropriate commands in a database management system, you could find all the children in a student database who have a given zip code, were born in a given year, and are also passing math about as fast as you could find one student's birth date alone (and that is very fast, indeed). Later in this chapter we will explore how such speed can turn a computer into a truly powerful educational tool.

Printing Database Reports

Having the capability to organize information and print it out in a report format is useful anytime you want to have a printed copy of the information you have gleaned from searching the database. It is especially useful when you want to organize the information you have gathered into a handy table or chart. Good database management software allows you to juggle the information to get it just like you want it and then turn it into a printed report.

Database Management Systems and Databases for School Use

In 1984, William Hedges described various types of database management software and discussed their relevance for school use. In that article, Hedges categorized existing software into three different levels by degree of sophistication and **user friendliness**. In 1984, it made sense to distinguish among different categories of software because they had uniquely different attributes, with the less sophisticated packages having little advantage over a nonelectronic filing system.

As this type of software developed, the categories described by Hedges became less meaningful. Less expensive and easy to use database management software packages are now available that have much of the power of the early sophisticated packages. Some specific examples will be discussed in the next section.

Common School-Oriented Database Management Systems

Six database management software packages have gained wide spread acceptance within the educational community. These systems have three features in common: (1) they are sophisticated enough to allow for real database power; (2) they are relatively easy to use; and (3) ready-made educational databases are available for them. Let's look now at some of the database management systems that are well accepted and well suited for school use.

Professional File   The most sophisticated database management systems we will mention in this chapter is Professional File. It is also the least educationally oriented. This database management system is only **compatible** with MS-DOS computers. It is a business- oriented product that is an update by Software Publishing Corporation of their original database management system called pfs File. We include it here because it is at a level of sophistication that works well for school administrators, teachers, and upper-level students and because educational databases distributed by Scholastic can be used with it.

With Professional File, Software Publishing Corporation has developed a database management program that is both powerful and easy to use. One powerful feature of this system is that it can "look-up" or retrieve data stored in databases developed with other database management systems such as dBASE. A feature that makes this package easy to use is a thorough help option. At any point in the program, the user can ask for help with the current task or any other task relating to the program. Useful and informational help messages are always available with the touch of a key.

pfs: file / report   Another Software Publishing Corporation product, pfs: file/report was licensed to, and is now marketed by Scholastic. It is much simpler, less powerful, and less flexible than its big brother, Professional File. pfs: file/report is packaged by Scholastic as educational software, and a variety of ready-made educational databases can be purchased along with it.

AppleWorks   While not the most powerful, the most popular database management system used in education today is AppleWorks. Three advantages make the AppleWorks database management system an excellent choice for classroom use:

1. *Integrated software:* The fact that the AppleWorks database management system is part of an **integrated software** package that also has a word processor and spreadsheet program allows students and teachers to use a database tool in the same working environment as their word processor and spreadsheet. A person using this database management system does not have to load a new software package when it is time to switch from word processing or spreadsheet work to database work. Once information has been gathered from a database, it can be transferred from a database to a word processing document. Specific concepts and commands used in the AppleWorks word processor and spreadsheet are relevant to using the database management system. There is a definite advantage to using integrated software packages in the classroom where they allow you to do the type of work you could do with several stand- alone or single-function software packages.

2. *Combination of power and user friendliness:* The AppleWorks database management system has much in common with the most sophisticated database management systems, yet it was designed with teachers and children in mind. Database concepts are in easy to understand terminology. The commands needed to drive the program are sensible and can be mastered with a reasonable expenditure of time and effort. An excellent on-screen help section is available at all times. Built-in prompts suggest what commands need to be used to take the next step in any database management sequence.

3. *Collection of databases and database templates:* Since AppleWorks is such a popular software package in schools, many educators have designed databases and database **templates** that they share with other educators. While the terms *database* and *template* are sometimes used interchangeably, a database is usually thought of as a file where all the necessary information has been entered and stored. A template, on the other hand, usually consists of the database design or the design with only a few sample records filled in. This sharing of databases and database templates saves time and increases the degree to which many teachers can use a computer to enhance their teaching.

Bank Street School Filer   One of a series of programs developed in conjunction with Bank Street College, Bank Street School Filer is now published by Sunburst Communications. While Bank Street School Filer lacks some of the power and flexibility of the AppleWorks database program, it does have some advantages. One feature Bank Street School Filer has that AppleWorks does not is the comment category (Bank Street School Filer uses the term *field* instead of *category*). This feature allows you to simply type text as one category for each record. The comments category is optional. If you choose to use it, you can type seven lines of free- form text. When conducting a search on the database, you can tell the computer to look for a given word in the comment category and it will show all the records where that word occurs.

An example of how the **comment category feature** could be helpful is when students are building a database for books they have read. In this database, categories such as title, author, type of book, and theme could be created. All these categories could be helpful in retrieving specific information from the database, but the information entered in each category would need to be precisely stated. A comment category could then be added that would allow a student to type in random notes about the book in a **free-form style**. Later, when the student wanted to find the book where a certain thought or passage had been read and no search of the specific categories brought about the desired result, the comment category could be searched using a key word. If the key word was included in the student's random comments, the book containing the desired thought or passage would be identified.

A second feature of Bank Street School Filer that has received praise from educators is the clear and easy method of searching for information in a database. The user is able to build a search sentence by choosing from **menu options**. A student might, for example, use a search sentence that asks the computer to find all the mystery books by English authors who lived before 1900. As you work with database management systems, you will gain an appreciation for the ease provided by this method of constructing a search.

Notebook Filer   This database program is advertised as "simple, yet flexible." Our assessment is that it lives up well to this claim. It is probably one of the best database management systems for use by young children. Even though Notebook Filer is easy to learn and simple to use, it is a true database management system because it can be used to create databases, add information to and delete information from a database, sort or rearrange the information in a database, search for specific information in the database, and print out reports containing information selected from the database.

MECC Dataquest Composer   A popular database management system used in education is MECC Dataquest Composer. The popularity of this package is largely due to the popularity of the MECC software in general.

MECC Dataquest Composer is not a very powerful database manager, but it is easy to learn, easy to use, and at the right level of difficulty for elementary and secondary school children. An advantage of this program is the fact that MECC also markets ready-made databases on a variety of subjects to be used with the database management system.

Databases for Schools

Ready-made databases allow you to take advantage of someone else's work and still have the power and flexibility of your own database management system. Although such databases are sold as complete and ready to use, some can be altered by adding or deleting information since they are managed by a separate database management system.

The strengths and weaknesses of any database depend in part on the strengths and weaknesses of the database management system being used. Both Scholastic and Sunburst market ready-made databases designed to be used with a variety of subject areas. Scholastic distributes ready-made educational databases on a learning activities disk that can be ordered along with pfs: file/report. These ready-made databases for classroom use can be used with either Professional File or pfs: file/report.

Sunburst lists a wide variety of educational databases that can be used with Bank Street School Filer. The following is a list of topics for which several databases are available:

Animal Life	Endangered Species
Space	Astronomy
North America	United States
Colonial Times	Minerals
Climate and Weather	

D.C. Heath markets some databases for Notebook Filer also. Called the *Heath Social Studies Data Files Disks*, these databases are compatible with Notebook Filer and come with a teaching plan, a student worksheet, and a data entry form for each file. The database titles include:

Regions Near and Far
The United States Past
The World Past
The World Today

AppleWorks Databases and Templates

The richest source of database learning materials revolve around AppleWorks. Much of this material can be obtained for a nominal fee. Both complete databases and templates are available. Nearly every major educational software producing company lists ready-made instructional databases to be used with AppleWorks. Osborne McGraw-Hill publishes a book of AppleWorks instructional templates authored by Flast and Flast (1986) titled AppleWorks Applications. Claris publishes a book (Bandura, 1988) called *The AppleWorks Resource Guide for Teachers and Parents*. This book includes not only instructional templates, but also sample lesson plans containing ideas and suggestions for integrating the templates into the curriculum.

Because AppleWorks enjoys such tremendous popularity among educators, collecting and sharing instructional templates is becoming popular. Various groups and organizations are forming to gather, organize, and make available collections of these instructional templates. One such organization is Teacher's Idea & Information Exchange (TI&IE). TI&IE publishes a news letter and catalog. The catalog lists hundreds of instructional templates that can be ordered for about the cost of the floppy disks.

ELECTRONIC SPREADSHEETS IN EDUCATION

In its simplest form, a **spreadsheet** is a **grid** with letters across the top that serve as labels for columns and numbers along the side as labels for rows. When we create a pronounced grid effect by drawing lines to separate the rows and columns, as in Figure 12.2, we can see that an entire page or sheet is divided into many cells. Each cell has a distinct name consisting of a letter and a number. For example, if you count down three rows

	A	B	C	D	E	F	G	H	I	J	K	L
1												
2												
3												
4												
5												
6												
7												
8												
9												
10												

FIGURE 12.2   A blank spreadsheet screen with lines.

and across five columns on Figure 12.2, you will be at cell E3. If you count down five rows and across three columns, you will be at cell C5.

Such grids, bound together to form ledgers, have been used for many years for bookkeeping purposes. In bookkeeping, the columns are usually labeled by time periods, such as days, weeks, months, or years. The rows are usually labeled with designated financial terms, such as income, taxes, and wages. The spreadsheet provides a very organized way of keeping track of numbers that have some relationship to each other.

The Electronic Spreadsheet

A story is told about how the electronic spreadsheet was first conceived. Dan Bricklin, a Harvard MBA student, was laboring over a set of financial cases using paper, pencil, and calculator to compute financial projections. As he labored, he began to ask an age-old question: Isn't there an easier way to do this? A logical answer to his question seemed to be to program the computer so it would do all of the "grunt work" for him.

Bricklin envisioned a program that would resemble an electronic chalk board. Labels, numbers, and formulas would all be visible, and changing any set of numbers would automatically cause the program to recalculate and adjust all other affected numbers.

After teaming up with an old friend, Bob Frankston, the idea became a reality. The first commercial spreadsheet software, VisiCalc, was born. Needless to say, these two young men became very wealthy (Alsop, 1982).

To get a glimpse of the power the creators of VisiCalc saw in the electronic spreadsheet, pretend that you decided to convert your paper and pencil personal budget to an electronic spreadsheet. The spreadsheet you see in Figure 12.3 was created using an electronic spreadsheet program. As you can see, three types of information can be entered into the **spreadsheet cells**: (1) numbers, (2) **spreadsheet formulas**, and (3) labels. The formulas in the spreadsheet tell the computer to carry out specified mathematical calculations on the numbers, and the labels consist of text used to explain or identify numbers and formulas.

The spreadsheet you see in Figure 12.3 was set up so that when you type numbers in the PAY CHECK and PARENT'S CHECK rows (rows 6 and 7), the computer automatically adds these two amounts together and inserts the total in the TOTAL INCOME row. Likewise, all the separate expense items are added and the total inserted in a cell designated to show TOTAL EXPENSES. The numbers in the SAVINGS row are automatically inserted by the computer and are the result of subtracting numbers in the TOTAL EXPENSES row from numbers in the TOTAL INCOME row.

This spreadsheet is very flexible. If you should decide you needed a separate category to keep track of your laundry expenses, you could

	JAN	FEB	MAR	APR	MAY	JUN	TOTAL
INCOME							
PAY CHECK 350	350	350					
PARENT'S CHECK	200	200	200				
TOTAL INCOME 550	550	550				1650	
EXPENSES							
CAR PAYMENT 150	150	150					
RENT 100	100	100					
FOOD 100	110	120					
TUITION 20	20	20					
BOOKS 10	10	10					
CLOTHING 30	15	30					
RECREATION 50	60	50					
OTHER 20	15	25					
TOTAL EXPENSES	480	480	505				1465
SAVINGS	70	70	45				185

FIGURE 12.3   Simple personal budget—electronic spreadsheet.

easily insert a new row labeled LAUNDRY EXPENSES. If you were to insert this category between the CLOTHING and RECREATION rows, the TOTAL EXPENSES row could be moved down to make room for the new row. When an amount was inserted in the new LAUNDRY row, the computer would include that amount in calculating the TOTAL EXPENSES.

When using an electronic spreadsheet, the computer becomes an automatic calculator. Anytime you change a number in a cell, the computer can automatically recalculate to provide updated totals.

Advantages of the Electronic Spreadsheet

Three advantages of an electronic spreadsheet turn the computer into an efficient and powerful number management tool. First, vast amounts of numerical data can be stored in a tiny space in **electronic memory**. Second, the spreadsheet can be edited, as in word processing, with rows and columns being inserted, deleted, or revised. Third, the heart of the electronic spreadsheet's power is its ability to perform instant automatic calculations on any or all of the numbers in its cells.

The instant and automatic recalculating characteristic of the electronic spreadsheet allows the computer user to do **forecasting**. Forecasting is the process of inserting hypothetical numbers into the spreadsheet to test certain theories or hunches. This has made the electronic spreadsheet an invaluable tool for business. A large company can test the effects on the profit margin of hundreds or thousands of different production costs. Forecasting can be thought of as a what-if game. A business person might ask, What if we save 5% of our labor costs by not working overtime and producing a smaller number of units? The answer to such a question can be obtained almost instantly by simply changing a couple of numbers in the spreadsheet. The entire spreadsheet is then automatically recalculated.

Let's look again at your imaginary Personal Budget, as shown in Figure 12.3, to get a clearer picture of how the what-if game works. Let's assume you want to have $500 saved by the end of June so that you can take a vacation. After three months of being on your budget, you only have $185. You don't have to be a student of economics to know that to make $315 available for savings during the next three months you have to either increase your income or decrease your spending.

To get an idea of how drastic the changes in your budget will need to be, you can project what will happen if you stay on the same level of income and spending. The spreadsheet program can easily be told to do this. As you can see in Figure 12.4, at your present rate you will only have $320 saved by the end of June.

Your challenge is to find some combination of percentage increase in income and decrease in spending that will result in increasing your savings to $500. The power of the electronic spreadsheet now comes into play. Even with a budget this small, there are many combinations of changes that could be made. For the Personal Budget spreadsheet to help us play the what-if game, we have added a new column to your spreadsheet as shown in Figure 12.5. The new column has been inserted between the March and April columns. At the top of the spreadsheet it is labeled *Pct. raise* (percent raise needed to save $500).

Another new column has been added in the expense section labeled *Pct. less spent* (percent less spent to save $500). In this spreadsheet, the PARENT'S CHECK, CAR PAYMENT, RENT, TUITION, and BOOKS lines are all fixed amounts. Therefore, the only way to increase your income is to get a pay raise. The only way to decrease your expenditures is to spend less on FOOD, CLOTHING, RECREATION, and OTHER.

Some formulas have been inserted into the spreadsheet that make it possible for you to use whole numbers representing the percentage pay raise and percentage decrease in spending you want to look at. The spreadsheet will then do all the necessary arithmetic on these percentages and balance the spreadsheet so that the total projected savings by the end of June will be shown.

Literally hundreds of different combinations of pay raises and decreased expenses could be examined. If you were sitting in front of a

	JAN	FEB	MAR	APR	MAY	JUN	TOTAL
INCOME							
PAY CHECK	350	350	350	350	350	350	
PARENT'S CHECK	200	200	200	200	200	200	
TOTAL INCOME	550	550	550	550	550	550	3300
EXPENSES							
CAR PAYMENT	150	150	150	150	150	150	
RENT	100	100	100	100	100	100	
FOOD	100	110	120	120	120	120	
TUITION	20	20	20	20	20	20	
BOOKS	10	10	10	10	10	10	
CLOTHING	30	15	30	30	30	30	
RECREATION	50	60	50	50	50	50	
OTHER	20	15	25	25	25	25	
TOTAL EXPENSES	480	480	505	505	505	505	2980
SAVINGS	70	70	45	45	45	45	320

FIGURE 12.4 Simple personal budget—project to end of semester.

	JAN	FEB	MAR	Pct. raise	APR	MAY	JUN	TOTAL
INCOME								
PAY CHECK	350	350	350	10	385	385	385	
PARENT'S CHECK	200	200	200		200	200	200	
TOTAL INCOME	550	550	550		585	585	585	3405
				Pct. less spent				
EXPENSES								
CAR PAYMENT	150	150	150		150	150	150	
RENT	100	100	100		100	100	100	
FOOD	100	110	120	10	108	108	10	
TUITION	20	20	20		20	20	20	
BOOKS	10	10	10		10		10	10
CLOTHING	30	15	30	15	25.5	25.5	25.5	
RECREATION	50	60	50	10	45	45	45	
OTHER	20	15	25	15	21.25	21.25	21.25	
TOTAL EXPENSES	480	480	505		505	505	505	2904.30
SAVINGS	70	70	45		45	45	45	500.75

FIGURE 12.5 Simple personal budget used to forecast saving $500.

computer with this spreadsheet in operation, you say to yourself, What if I get a 5% pay raise, decrease what I spend on food by 7%, decrease what I spend on clothing by 10%, decrease what I spend on recreation by 7%, and decrease my other expenses by 6%? Just as you typed in the 4 to represent the percentage of decreased spending for the OTHER, you would see the TOTAL SAVINGS cell change to $421.70. At this rate, you will be $78.30 short of your goal. So, you try a little larger pay raise and you try more drastic cuts in spending. Finally, you find a combination of changes that will result in $500 saved by the end of June and that seems realistic to you.

Figure 12.5 shows just one of many combinations that might qualify. A 10% raise seems high, but you have worked hard, you feel you deserve it, and you make up your mind to go for it. If only solving the national debt were so easy!

The Electronic Spreadsheet as an Educational Tool

The electronic spreadsheet would have little place in education if all it could be used for was managing a personal budget. As we suggested earlier, the spreadsheet is beginning to be viewed as an important teaching and learning tool. A report by Wilson (1985) is typical of the enthusiasm some educators show when they begin to appreciate the power of this new educational tool. According to Wilson, the spreadsheet

> can be a valuable tool in science, mathematics and social studies by developing and reinforcing skills in problem solving, generalizing, predicting, decision making and hypothesizing. Students can gain practice in setting up mathematical formulas, which can be used to find totals, subtotals, differences, percents, etc.; they can predict what would happen if an entry were changed. Deciding which entry to change and how to change it provides practice with decision making. (p. 30)

One example of how to put a spreadsheet to work in a social studies class was reported by Pogge and Lunetta (1987). These teachers designed a spreadsheet template that would project population growth. The formulas in the spreadsheet were based on an exponential population equation.

Students can use the spreadsheet to investigate a variety of social issue questions. One such question might be, When will city X reach a critical water shortage? The students would then conduct library research to obtain the statistics called for in the spreadsheet template or be provided with invented data for a fictitious city. Once the statistics were entered, population growth could be projected and correlated with available water supply, and a report could be written suggesting the year when the available water resources would not be adequate to meet the city's needs.

John Turner (1988), a professor at the U.S Naval Academy, sees the electronic spreadsheet as a valuable tool in teaching undergraduate mathematics. He provides his students with enough expertise in one session to start them on their way to using the spreadsheet in solving problems and exploring concepts. For example, Turner encourages his students to test new formulas. They do this by plugging the formula into the spreadsheet and then entering diverse numbers. Thus, they gain a feel for how the different variables in the formula affect the final answer.

The way Turner is using the spreadsheet is similar to the way a teacher might use a computer simulation program. Actually, any concept that involves numbers can be simulated with a spreadsheet. An example would be the concept of compound interest. After you have explained what compound interest is and how it works, you could have your students sit down at the computer with a spreadsheet and experiment with different numbers. They could take out imaginary loans with compound interest. The length of time of the loan and the interest rate could be changed, and students would be able to see how these two variable affect the monthly payment and the total amount of interest paid.

School-Oriented Spreadsheet Programs

The use of spreadsheets in schools has been largely limited to the spreadsheet portions of two popular integrated software packages, AppleWorks and Microsoft Works. These two spreadsheet programs are briefly discussed next.

AppleWorks   Since AppleWorks is one of the most widely used software packages in education, it stands to reason that the AppleWorks spreadsheet is the most popular spreadsheet program in the schools. The AppleWorks spreadsheet enjoys great popularity as an educational tool for the same three reasons the database management portion of the integrated package is popular: (1) it is part of an integrated software package where data can be quickly and easily interchanged, (2) it combines power and user friendliness, and (3) a large number of spreadsheet templates are available.

Microsoft Works   Beginning in 1989, IBM Corporation made a major effort to gather a larger share of the educational computer market. With this effort, many secondary level schools began installing MS-DOS computers. An integrated software package that is MS- DOS compatible and has similar advantages to AppleWorks is Microsoft Works. Microsoft Works, unlike AppleWorks, has not spawned a collection of compatible instructional templates. We believe, however, that the increased use of MS-DOS machines in education and the popularity of using integrated software packages in education will result in collections similar to those available for AppleWorks.

Spreadsheet Templates for Schools

Since AppleWorks is an integrated program, those who develop instructional templates using the database management system also develop instructional templates using the spreadsheet. Therefore, most sources of AppleWorks instructional templates will list spreadsheet templates. Again, *The AppleWorks Resource Guide for Teachers and Parents (1988) and AppleWorks Applications* (1986) are good sources of information.

MECC markets what they call *Spreadsheets for Mathematics and Science: AppleWorks Sampler*. The disk containing the sampler consists of a variety of spreadsheet activities to help students understand and appreciate certain mathematical concepts, sample lesson plans, and ideas and suggestions for integrating the templates into the curriculum. The Teacher's Idea & Information Exchange can also provide numerous instructional spreadsheet templates.

SUMMARY

As with many computer applications that are now viewed as educational tools, the database and the spreadsheet were first developed and accepted by business. These applications are general and flexible enough to be very effective teaching and learning tools. In this chapter, you have read about database management and spreadsheet software. You have been exposed to the necessary terminology for understanding and becoming conversant about these two types of applications software. You learned that a database management system is a program that can be used to organize, sort, rearrange, and exchange information at very rapid speeds. You have also learned that an electronic spreadsheet is a program that allows you to organize numbers and formulas into a visible pattern where changing any set of numbers will automatically cause the program to recalculate and adjust all other affected numbers. You have read about some of the common database management and spreadsheet programs used by teachers and have been exposed to educational examples of their use.

LOOKING AHEAD

You should now have knowledge of how databases and spreadsheets can be applied to the field of education. The main emphasis of this chapter has been the use of the computer as a tool. While spreadsheets and databases constitute two ways of turning the computer into an educational tool, there are many other ways. Some software is designed specifically for the purpose of developing student's problem-solving skills. The next chapter explores the possibilities of using the computer to teach problem solving and emphasizes the research on the effectiveness of this proposition.

SOME QUESTIONS TO CONSIDER

1. Why are database management and spreadsheet programs considered new educational tools?
2. What are some lessons that could be taught more effectively using an electronic database or spreadsheet?
3. What are some of the problems associated with getting teachers to take advantage of these new educational tools to enhance their teaching?

RELATED ACTIVITIES

1. Go to a place of business in the community and ask someone who works there to demonstrate a database or spreadsheet to you and then obtain a printout that illustrates how one of these applications is used.
2. After viewing the database or spreadsheet demonstration, show how that application could be used as a teaching tool in your educational field of study.
3. Interview a public school teacher, explain some of the ways databases and spreadsheets or being used to help teachers and, together with the teacher, explore some ways that he or she could use either a database or a spreadsheet to enhance a lesson.

SUGGESTIONS FOR ADDITIONAL READING

Matthews, C. B. (1985). *AppleWorks made easy*. New York: McGraw-Hill.

Hoelscher, K. (1988). Making it in America. *Computers in the Schools*, 5(1/2), 179–185.

Szymona, M. L. (1988). The *Immigrant* experience withintegrated tool software. *Computers in the Schools*, 5(1/2), 187–192.

SOFTWARE PRODUCTS CITED IN TEXT

Professional File, *Software Publishing Corporation*, P.O. Box 7210, 1901 Landings Drive, Mountain View, CA 94039.

pfs: file/report, Scholastic Inc., 2931 East McCarty Street, P.O. Box 7502, Jefferson City, MO 65102.

AppleWorks, *CLARIS Corporation*, 440 Clyde Avenue, Mountain View, CA 94043.

Bank Street Filer, *Sunburst Communications*, 101 Castleton Street, Pleasantville, NY, 10570.

Notebook Filer, *D.C. Heath and Company*, School Division, 125 Spring Street, Lexington, MA, 02173.

MECC Dataquest Composer, *MECC*, 3490 Lexington Avenue North, St. Paul, MN, 55126.

Microsoft Works, *Microsoft Corporation*, 16011 NE 36th Way, Box 97017, Redmond, WA 98073.

REFERENCES

Alsop, S. (1982). Software Arts wrote the first best-seller. *INC*, January, pp. 71–74.

Bandura, S. (ed.) (1988). *The AppleWorks resource guide for teachers and parents.* Mountain View, CA: Claris.

Flast, L., & Flast R. (1986). *AppleWorks applications*. Berkeley, CA: Osborne McGraw-Hill.

Hedges, W. D. (1984). The database and decision making in public schools. Computers in the Schools, *1*(3), 91–100.

Pogge, A. F., & Lunetta, V. N. (1987). Spreadsheets answer "what if . . . ?". *Science Teacher, 54*(8), 46–49.

Turner, J. C. (1988). The use of spreadsheets in teaching undergraduate mathematics. *Computer Education, 12(*4), 535–538.

Willson, J. W. (1985). VisiCalc in the elementary school. *Computing Teacher, 12*(9), 29–30.

13

Problem-Solving Software

GOALS AND OBJECTIVES

Goal: To become aware of the controversies surrounding the teaching of problem-solving skills, and to learn some of the useful facts known about this topic.

When you finish studying this chapter, you will be able to:

1. Write a paragraph listing at least two of the controversial issues involved in teaching students problem-solving skills.
2. List the four stages of problem solving identified by Polya.
3. Compose a paragraph explaining the term domain-specific as it relates to problem-solving skills.
4. List the six categories of cognitive domain objectives as identified by Benjamin Bloom and tell how they might be used to plan a problem solving curriculum.
5. Tell why domain specific is probably preferable to nondomain specific software.

KEY TERMS

affective domain
affective variables
analysis
application
Bloom's taxonomy

cognitive domain
comprehension
concrete thinking
domain specificity
domain specific software

evaluation
executive skills
factual knowledge
formal operational
   thinking
hierarchy
higher-order thinking
   skills
HOTS
IDEAL
idea processors
lower-order thinking
   skills

metacognitive skills
nondomain specific
software
Polya
problem solving
psychomotor domain
rote computational
habit
synthesis
transfer

Many educational computing advocates believe that computers can play an important role in teaching children to be better at problem solving. This chapter will discuss current and future attempts to use the computer for this purpose. We begin by discussing some of the accepted definitions of problem solving and then move on to a review of research on the teaching of problem solving. We then present a section on Bloom's taxonomy of educational objectives and discuss how his categories can help us in developing a problem-solving curriculum across grade levels. We provide a review of different types of commercial problem solving software and we conclude with some recommendations about computers and the teaching of problem-solving skills.

THE NATIONAL CONCERN ABOUT PROBLEM SOLVING

Recently, education has been the target of intense criticism from diverse sources. This criticism has frequently concentrated on the perceived lack of success of schools in teaching effective problem-solving skills to children. Many educational observers have deplored the overemphasis on facts and rote learning in the curriculum and the underemphasis on critical thinking and problem solving. A report of the National Assessment of Educational Progress points out the following:

> *One of the consequences of students learning mathematical skills by rote is that they cannot apply the skills they have learned to solve problems. In general, NAEP results showed that the majority of students at all age levels had difficulty with any non routine prob-*

lem that required some analysis or thinking. It appears that students have not learned basic problem-solving skills. *(Corbitt, 1981, p. 146)*

Sprinthall and Sprinthall (1990) have pointed out that science teachers and the writers of science textbooks wrongfully assume that most high school students are capable of advanced problem-solving ability, even though studies have shown that only between 18% and 33% of students in grades 9 through 12 are able to apply formal operational thinking (advanced conceptual thinking needed for problem solving) to scientific problem solving (Renner and others, 1976). Sprinthall and Sprinthall (1990) go on to suggest that research shows that "The great majority of pupils have difficulty in understanding the basic assumptions of the science curricula in secondary schools" (p. 121).

They suggest that the picture in the humanities is no more encouraging. The Project Talent study, for example, determined that only 8% of a random sample of over 500,000 teenagers could understand passages from Jane Austen, and only 33% could understand passages from Stevenson's Treasure Island (Flanagan, 1973).

Deficiencies such as these have recently been highlighted in a number of commission reports that conclude that there are major problems in U.S. schools. These reports have been given wide coverage in the media and are a source of concern to politicians, educators, and the general public.

WHERE SHOULD A DISCUSSION OF PROBLEM SOLVING BEGIN?

Deciding where to begin a discussion of problem solving is difficult in the extreme. After all, in a general sense, skill in problem solving is the ultimate goal of education at all levels. It is even possible to argue that problem solving is the principal activity of human beings and the single ability that most clearly distinguishes our activities from those of other animals. Entire books have been written on the topic.

Adding to the dilemma is the fact that the subject is controversial. There is little agreement about what constitutes problem solving, whether or how it should be taught, and whether or not problem-solving skills learned in one domain can be transferred to problems in another context.

Thus, the task of writing this chapter is a bit intimidating (and also a bit presumptuous, given the scope and complexity of the topic). Nevertheless, even though we recognize many problems, we are excited about the potential of computing as an aid to the teaching of problem-solving skills. Therefore, we will begin the formidable task of writing a chapter on problem solving in computing by considering the definition of problem solving itself.

WHAT IS PROBLEM SOLVING?

Defining **problem solving** is not as easy as it sounds. Some experts attempt to define problem solving itself, while others elect to discuss characteristics of problems or of problem solvers. Flake, McClintock, and Turner (1990) describe problem solving as follows:

> *Problem solving involves intellectual curiosity. It is wanting to find out: to find answers to questions, to find ways to overcome difficulties, to find solutions to puzzles, and to find ways of accomplishing goals . . . . This problem-solving attitude is a part of the person's personality pattern. (p. 97)*

Polya (1957), a writer and researcher who has concentrated on problem solving, describes it as a goal-directed activity involving a sequence of stages. (Although not all authorities on problem solving agree on what constitutes the stages of problem solving, most have described stages or sequences in the solution of problems.) Polya (1957) suggests that problem solving involves (1) understanding the problem, (2) formulating a plan, (3) carrying out the plan, and (4) looking back, or evaluating the results.

Similarly, Kinzer, Sherwood, and Bransford (1986) describe a five-stage process making use of the mnemonic aid **IDEAL**. (The five stages can be remembered by recalling each letter in IDEAL.) These stages are (1) identifying the problem, (2) defining the problem with precision, (3) exploring some possible strategies, (d) acting on these strategies, and (5) looking at the results.

Gore prefers "skills in critical thinking and/or logic," a general definition that would be applicable to a wide range of disciplines (Gore, 1988, p. 172). She goes on to define what constitutes a problem by endorsing a nontechnical definition by Moursund (1985), who suggests that a problem has three parts:

1. *How something actually is (initial state)*
2. *How you would like the thing to be (goal state)*
3. *What you can do about the situation (allowable types of actions to move from the initial state to the goal state) (p. 3)*

Moursund (1985) goes on to suggest that (1) problem solvers must be motivated to solve the problem, (2) they must have an extensive foundation of knowledge and experience, (3) they must possess a feeling of power and a repertoire of possible actions, and (4) they must have the ability to act and to evaluate their actions.

Vockell and van Deusen (1989), who wrote an entire book on using computers to teach higher-order thinking skills (**HOTS**), suggest that such skills "may be arranged into several overlapping sets of categories" (p. 3). These categories include (1) **metacognitive** or **executive skills** (awareness of our own thinking and the ability to use that awareness to improve performance); (2) critical and creative thinking; (3) thinking processes including problem solving, concept formation, principle formation, comprehension, decision making, research, composition, and oral discourse; and (4) core thinking skills. [These writers suggest that the distinction between core thinking skills and thinking processes is fuzzy, but that the former "can often be taught much more directly than the more global thinking processes" (p. 10).]

Flake, McClintock, and Turner (1990) suggest that a problem is one of the following:

1. A question for which the answer is not easily obtained and for which the problem solver must search for, deliberate on, and create a valid answer.
2. A difficulty that must be overcome for which resources must be marshalled or created and for which the resolution must be invented (a strong desire is present for overcoming the difficulty).
3. A goal that is obstructed, but for which motivation is present. To achieve the goal, the problem solver must creatively develop a way of overcoming the obstacle. (p. 98)

It should be evident from this short discussion that problem solving means various things to various people and that no hard and fast definition exists.

THE RESEARCH ON PROBLEM SOLVING

We briefly discussed research on problem solving in both Chapters 2 and 4. As we mentioned at that time, there is considerable controversy about whether there exists a set of generic problem-solving skills that can be taught. If such skills exist, then constructing a problem-solving curriculum makes sense. Activities promoting such skills could be identified, and children would spend a portion of each day engaging in such activities. Then, when these skills were learned, children would be able to apply the skills to problems encountered in any subject in everyday life, in a job, and so on.

This controversy actually involves the question of whether or not there are generalizable problem-solving skills. If a child learns skills that help to solve problems in one area (domain), will these skills generalize or **transfer** to another area (domain) and improve the problem-solving ability of the individual in the new area? For example, will learning to be a better problem solver in math automatically improve one's problem-solving ability in social studies?

As you may suspect, this question has troubled educators and researchers long before computers began to find their way into schools. [Readers who are interested in this research, especially as it applies to computing, will be interested in reviews by Tetenbaum and Mulkeen (1984), Linn (1985), Perkins and Salomon (1987), and Burton and Magliaro (1988).]

Although there is no universal agreement about what research tells us about the transferability of problem-solving skills, most knowledgeable observers agree that problem-solving skills have been shown to be relatively **domain specific** (Frederiksen, 1984; Krasnor and Mitterer, 1984). In other words, skills learned in one domain probably do not automatically or easily transfer to other domains.

Frederiksen (1984) concluded that "There appears to be little if any transfer from one domain to another" (p. 391), while Ginther and Williamson (1985) observed that "decades of research on problem solving, with both animal and human subjects, has shown that transfer of general problem-solving skills is difficult to achieve" (p. 76). Judah Schwartz, codirector of Harvard's federally funded Educational Technology Center (ETC), took a similar position when he was interviewed recently for an article in Computers in the Schools (Johnson, Maddux, and O'Hair, 1988):

> *I, for one, fall very much on the side of domain specificity. . . . To talk about problem solving in a kind of undifferentiated way and then look for transfer and domain generality seems to me to be much too hard a task. (p. 14)*

Cyert (1980) suggests that teachers have traditionally hoped to develop higher-order cognitive processes in children, but have been largely unsuccessful. Tetenbaum and Mulkeen (1984) agree and point out that computer educators hope the computer can succeed where other methods and materials have failed in developing problem-solving skills, even though there "is little evidence to support this supposition" (p. 17).

As we have shown, most authorities do not believe in the automatic transfer of problem-solving skills. However, we believe that the most important word in the previous sentence may be "automatic." Even the most optimistic of writers and researchers emphasize that if transfer is possible it must be nurtured through proper teaching strategies.

Vockell and van Deusen (1989), in their book on the teaching of higher-order thinking skills, suggest that such skills can be taught if specific teaching steps are taken. Glover, Ronning, and Bruning (1990), in discussing programs for teaching general problem-solving skills, provide a cautious endorsement given proper usage:

> *Intuitively, it seems that teachers using such programs must carefully show their students how skills learned from the programs can be used to help acquire new domain-specific information... Of course, confidence that these programs will enhance problem solving in domain-specific areas of problem solving awaits further research. (p. 180)*

Similarly, Burton and Magliaro (1988), while generally pessimistic concerning automatic transfer, conclude:

> *One area of research that offers some hope to this transfer dilemma is the* explicit *instruction of strategic knowledge within the domain. . . . While this hypothesis needs further study, the general idea of teaching explicitly how to analyze, for example, the relevant features of problem domains and identify those features seems to be a promising avenue. (p. 68)*

We will give some suggestions for maximizing transfer at the the end of this chapter.

BLOOM'S TAXONOMY AND ITS RELEVANCE TO PROBLEM SOLVING

If this discussion has led you to the conclusion that there is a bewildering array of ways to think about problem solving and that teaching methods will vary greatly according to which of these ways is selected, you are correct. In addition, research on the topic is in its infancy and has provided few definitive answers.

Although there is much of interest and value in all the conceptualizations of problem solving discussed so far, we find the observations of Benjamin Bloom (1956) to be particularly appropriate and useful.

Bloom felt that a major educational problem was the lack of consensus among educators concerning the goals of schooling. To help resolve the problem of selecting educational goals and then defining how these goals will be achieved and evaluated, he developed a taxonomy for educational goals and objectives in the **cognitive** (intellectual), **affective** (attitudinal), and **psychomotor domains**. These taxonomies consist of a **hierarchy** of objectives. (A hierarchy is a listing in order of rank, grade, or the like. Bloom's taxonomy is ordered from simple to complex, from concrete to abstract.)

In the **cognitive domain** (the domain of most relevance to problem solving), **Bloom's taxonomy** includes (1) **factual knowledge**, (2) **comprehension** (understanding), (3) **application** (applying skills), (4) **analysis** (reduction of a solution into component parts), (5) **synthesis** (arriving at a solution by combining component parts), and (6) **evaluation** (judging). The first three of these categories are sometimes referred to as **lower-order thinking skills**, while the last three are said to be **higher-order thinking skills**, sometimes abbreviated HOTS (Church and Bender, 1989). It is these latter skills that are usually thought of when problem solving is discussed.

Sprinthall and Sprinthall (1990) point out that, while Bloom has never equated his taxonomy with developmental stages, the first three of his categories are consistent with and can be accomplished through Piagetian **concrete thinking** (nonabstract thinking available to children of elementary school ages), while the final three require **formal operational thinking** (abstract thinking available to secondary and adult ages).

This is an interesting observation for several reasons. First, it suggests that elementary schools should emphasize the objectives of basic knowledge, comprehension, and application (lower-order thinking skills), while middle schools and secondary schools should emphasize analysis, synthesis, and evaluation (higher-order thinking skills). Additionally, it suggests a continuum of skills in any specific content area, with the lower-order skills being, to some extent, prerequisite to the higher-order skills.

Following this line of thinking, it would be unrealistic to expect students to become expert at evaluation, the most advanced, abstract goal in the hierarchy, if they have not mastered the lower-level objectives, including (1) acquisition of basic knowledge and facts, (2) understanding of those facts, and (3) application of their knowledge to real situations. Furthermore, acceptance of these ideas suggests that effective teaching of problem solving must involve attention to goals from all six levels of the taxonomy and that neglect of any of these six levels could render ineffective any attempts to teach problem-solving skills.

DETERMINING WHAT TO TEACH

Bloom's taxonomy is useful in helping us to classify goals for children and in reminding us not to neglect any of these categories of goals. Furthermore, even a superficial general knowledge of the sequence of stages hypothesized in Piagetian developmental psychology gives clues about when to emphasize each goal. Such cursory and superficial knowledge, however, does little to simplify the task of deciding exactly what and how to teach.

Unfortunately, we cannot provide a simple formula to solve this ubiquitous teaching problem. As you have seen, there are simply too many different ideas about the nature of problem solving, and research is too mixed on the transferability question to permit hard and fast prescriptions.

The best advice we can give is to invest a great deal of time and energy in becoming familiar with a number of the theoretical approaches to problem solving. We recommend that you look back over the part of this chapter in which we reviewed some of the definitions of problem solving. Perhaps one or more of these approaches (or some other approach we have not mentioned) appeals to you as particularly compatible with your own knowledge, attitudes, and skills. As you study a specific approach, you will find that the theory will provide a path that will lead you to try specific methodologies with specific content. The more you learn about the theory, the more sophisticated these methods are likely to become, and the more likely they are to be successful methods. (We believe this process of intensive study of theory, which then leads to generation and refinement of methodology, is the essence of our professionalism and the mark of the master teacher.)

However, we recognize that teachers must often make teaching decisions before they have the time or energy to invest in such intensive study. Therefore, at the end of this chapter we provide some recommendations with the understanding that they are tentative, and are intended only as a temporary solution to a problem that will best be uniquely solved by each teacher over a long period of time.

COMMERCIAL PROBLEM-SOLVING PROGRAMS

Problem-solving software is appearing in ever-increasing quantity (Burton and Magliaro, 1988; Lockard, Abrams, and Many, 1987). Several different types of computer software are often advertised as problem-solving software:

1. *Computer programming languages:* We have discussed this kind of software and its potential to teach problem solving in Chapters 4 and 11. In addition, we will deal further with this topic in Chapter 14 at the end of this chapter.

2. *Domain-specific problem-solving software:* **Domain-specific software** is intended to make better problem solvers within a specific subject such as science or math. Examples of software advertised as domain-specific include that offered by Sunburst Communications (101 Castleton Street, Pleasantville, NY 10570-3498, 800- 628-8897). For example, Sunburst advertises four programs as part of their Problem Solving & Science collection for grades K–8. These include The Incredible Laboratory, Color Keys, M-ss-ng L-nks Science Disk, and Ant Farm. Sunburst's Problem Solving & Math series includes 36 programs such as Teasers by Tobbs, The Factory, and The King's Rule.

A caution is in order concerning such software, however. Sunburst advertises The Incredible Laboratory as a science problem-solving activity, since the skills emphasized in the program are skills that are often identified as important in science (trial and error processes, note taking, and making organized lists). However, we do not agree that this software should be listed as science software, since it makes use of no actual science content.

In The Incredible Laboratory, users are presented with a list of imaginary chemicals that can be added to a beaker. Each ingredient produces a specific feature in a monster that is supposedly "produced" by the chemical mixing. Since there is no actual science content, The Incredible Laboratory should be classed as nondomain-specific problem-solving software. The authors apparently believe that skills learned while using this software to construct imaginary monsters from imaginary chemicals will automatically transfer to real science problem solving. As we have already pointed out, this is an unsubstantiated assumption. Although children enjoy The Incredible Laboratory, we would prefer software that makes use of actual science content.

Also included in the category of domain-specific problem-solving software are tool software such as Judah Schwartz' Semantic Calculator, which is marketed by Sunburst Software as *SemCalc*. This software is described in some detail in Chapter 2. Briefly, the Semantic Calculator is used as an aid in solving story problems in mathematics. It is intended to combat the development of a **rote computational habit** in which children focus improperly on numbers and computation and neglect the sense of the problem.

The author of this software is currently developing another program that will be called The Algebraic Proposer, and is intended as a modeling environment for the making of algebraic models in fields such as physics, industry, economics, and accounting. We find software such as SemCalc and The Algebraic Proposer to be truly domain specific and highly promising.

Also included in this category are the various tool programs to aid writing. These include **idea processors** designed to allow writers to make use of an outline (see Chapter 10) and the various tutorial programs designed to aid writers by asking critical questions at strategic points in the writing process. Again, many of these programs are exemplary, since they do a good job of helping students learn domain-specific problem-solving skills.

3. *Nondomain-specific, general problem-solving programs:* **Nondomain-specific software** is based on the premise that general problem-solving skills can be taught and that, once learned, such skills can be applied to problems in other domains. An example in this category is Broderbund Software's *Where in the World Is Carmen Sandiego?* detective simulation series (Broderbund, Inc., 17 Paul Drive, San Rafael, CA 94903-2101). (See Chapter 4 for a short description of this program.)

Rocky's Boots is another example in this category (IBM Corp., PO Box 1328-S, Boca Raton, FL 33432). This software involves constructing a simulated electric logic machine in specific game formats.

SOME RECOMMENDATIONS CONCERNING PROBLEM-SOLVING SOFTWARE

There is much more to be said about problem solving than we have included in this short chapter and much is yet to be learned about this topic. Programs for teaching problem solving, whether or not they involve computers, are still in the experimental stage. We agree with the following assessment by Hyde and Bizar (1989):

> *We have carefully reviewed the many programs and have concluded that they are each valuable but incomplete. Each seems to stake out only a section of the territory on what might be considered key intellectual processes. In promoting his program, each author exaggerated the importance of the* kind of thinking *encouraged by his program, as if that is all there is or should be to thinking. A few programs attempt to be more complete or comprehensive, to encompass the many varied kinds of thinking. However, these seem to be like a smorgasbord of processes, without a clearly defined theoretical model that shows teachers how they fit together. (pp. 15–16)*

Although the state of the art in teaching problem solving is in its infancy, we believe there is presently enough evidence available to permit some useful conclusions. With the above qualification in mind, we recommend the following:

1. *Although problem solving is an important goal at all levels, elementary schools should emphasize lower-order thinking skills, while middle schools and secondary schools should emphasize higher-order thinking skills.* While emphasizing lower- or higher-order skills, however, teachers at all levels should remember that effective teaching of problem solving must involve attention to goals from all six levels of the taxonomy, since lower-order skills seem to be prerequisites for higher-order skills.

2. *Computer programming should not be taught exclusively with the hope of teaching generalizable problem-solving skills, since research remains unclear as to its potential to accomplish this goal.* We believe that there are other good reasons to teach programming, however, and Chapters 4, 11, and 14 present those reasons. Chapter 14 also presents recommendations generated from research and from experience that we think will maximize the likelihood of transfer of skills learned. Furthermore, as we discuss in Chapter 14, we believe that the Logo computer language is the most appropriate for use with children.

3. *Domain-specific problem-solving software should be chosen over nondomain-specific software.* Bransford and Stein (1984), in their book on problem solving, assert that knowledge is a necessary tool in problem solving and that good problem solving requires the development of the ability to acquire new knowledge. Kinzer, Sherwood, and Bransford (1986) echo this assertion:

> *We argued earlier that it is difficult to significantly improve problem solving by emphasizing only general strategies such as trying to identify potential problems, defining problems carefully, and so forth. The ability to solve problems requires specific knowledge that can function as a conceptual tool. If we want to solve problems about population control, for example, we need information about biology, and if we want to make informed decisions about a journey (e.g., along the Oregon Trail), we need information about resources and potential hazards. (p. 175)*

Therefore, we believe that exemplary problem-solving software is domain specific and knowledge intensive.

4. *Nondomain-specific software should be used only if the goal is to influence attitudes toward problem solving or if the specific skills taught are valuable in and of themselves, rather than as a vehicle to teach transferable problem-solving skills.* If you look back over the beginning section of this chapter in which we presented various definitions related to problem solving, you may note that many authorities refer to the importance of **affective variables** such as intellectual curiosity, wanting to find out, problem-solving attitudes, motivation, belief in one's potential to solve problems, and a feeling of power. We also believe in the importance of these affective variables. Therefore, we can endorse the use of nondomain-specific software such as The Incredible Laboratory, Rocky's Boots, or Where in the World Is Carmen Sandiego? if they are chosen because they are interesting and enjoyable and because the teacher wants to foster affective attributes such as those listed above. Once such attributes are established, however, we suggest emphasizing domain-specific problem solving software. (Nondomain-specific software might also be chosen to teach specific knowledge or skills. For example, Where in the World Is Carmen Sandiego? teaches the use of the World Almanac and certain concepts and skills in geography. If such knowledge and skill are considered important, we see no reason why such software should not be used.)

5. *Teachers should keep an open mind concerning the issue of teaching transferable problem-solving skills, and they should watch for research reports that may shed light on this cloudy issue. In addition, whether domain-specific or nondomain-specific problem-solving software or computer programming is chosen, teachers should use those teaching techniques that have shown promise of maximizing the chances of transfer.* For example, Krasnor and Mitterer (1984) attempt to convert research findings into specific recommendations. They suggest that teachers keep in mind that research shows that (1) transfer requires that some of the knowledge or skills be identical across domains, (2) the learner should be helped to recognize how the new problem is similar to the old one, (3) transfer may depend heavily on the completeness of the original learning, and (4) it is probably important for the child to be exposed to many situations where the specific skill is useful in more than one domain.

With regard to programming as a vehicle to teach transferable problem solving, McCoy (1989–1990) suggests that success has been limited because programming is often poorly taught. She recommends:

> *In order to promote problem solving, there are three essential components that must be taught in computer programming classes: metacognition, planning, and debugging. (p. 46)*

SUMMARY

American schools have recently been criticized for emphasizing rote learning and neglecting to teach higher-order thinking skills such as problem solving. One problem in addressing this criticism is that the subject is controversial and research results are mixed. It is, for example, unclear whether or not general problem-solving skills can be taught, although most authorities believe that problem solving is relatively domain specific and will not automatically transfer to other subjects.

There is preliminary evidence that transfer may be accomplished through proper teaching strategies. One promising technique is for teachers to carefully point out to students how skills learned in one domain can be used to solve problems in other domains.

Bloom's taxonomy of educational objectives can be helpful in providing clues about the teaching of problem solving. Lower-order objectives should be emphasized in the elementary schools, while higher-order objectives should be emphasized in middle schools and secondary schools.

Commercial problem-solving software includes (1) computer programming languages, (2) domain-specific packages, and (3) nondomain-specific programs. Recommendations for use of such software include (1) making use of the elementary–secondary dichotomy of the goals explained above, (2) teaching of computer programming to achieve goals other than those related to problem solving, (3) choosing domain-specific over nondomain-specific problem-solving software, (4) using nondomain-specific software only to achieve affective goals or because the specific skills taught are considered important for their own sake, (5) keeping an open mind and staying up to date on the latest research on teaching problem solving, and (6) regardless of the type of problem-solving software chosen, using techniques that have shown promise of promoting transfer.

LOOKING AHEAD

As you have probably realized by now, there are many unresolved issues related to the teaching of problem-solving skills. One of these issues concerns the teaching of computer programming and whether the learning of programming skills improves general problem-solving or other cognitive skills. This question has sparked a heated controversy in educational computing and psychology. Although many different computing languages are sometimes suggested as vehicles for learning problem solving, the controversy is especially heated with regard to the Logo language. The next chapter will deal with this topic.

SOME QUESTIONS TO CONSIDER

1. The chapter presents several ways of thinking about problem solving, problems, and problem solvers. Which of these ways do you find the most personally meaningful? Tell why.
2. Kinzer, Sherwood, and Bransford (1986) describe a five-stage problem-solving process symbolized by the mnemonic aid IDEAL. Tell what each letter stands for and describe a lesson in a specific subject using these stages. Be sure the lesson is domain specific and knowledge intensive.
3. Choose one of Bloom's six categories of goals in the cognitive domain. Write a goal for a short lesson in some specific subject. Be sure the goal will fit in the category you choose. Then outline a brief lesson aimed at that goal using the Kinzer, Sherwood, and Bransford stages (IDEAL).
4. Suppose a software company advertised a piece of math problem-solving software in which children listened to melodies with miss-

ing notes and then had to supply the notes necessary to complete the tune. If the software company advertised that this taught an important math skill, that of identifying patterns, would you agree that (1) it is domain-specific software and that (2) such software is highly useful? Explain your answers fully.

5. Can you imagine any circumstances in which the software in question 4 could be useful?

6. Identify activities you might use to convince your students that they have the power to solve problems.

RELATED ACTIVITIES

1. Obtain a copy of *Taxonomy of Educational Objectives* (Bloom, 1956) and read more about the cognitive domain. Then select one teaching topic related to computing (such as learning to move text around in a word-processing document). Prepare a one-paragraph summary of each of six lessons on that topic. Each lesson should be aimed at one of the six cognitive-domain goals identified by Bloom. For each paragraph, include a brief statement explaining why you think the lesson could achieve that goal.

2. In Bloom's text (1956), read about educational goals in the affective domain. Then prepare a brief (two- to three-page) paper in which you explain whether or not (and why) you think these affective goals could be useful in computer education.

3. Locate a commercial educational software catalog. (Visit your college of education computer lab or a retail store that sells software.) See if the catalog advertises software intended to teach problem solving. If so, select one program and tell whether it appears to be domain specific or nondomain specific problem-solving software. Tell why. If possible, locate the software and run it on a computer to help you decide.

REFERENCES

Bloom, B. (ed.). (1956). *Taxonomy of educational objectives, Handbook 1: Cognitive domain*. New York: McKay.

Bransford, J. D., & Stein, B. S. (1984). *The IDEAL problem solver*. San Francisco: W. H. Freeman.

Burton, J. K., & Magliaro, S. (1988). Computer programming and generalized problem-solving skills: In search of direction. *Computers in the Schools, 4*(3/4), 63–90.

Church, G., & Bender, M. (1989). *Teaching with computers*. Boston: College-Hill.

Corbitt, M. K. (1981). *Results from the second mathematics assessment of the National Assessment of Educational Progress*. Reston, VA: National Council of Teachers of Mathematics.

Cyert, R. M. (1980). Problem solving and education policy. In David T. Tuma and Frederick Reif (eds.), *Problem solving and education: Issues in teaching and research*, pp. 3–8. Hillsdale, NJ: Lawrence Erlbaum.

Flake, J. L., McClintock, C. E., Turner, S. (1990). *Fundamentals of computer education*. Belmont, CA: Wadsworth.

Flanagan, J. (1973). Education: How and for what? *American Psychologist, 28*(7), 551–556.

Frederiksen, N. (1984). Implications of cognitive theory for instruction in problem solving. *Review of Educational Research, 54*(3), 363–407.

Ginther, D. W., & Williamson, J. D. (1985). Learning Logo: What is really learned? *Computers in the Schools, 2*(2/3), 73–78/

Glover, J. A., Ronning, R. R., & Bruning, R. H. (1990). *Cognitive psychology for teachers*. New York: MacMillan.

Gore, K. (1988). Problem-solving software to implement curriculum goals. In W. M. Reed & J. K. Burton (eds.), *Educational computing and problem solving*, pp. 171–178. New York: Haworth Press.

Hyde, A. A., & Bizar, M. (1989). *Thinking in context: Teaching cognitive processes across the elementary school curriculum*. White Plains, NY: Longman.

Johnson, D. L., Maddux, C. D., & O'Hair, M. M. (1988). Are we making progress? An interview with Judah L. Schwartz of ETC. *Computers in the Schools, 5*(1/2), 5–21.

Kinzer, C. K., Sherwood, R. D., & Bransford, J. D. (1986). *Computer strategies for education: Foundations and content-area applications*. Columbus, OH: Merrill.

Krasnor, L. R., & Mitterer, J. O. (1984). Logo and the development of general problem-solving skills. *Alberta Journal of Educational Research, 30*(2), 133–144.

Linn, M. C. (1985, May). The cognitive consequences of programming instruction in classrooms. *Educational Researcher*, pp. 14–16, 25–29.

Lockard, J., Abrams, P. D., & Many, W. A. (1987). *Microcomputers for educators*. Boston: Little Brown.

McCoy, L. P. (1989–1990). Computer programming can develop problem-solving skills. *Computing Teacher, 17*(4), 46–49.

Moursund, D. (1985). Problem solving: A computer educator's perspective. *Computing Teacher, 12*(5), 2–5.

Perkins, D. N., & Salomon, G. (1987). Transfer and teaching thinking. In D. N. Perkins, J. D. Lockhead, and J. C. Bishop (eds.), *Comprehension instruction: Perspectives and suggestions*. White Plains, NY: Longman.

Polya, G. (1957). *How to solve it*. Garden City, NY: Doubleday.

Renner, J., Stafford, A., Lawson, J., McKimmon, J., Friot, F., and Kellogg, D. (1976). *Research, teaching, and learning with the Piaget model*. Norman, OK: The University of Oklahoma Press.

Sprinthall, N. A., & Sprinthall, R. C. (1990). *Educational psychology* (5th Ed.). New York: McGraw-Hill.

Tetenbaum, T. J., & Mulkeen, T. A. (1984, November). LOGO and the teaching of problem solving: A call for a moratorium. *Educational Technology, 24*(11), 16–19.

Vockell, E., & van Deusen, R. M. (1989). *The computer and higher-order thinking skills*. Watsonville, CA: Mitchell Publishing.

14

Logo: A Unique Computer Language

GOALS AND OBJECTIVES

Goal: To know the nature and history of the Logo computer language, to become familiar with some of the educational issues surrounding the language, and to become familiar with a methodology for teaching Logo to students.

When you finish studying this chapter, you will be able to:

1. Compose a brief explanation of how Papert's involvement with gears led to the development of Logo.
2. Write a sentence defining "mathophobia" and tell how Papert believes Logo can be used to alleviate this problem.
3. Write a paragraph explaining Papert's rationale for believing that learning to program in Logo can lead to lowering the boundary between child and adult thinking.
4. Explain why the Bank Street Studies do not prove that Logo will not promote transferable problem solving skills.
5. Explain the authors' three-part strategy for teaching Logo.

KEY TERMS

artificial intelligence	concretizing the abstract
affective learning	differential
backlash	discovery learning
Bank Street Studies	formal operational thinking
cognitive amplifier	graphics

interactive programs	mathophobia
LISP	mental rigor
list processing	metacognition
Logo	point in space
Logo list	transfer
Logo turtle	turtle graphics
Logo word	variable

It has been said that anyone who is uncomfortable with controversy should avoid education. We would agree, and we would add that such individuals should especially avoid educational computing in general and Logo in particular.

We make that suggestion because some of the most heated controversies in the controversial field of educational computing center around the teaching of the Logo computer language to children. For example, experts disagree about whether or not Logo should have a place in the school curriculum, how the language should be taught, the age at which students should be introduced to Logo, and, most of all, the effect that learning Logo programming has on students. In fact, just about everything connected with Logo in schools is controversial.

If you become a teacher who makes extensive use of computers, you will almost certainly make some decisions about the teaching of Logo. This chapter is designed to help you make those decisions.

We first discuss the history of Logo and Logo's present status in education. We present the arguments that Logo advocates use to justify their advocacy, and we attempt to evaluate these claims. We discuss selected Logo research and we present our conclusions (based on our interpretation of that research and our experiences with Logo) about the advisability of teaching this language. Finally, we discuss specific teaching methods and a sample Logo lesson.

HISTORICAL OVERVIEW

Logo is widely taught. In fact, Becker (1987) reported that in 1985 more than 40,000 educators in the United States were teaching Logo. Many other educators in other countries also teach the language. In many ways, Logo is a unique computer language. For example, it is the only language that has been developed specifically for use with children. It is also the only language to be based on an accepted theory of human cognitive development.

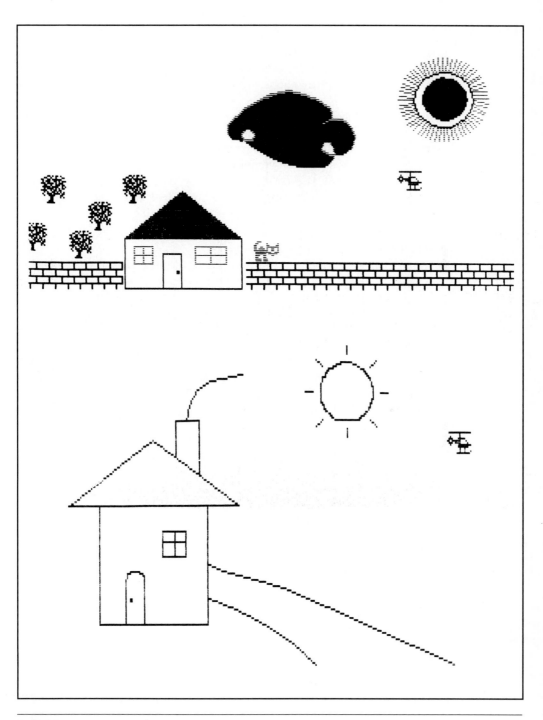

FIGURE 14.1 Logo graphic.

Logo's Roots

Logo was developed by Seymour Papert, a computer scientist and mathematician at the Massachusetts Institute of Technology (MIT). Papert (1980) presents his ideas about children, schools, computers, mathematics, learning, and Logo itself in a book entitled *Mindstorms: Children, Computers, and Powerful Ideas*. Papert's articulate and compelling writing style, coupled with his clear expertise in computing, mathematics, and learning theory, captured the imagination of many educators and sparked the beginning of the Logo movement.

We believe that *Mindstorms* should be read by anyone who is interested in computer education. Indeed, we feel that the book ranks among the 10 best educational books we have read.

A Thumbnail Sketch of Logo's Developer

Seymour Papert was born and educated in South Africa. At the university, he decided to major in philosophy, probably because he had a long-standing interest in thought processes. However, he soon tired of philosophy and switched his major to mathematics. Eventually, he joined the faculty of the Massachusetts Institute of Technology, where he became interested in **artificial intelligence**.

In the 1950s, Papert sensed that computers had potential as teaching and learning tools. However, before he could begin developing such tools, he believed he needed to know more about how children think and learn. Therefore, he spent five years (from 1958 to 1963) at the University of Geneva, studying with the imminent child psychologist, Jean Piaget. During this time, he became convinced that the computer could be turned into an object that could help children to think. However, he believed that this would only be possible if communication between child and computer could be simplified. He also believed that such communication should be interactive and natural. He envisioned a computer language that children could learn in the same way that they learn to speak their native tongues. In other words, he wanted his language to be learned incidentally (through normal daily interaction and without the necessity of formal instruction).

In 1963, Papert returned to the artificial intelligence laboratory at M.I.T. where he put together a team of individuals that eventually produced the Logo language.

Papert's Rationale

Papert's book *Mindstorms* does an excellent job of presenting the rationale for Logo and for the kind of schools and the kind of teaching that Papert endorses. In the foreword, he relates a critical childhood experience. As a boy, he was fascinated by automobiles. At an early age he played with two sets of automobile gears: one from a transmission, another from a

differential (the part that transfers energy from the drive line to the rear wheels). At first, his pleasure derived merely from predicting, from the movement of the first gear, the movement of the last gear in the chain. He then became fascinated with the functioning of the differential gear, since it illustrated a nonlinear chain of causality. That is, it distributed motion from the transmission shaft differentially, depending on the resistance offered by the wheels:

> *I remember quite vividly my excitement at discovering that a system could be lawful and completely comprehensible without being rigidly deterministic. (p. vi)*

For Papert, gears became models for understanding a variety of difficult concepts:

> *Gears, serving as models, carried many otherwise abstract ideas into my head. I clearly remember two examples from school math. I saw multiplication tables as gears, and my first brush with equations in two variables (e.g., 3x + 4y = 10) immediately evoked the differential. By the time I had made a mental gear model of the relation between x and y, figuring how many teeth each gear needed, the equation had become a comfortable friend. (p. vii)*

Thus, Papert's fascination with gears evolved into a versatile tool with which old knowledge was used to help acquire new understanding. Additionally, Papert suggests that his experiences with gears, which led to an understanding of mathematics, helped instill a positive attitude toward mathematics.

Papert sums up his ideas about learning as follows:

> *Slowly I began to formulate what I still consider the fundamental fact about learning: Anything is easy if you can assimilate it to your collection of models. If you can't, anything can be painfully difficult . . . . What an individual can learn, and how he learns it, depends on what models he has available. (p. vii)*

Thus, Papert designed Logo as a thinking tool that provides children with powerful models that will assist them in understanding new concepts.

To fully understand Papert's ideas, it is necessary to pay particular attention to what he says about the **affective** (emotional) aspect of **learning**. The model of the gears was effective for him, not only because it was a powerful model, but because, as he says, he "fell in love with the gears."

This affective component is obviously highly unpredictable, highly personal, and highly individual. All children do not "fall in love" with the same objects. The necessity for an emotional connection to an effective model would make it ineffective to provide each child with a mass-produced set of gears. Since an emotional connection would not occur for most children, such a set of gears would not be a useful cognitive tool for most children.

Papert sums up his vision for Logo as follows:

> *What the gears cannot do the computer might. The computer is the Proteus of machines. Its essence is its universality, its power to simulate. Because it can take on a thousand forms and serve a thousand functions, it can appeal to a thousand tastes. This book is the result of my own attempts over the past decade to turn computers into instruments flexible enough so that many children can each create for themselves something like what the gears were for me. (p. viii)*

Mindstorms goes on to fully develop Papert's rationale for teaching Logo to children. In that volume, Papert makes one of the most startling educational suggestions we have encountered. He suggests that using the **discovery method** of teaching children to program in Logo, coupled with sweeping changes in school policies and procedures, can result in a lowering of the boundary between child and adult thinking. (Piagetian discovery learning involves the teacher serving as facilitator to help children discover things for themselves. This teaching role is in opposition to traditional teaching, in which the teacher serves as lecturer or disseminator of knowledge.)

In making this claim, Papert departs from traditional Piagetian thinking. As you may know, Piaget believed that children pass through four stages of cognitive development. He believed that the time spent in each stage varies from person to person, and he emphasized the importance of the environment in facilitating this progression. Although Piaget never maintained that no other sequence was possible, most Piagetian psychologists have concluded that the order of progression through the stages are part of the human genetic heritage and are invariant in their sequence.

Another way of expressing this is to say that Piagetian psychologists believe that the order in which people develop different intellectual abilities is part of the human condition and is relatively insensitive to cultural or environmental variables. In support of this contention, research has consistently shown that children in different Western cultures do not vary in the sequence of stages as they mature (Wadsworth, 1989). Likewise, research on handicapped children has failed to find any other sequence of development (Brekke, Johnson, and Williams, 1975).

Piaget suggested that **formal operational thinking** (adult thinking) is unavailable to children younger than about 12 years of age because (1) the logical structure of such tasks is too complex, and (2) the necessary neurological structures are not sufficiently mature.

Papert agrees that these two variables play a role. On the other hand, he suggests that the order in which these intellectual abilities are acquired is more responsive to the environment than Piaget suspected. Specifically, he suggests that some developmental differences may be due to our culture's lack of materials that serve as the foundations of advanced intellectual structures. Papert's position, therefore, is that computers in general, and Logo in particular, can make the tools and models available from which prepubescent children can build ways of thinking that Piaget thought were available only from puberty onward. In other words, Papert suggests that Logo can make children capable of adult thinking.

Papert goes on to suggest that Logo can be used to dispel **mathophobia**, or the unreasonable fear and hatred of mathematics that currently pervades our culture. In this regard, Papert asserts that Logo should be used to introduce math, specifically geometry, to children. We will return to this idea later in this chapter.

Implementation of Logo

The first school field testing of Logo took place during the 1968—69 school year in a junior high school in Massachusetts. The language was installed on a minicomputer, and the version being tested did not include the capability of constructing **graphics** (computer pictures). This latter point was probably due to the fact that Logo was originally based on **LISP** (for list processing), a computer language that also had no graphics capability. (This lack of graphics capability is ironic in that today Logo is often erroneously characterized as being exclusively a graphics language. Actually, Logo's present graphics capabilities were added later.)

After this first successful field testing, the Logo group added the concept of the turtle. At first, Logo turtles were called tortoises, and were small, dome-shaped floor robots. These robots, built in the 1960s by Grey Walter, a British neurophysiologist, could be directed to move around the floor by typing commands on a computer keyboard (Abelson and diSessa, 1980). These robots were fitted with markers and could thus draw designs on paper fastened to the floor. (Logo robot turtles can now be purchased for several hundred dollars from companies such as Harvard Associates, 260 Beacon Street, Somerville, MA 02143, 617-429-0660, FAX-1-800-776- 4610. Slesnick [1984] reviews seven programmable robots and lists addresses, compatibility, languages, and cost for each machine.)

Eventually, the three-dimensional robot was transformed to a two-dimensional turtle (usually a small triangle or simple turtle shape) that could be moved around a computer screen, thus drawing designs (graphics) on the screen. The purpose of the **Logo turtle** is a specific example of the general role Papert envisions for computers in education. He believes computers can be used to make difficult, abstract ideas more concrete and, therefore, more understandable to children. He refers to this general goal as using computers to **concretize the abstract** (Papert, 1980, p. 21).

Earlier, we alluded to Papert's assertion that the Western world suffers from mathophobia. He suggests this unreasonable fear and hatred of mathematics and, to a lesser extent, fear of learning in general is primarily the result of the way mathematics and other subjects are taught in schools. He suggests that school math is a corruption of true mathematics, and he makes many suggestions for reforming schools, including, among others, the suspension of grading, the adoption of Piagetian discovery learning, and the provision of a computer for every student. With respect to the teaching of mathematics, one of Papert's suggestions is that school children should receive their introduction to mathematics through geometry.

This is a radical suggestion, since traditional wisdom holds that geometry is too abstract for young children to understand. After all, when Euclid formulated his geometry, he made use of a number of fundamental concepts, one of which is the **point in space**. This concept is the quintessential abstraction. Since it is totally imaginary, it has no shape, no color, no heading, no physical characteristics whatsoever. The Logo turtle is analogous to Euclid's point in space, and is Papert's attempt to concretize that abstraction, thereby making it available for young children.

Designs constructed with the turtle are called **turtle graphics**. In addition to turtle graphics, Logo retains full **list processing** (the ability to handle words) and mathematical capabilities.

The Logo group continued to refine the language until 1978, when the availability of microcomputers made it possible to make the language widely available to schoolchildren. The MIT Logo group and personnel from Texas Instruments developed an excellent commercial version of Logo that ran on the ill-fated 99/4-A microcomputer. An Apple II version quickly followed. Eventually, many other dialects of the language were developed. Today, there are versions of Logo that run on all popular microcomputers.

A Logo Advocacy Becomes Established

Papert published *Mindstorms* in 1980. The book was an immediate success and created a sensation in education. The entire August 1982 issue of *BYTE* (a prestigious, semi-technical computing periodical) was devoted to Logo, creating further interest among computer professionals and hobbyists alike.

An international conference for those interested in Logo was held in 1984. In 1985, a special issue of *Computers in the Schools* dealt with Logo and was later issued in both hard and soft cover. By this time, scores of books about Logo had been published, and The National Logo Exchange began publishing a journal. (Today, this journal is *Logo Exchange*, the journal of the International Society for Technology in Education Special Interest Group for Logo-using Educators (or SIGLogo). Information about the journal can be obtained by writing ISTE, University of Oregon, 1787 Agate Street, Eugene, OR 97403-9905.)

Soon after publication of *Mindstorms*, a vocal advocacy for Logo began to form. Many educators were fascinated, and, in their zeal, they began making continually more outlandish and undocumented claims for benefits to be gained by teaching children to program with Logo.

Although these advocates were well intentioned, they made the common error of claiming more for an educational innovation than could be documented. At times, their fervor became almost religious in nature, as in this quote from Marvin Minsky:

> *Seymour Papert is the greatest of all living educational theorists. He puts into the hands of the child new conceptual tools and thus changes the learning experience from a matter of discipline and suffering into one of discovery and excitement. (Marvin Minsky, quoted from back cover of* Mindstorms, *Papert, 1980)*

Inflated claim followed inflated claim, as typified by an article by Judd (1983). In that article, the author claimed that Logo was effective in developing number, letter, and color recognition, symbol association, directionality, decision making, following instructions, memory recall, spatial awareness, sequential thinking, creativity, and computer awareness. The author went on to suggest that teaching Logo will cause children to develop an improved self-image; pay attention to detail; enhance both divergent and logical thinking; improve decision making, spelling, math, and communication skills; and develop an awareness of the computer as a tool. Furthermore, Judd (1983) suggests that these benefits are available to both gifted and handicapped children.

The Backlash against Logo

Such claims are, in the long run, detrimental to the field of educational computing and to Logo, because exaggerated claims lead inevitably to a **backlash** of public and professional opinion. Why Logo became the object of a cadre of true believers is unknown. There are probably many reasons. Perhaps it is partly because education, for the last few years, has been the target of widespread attacks by both professional and lay people. Another reason may be that educational computing in its infancy has been dominated by Type I applications that are so boring, repetitive, and disappointing that Logo may have seemed even more promising than it ordinarily would have.

Logo as a Cognitive Amplifier

None of the many claims for Logo have proved as controversial as the claim that Logo can somehow improve cognitive functioning such as general problem solving. Although the issue is far from settled, much of the research on problem solving seems to show that such skills are more discipline specific than many teachers would hope. In other words, if a child learns to solve Logo programming problems, he will not necessarily be better at solving problems in other areas.

Although the question of whether programming cultivates transferable problem-solving skills is relatively new, the question of **transfer** itself is quite old. For example, it was once common for schools to teach Latin on the grounds that it improved general reasoning ability or resulted in increased **mental rigor**. When this contention could not be proved, Latin was dropped from many programs.

If skills learned in one domain carry over into some other domain, these skills are said to transfer. But skills learned in Logo do not necessarily transfer to other domains. At least such transfer does not automatically occur. There is some evidence, however, that transfer can occur, given the proper conditions. Black, Swan, and Schwartz (1988), for example, were able to document transferable problem-solving skills in a Logo project involving 133 subjects in fourth through eighth grades. This study was carefully controlled and well thought out, and the researchers included several features designed to overcome the shortcomings of other Logo research:

1. Due to the failure of nondirective, discovery methods of teaching Logo, the researchers included well-structured activities.
2. Since other studies have focused on children at all ages, the researchers used subjects in middle and junior high school, the ages at which formal operational thinking (abstract or adult thinking) is thought to emerge.
3. Many other researchers have not defined problem solving and have directed their studies merely at solutions, rather than problem-solving strategies leading to solutions. Black, Swan, and Schwartz identified six problem-solving strategies judged useful in programming, including (1) subgoal formation, (2) forward chaining, (3) backward chaining, (4) systematic trial and error, (5) alternative problem representation, and (6) analogical reasoning. Instruction and assessment were developed around these strategies.
4. Other researchers have not emphasized the importance of **metacognition**, defined as the awareness of one's systematic

thinking strategies that are required for learning (Lerner, 1989, p. 188). Therefore, Black, Swan, and Schwartz made efforts to model such metacognitive strategies and to help children develop metacognitive habits.

5. Most previous researchers have restricted the teaching of Logo to the turtle graphics capabilities of the language. Black, Swan, and Schwartz blocked on this variable, instructing one subgroup in graphics only, one in graphics and list processing, and one in list processing only.

More high-quality research such as this is obviously needed.

The Bank Street Studies   Space will not permit an exhaustive review of Logo research. (For a comprehensive review of this research, see Maddux and Johnson, 1988, and Maddux, 1989.) However, we feel compelled to mention a series of well-known research studies that are often called the **Bank Street Studies** (Kurland and Pea, 1983; Pea, 1983; Pea and Kurland, 1983a, 1983b; 1983c; Pea and Kurland, 1984).

These studies are popularly (and erroneously) believed to have proved that Logo does not improve transferable problem solving skills. However, we believe that this research is so flawed that it cannot be interpreted. There were many errors made in this research, but we believe the fatal flaw is that Pea and Kurland themselves admitted that the children in the study did not master Logo programming skills. Therefore, the failure to find improved, transferable problem solving skills among the "Logo group" should not be interpreted as a reflection of Logo's lack of power to produce such results. The researchers should have tested their subjects on Logo programming skills, and, before testing for transfer, they should have disqualified any who failed to show Logo mastery.

Other researchers have found benefits for Logo. Roblyer, Castine, and King (1988), in their meta-analysis, included 11 studies examining the results of teaching Logo on problem-solving and general thinking skills and three studies on the effects of problem-solving CAI. They reported "A fairly substantial and homogeneous effect for Logo in enhancing problem-solving skills" (p. 105). They summarized their findings as follows: "Logo shows promise as a method of enhancing cognitive skills of various kinds, and looks especially good in comparison with unstructured, discovery-learning CAI applications." (p. 105).

Some Recommendations Concerning Logo

The discussion to this point has given you a brief exposure to Logo and to some of the controversies involving its educational use and value. These controversies, together with unrealistic and inflated claims for Logo, have led to the current backlash against educational use of the language.

The danger with any backlash is that it will result in "the baby being thrown out with the bath water." Logo advocates should refrain from making promises that cannot be documented, and we should encourage more and better research into Logo's power as a **cognitive amplifier**.

Why Teach Logo?

We are often asked if we think Logo should be taught in schools. The answer is yes. We are Logo advocates, although we have already explained that we are opposed to the unscientific discipleship that has formed around the language. Even though research has yet to establish whether Logo has value as a cognitive amplifier or whether it can be used to lower the boundary between child and adult thinking, we believe there are other, less controversial reasons to teach Logo. These include the following:

1. Logo can provide an area of success for children, some of whom seldom have such an experience in a school setting.

2. Programming permits trial and error problem solving. Thus, it is somewhat self-correcting. This can be beneficial for children who have become highly sensitive to adult correction.

3. Because Logo (unlike other languages such as BASIC) requires only a small investment of time and effort before interesting things can be accomplished, many children are motivated to continue practicing their programming skills. This can be important for children who have seldom had the experience of persevering to mastery in any school activity.

4. Logo graphics provides practice in spatial relationships. This can be beneficial to students who have deficits in spatial relations.

5. Many children are distractible. Distractibility interferes with many academic tasks that require long periods of uninterrupted effort (long division, for example). However, Logo programming sessions can be interrupted and resumed later with little or no impairment in efficiency.

6. Peer tutoring and cooperative learning can be made part of Logo teaching strategies. These methods can facilitate social status and peer relations for children who experience difficulty in such areas.

7. Logo provides an interesting, relevant reason to use mathematics in a setting that is free of unpleasant associations. Thus, Logo may prove useful in reversing the trend toward mathophobia.

How Should Logo Be Taught?

Pending more definitive research, we can recommend the following based on our own experiences in teaching Logo and on our interpretation of the growing body of Logo literature:

1. *Logo should be taught using structured discovery methods* in addition to open-ended methods. Otherwise, few children will achieve programming mastery.

2. *Very young children (younger than grade three) should not be given formal Logo instruction.* For such children, a variety of social and academic tasks are probably more valuable than learning to program, and programming mastery probably requires greater intellectual maturity than is commonly found prior to this time. Intensive Logo instruction should probably not begin until around age 12.

3. *Do not expect the teaching of Logo to lower the boundary between child and adult thinking.* Papert himself called for sweeping changes in schools and in educational practices. Changes such as providing a computer for every child and eliminating grading are not currently economically or politically realistic.

4. *The jury is still out on Logo's ability to train transferable problem-solving skills.* Preliminary indications are that it may be possible to teach Logo in a way that achieves this goal. It is clear, however, that transfer does not automatically occur when Logo is taught to any group of children, for any length of time, using any teaching method.

Teaching to Facilitate Transfer

Four articles provide excellent clues for how to facilitate transfer. These include Black, Swan, and Schwartz (1988), Burton and Magliaro (1988), Rieber (1987), and Krasnor and Mitterer (1984). Here is a list of recommendations for facilitating transfer. We have distilled these recommendations from these and other articles, as well as from our own experiences:

1. Teachers should continually point out to students how Logo problems and solutions are similar to problems and solutions in other domains.

2. Teachers must ensure that students achieve Logo programming mastery. Students should be tested frequently and areas of individual confusion should be remediated.

3. Logo teachers must themselves be Logo experts.

4. Logo teachers should emphasize the entire language, including arithmetic and list processing. Instruction in Logo graphics alone is insufficient.

5. Programming courses should be extensive. The usual 20 to 40 hours of instruction are not enough.

6. Debugging should be used extensively in courses. Experimenting with flawed programs is a powerful way to learn programming skills.

7. Teachers should emphasize structured programming (see Chapter 8 for a full explanation of structured programming).

8. Teachers should minimize the negative consequences of errors.
9. Preschool and primary grades are too early to begin intensive Logo instruction.

SPECIFIC TEACHING METHODS AND A SAMPLE LOGO LESSON

Space will not permit us to provide a comprehensive orientation to the Logo computer language. Readers who desire such an orientation are directed to the technical manual for the specific dialect they choose and to our earlier volume (Maddux and Johnson, 1988). The first half of that book presents the theory, philosophy, and research base for teaching Logo, while the second half presents teaching methods and daily lesson plans. We will make suggestions for additional reading and list them at the end of this chapter.

General Teaching Suggestions

We have already mentioned that Papert strongly asserts that Logo should be taught using nondirective, discovery learning. However, this assertion presents a dilemma in light of the recent research evidence that when children are taught Logo through the use of such methods many fail to achieve programming mastery. The dilemma is the difficulty of finding a way to teach Logo that is structured enough to ensure that many children achieve mastery, while allowing enough freedom and experimentation so that Papert's underlying theory and philosophy are not compromised.

Classroom Equipment Requirements

We feel that the ideal lab arrangement includes at least one computer for every two students and a large-screen monitor so that teacher demonstrations will be visible to the students. (There is some evidence that having two students share a computer can improve social skills and peer relations and encourage thoughtful problem solving.)

To facilitate teacher demonstrations, signal-splitter devices are available for use with large-screen monitors. These are excellent since they permit the computer to be plugged into a regular monitor that faces the teacher as well as the large-screen monitor that faces the class. This arrangement permits the teacher to face the class while typing on the computer.

An even better arrangement involves the use of a device that makes it possible to project the computer display through a standard overhead projector while simultaneously using a standard monitor. When these devices first came on the market, they were frustrating to use since they developed hot spots that obscured the display after only a few minutes of use. The state of the art has improved considerably, however, and the current crop of display devices does not suffer from this problem.

A Three-Part Daily Plan for Teaching Logo

Because of the structure versus discovery dilemma, we have modified a scheme suggested by Leron (1985). We described this strategy in our earlier book (Maddux and Johnson, 1988):

> *Each Logo session should have three distinct parts. The first part should be a structured, organized activity, usually including a demonstration and simultaneous student hands-on activities . . . . The second part should be a supervised, rather open-ended work period in which the demonstrated features of the language are put to use to complete an assigned activity. In part two, each child works independently at his or her own machine, or in groups of two children to each computer. Part three of each day's activity is experimentation and exploration of a self-directed nature. Children work on individual projects of their own choosing or simply engage in free Logo exploration. (p. 103)*

If, for example, we decided to spend 50 minutes on Logo, we would allocate 25 minutes, 15 minutes, and 10 minutes to parts 1, 2, and 3 respectively.

A Sample Lesson on Interactive Projects

The following demonstration Logo lesson does not involve any graphics whatsoever. We have chosen an interactive, list processing project to emphasize that Logo has capability other than graphics capability. In reality, we can do anything with Logo that can be done in any other language. (Throughout this chapter we will present examples written in the *LogoWriter* dialect of Logo, the dialect that we recommend to teachers. This dialect is available for use with Apple II and IBM-compatible computers and has become the most popular of the many available dialects. The popularity is probably due to the attractive cost of the LogoWriter packages available. A single copy of LogoWriter is $169, a lab pack is $299, and a site license with the right to make unlimited copies is $450. A home-use addition to the site license is an additional $150 and allows a site to loan LogoWriter disks to students to use at home or for a research project off campus. For more information, contact Logo Computer Systems Incorporated, P.O. Box 162, Highgate Springs, VT 05460, 800-321-LOGO.)

Part 1

In part 1, the teacher should explain that some programs are interactive. In **interactive programs**, the program asks questions and allows the user to type in answers. The teacher should then demonstrate an interactive Logo program or two. After demonstrating, the teacher should point out that, for interactive projects to work, there must be a command that tells the computer to stop executing program lines and pause to let the user respond. In the most popular dialect of Logo (LogoWriter), this command is READLIST (abbreviated RL). READLIST causes a Logo program to pause, allows the user to enter something from the keyboard, and causes that entry to become a Logo list.

Before proceeding, the teacher should review the differences between **Logo words** and **lists**. This has been the subject of a previous lesson. Briefly, words are one or more characters without spaces between characters. Lists are one or more words with spaces between words.) Words are designated as such by preceding them with opening quotation marks such as

```
"MARY
```

Lists are designated by enclosing them in brackets:

```
[MARY IS A GIRL]
```

The first element of the word MARY is the letter M, while the first element of the list MARY IS A GIRL is the entire first word MARY.

Students should be asked to predict what will happen if we type

```
PRINT FIRST "MARY
```

(We will omit instructions to press ENTER or RETURN and will assume that this is understood.) PRINT is a command that has been previously taught and instructs Logo to PRINT whatever follows on the screen. FIRST has also been taught, and students should be reminded that the FIRST command returns the first element of a word or a list.

Logo will print the letter M, since M is the first element of the word MARY. Then ask the students what will happen if we type PRINT FIRST [MARY]. (Logo will return the word MARY, since MARY is the first and only element of the list MARY.)

The students should then be reminded that the MAKE command can be used to create a **variable** and assign a value. This can be demonstrated in the immediate mode by typing the following:

```
MAKE "X "MARY
```

This creates a variable named X and assigns the word MARY to that variable. The students should be asked to predict what will happen if we type

```
PRINT :X
```

(The X variable is now referred to as :X rather than "X, since quotation marks are used only when a variable is created.)

```
PRINT :X
```

will return MARY. MARY is a word rather than a list since the X variable was created with opening quotation marks preceding MARY rather than with surrounding brackets. We can determine whether a variable has stored a word or a list by using the FIRST command. If we ask for the first element of the word MARY, Logo will return M, since individual characters are the elements of a word. If we ask for the first element of the list MARY, Logo will return MARY, since individual words are the elements of a list. Students should be asked to predict what will happen if we type

```
PRINT FIRST :X
```

Since the value of the X variable is the word MARY, Logo will return the first element of that word (the letter M).

The students should be asked if they can deduce how to create a variable named Y that is assigned the list MARY. Someone may suggest

```
MAKE "Y [MARY]
```

They should then be asked how to prove that X and Y have different values:

```
PRINT FIRST :X
```

This should return the letter M.

```
PRINT FIRST :Y
```

This should return the word MARY.

So far, everything we have done has been a review of previous lessons. The students should again be reminded that READLIST is the command that stops a Logo program, allows the user to type in characters from the keyboard, and makes the user response into a Logo list. To this point, we have used the MAKE command to create variables, but it is also possible to use READLIST to do so. If we wish to create a variable named Z and assign a list consisting of whatever the user types in, we could use

```
MAKE "Z READLIST
```

This can be tried in immediate mode. Have the students type the above line on their computers. They will notice that when they press ENTER (or RETURN), nothing happens. This is because Logo is waiting for the user response to be typed in so that it can be assigned to the Z variable. The students should now type

```
COMPUTERS ARE EDUCATIONAL TOOLS
```

The students should be asked to predict what will happen if they type

```
PRINT :Z
```

and

```
PRINT FIRST :Z
```

Logo will return COMPUTERS ARE EDUCATIONAL TOOLS and COMPUTERS, respectively. The teacher should now suggest that READLIST can be used in a procedure. Students can FLIP (OPEN-APPLE-F on Apple II computers and CTRL-F on IBM and Commodore computers) and enter the following procedure:

```
TO STORENAME
 PR [WHAT IS YOUR NAME, PLEASE?]
 MAKE "N READLIST
 PRINT [HELLO,]
 PR :N
END
```

Students should be reminded that RL can be used as an abbreviation for READLIST and PR for PRINT. They should again be reminded that opening quotation marks are needed when creating a variable (MAKE "N READLIST), while a colon must precede the variable name when you are referring to the value of the variable (PR :N).

Students should then run the program (first FLIP back with OPEN-APPLE-F or CTRL-F), typing in CLARK KENT when asked for their name. The program will respond with

```
HELLO,
CLARK KENT
```

The procedure works as intended, but it would be more natural if the entire response were on the same line. This can be done easily. The teacher should type the following line in immediate mode:

```
(PRINT [HELLO,] :N )
```

Logo will return

```
HELLO, CLARK KENT
```

The parentheses around the entire line are necessary because a PRINT command can handle only one input. PRINT [HELLO] would work fine, since the input to PRINT is only one thing (one list). PRINT :N would also work, since the input to PRINT is only one thing—whatever is assigned to the variable N. But to cause PRINT to handle both the list HELLO and the value assigned to :N requires parentheses around the PRINT command and the multiple inputs to that command.

The students should be asked to modify the STORENAME procedure so that it will print the word HELLO and the user's name on the same line. Here is one solution:

```
TO STORENAME
  PR [WHAT IS YOUR NAME, PLEASE?]
  MAKE "N READLIST
  (PRINT [HELLO,] :N )
END
```

The students should then be allowed to experiment with the procedure using a variety of names, including their own, their friends, celebrities, and so on. They should also be told that this is a useful procedure since it stores the user's name as variable N, and that name can be used later, if desired. For example, a line could be added just before the end:

```
(PRINT [IT'S BEEN NICE MEETING YOU,] :N )
```

In fact, the N variable will continue to store the user's name until its contents are changed or until the computer is turned off.

Part 2

During part 2, the students should work in pairs, writing a few simple interactive procedures involving the READLIST command. Here are some assignments that might be handed out on worksheets:

1. Write a short procedure that asks the user for his/her favorite color. The procedure should store the answer in a variable named C. Then the procedure should respond "_____ IS A PRETTY COLOR", with the user's favorite color in place of the blank.

2. Write a procedure asking the user to enter both first and last names (in that order). Store the user response in a variable called N. Have the procedure respond NICE TO MEET YOU, _____, with the first name only in place of the blank. *HINT*: Use of the FIRST command will be necessary.

Part 3

During part 3, the students will be allowed 10 minutes of free Logo exploration.

SUMMARY

Logo has become a controversial topic in educational computing. Although it is widely taught in schools, experts disagree about its value and about which teaching methods are most desirable.

Logo was developed by Seymour Papert, an M.I.T. mathematician and computer scientist. The language was developed for use by children after Papert spent five years studying child psychology with Jean Piaget. Papert believes that the teaching of Logo, coupled with sweeping changes in schools, can provide children with a thinking tool that could, in turn, lower the boundary between concrete operational (child) and formal operational (adult) thinking.

Although Logo is a general-purpose computer language that can be used to do anything that can be done in any other language, it is best known for its graphics capabilities. Logo graphics involve use of the turtle, a small figure that can be moved around the computer screen. As the turtle moves, it leaves a line in its path. The Logo turtle is Papert's effort to concretize the abstract. The turtle is analogous to the Euclidean point in space. Unlike the point in space, however, the Logo turtle has concrete physical properties such as shape, color, and heading. Because the highly abstract concept of the point in space can be concretized through use of the Logo turtle, Papert believes that geometry, introduced through Logo, should be a child's introduction to mathematics.

After Logo became available for use with microcomputers, it quickly gained educational advocates. Although these advocates meant well, they damaged the Logo movement by making unsubstantiated, unlikely, and exaggerated claims concerning the benefits to be gained by teaching children to use Logo.

One of the most controversial claims is that Logo can act as a kind of cognitive amplifier, improving thought processes such as general problem-solving skills. Those who endorse this idea believe that if children learn to solve Logo programming problems they will improve their ability to solve problems of other kinds. In other words, these advocates claim that Logo can teach transferable problem solving skills.

Research on this topic is in its infancy. We do know that transfer does not automatically occur across problem-solving domains. If there is to be transfer, the teacher must facilitate that transfer through teaching methodology.

Although the jury is still out on Logo and transferable problem solving, there are other, more down-to-earth reasons to teach the language. For example, one reason is that Logo can provide a success environment for children who do not often succeed at school. Other reasons are that Logo is self-correcting, it is highly motivating, it provides practice in spatial relationships, distractible children can succeed, it can improve social skills and peer relations, and it provides a reason to use mathematics in an arena free of negative associations and experiences.

The authors of this text recommend that Logo be taught using structured teaching methods, that preschool and primary age children not be given intensive Logo instruction, that teachers should not expect Logo to make children into adult thinkers, and that specific techniques must be used to facilitate the transfer of problem-solving skills.

The authors of this book recommend a three-part teaching strategy designed to resolve the dilemma of using teaching methods with sufficient structure that learners will achieve programming mastery without sacrificing the theoretical and philosophical foundations upon which the language is based. This strategy involves a structured demonstration and discussion stage, a stage in which children work in pairs or alone to arrive at individual solutions to assigned Logo problems, and a final stage of free Logo exploration.

LOOKING AHEAD

This concludes the section of this textbook dealing with Type II educational computing applications. As we have emphasized throughout this book, we believe that these applications represent the most powerful potential for computers to contribute to teaching and learning.

After reviewing a draft copy of the manuscript for this book, one of our graduate students made a comment we find particularly perceptive and encouraging. This student remarked that as she read the book she was struck by how much the success of educational computing depends not on what software or hardware developers accomplish, but on how educators choose to use the computing tools available to them.

We agree, and we believe this observation an appropriate note on which to conclude this section of the text. In part Four, we will present some material on software evaluation and indulge in a bit of speculation about what the future holds for computer education.

SOME QUESTIONS TO CONSIDER

1. If Papert is correct about Logo lowering the boundary between child and adult thinking, what would be the curriculum implications?
2. In what ways do Papert's ideas conflict with Piaget's?
3. What lessons can be learned from examining the effects of Logo advocacy on educational computing?

RELATED ACTIVITIES

1. Locate at least three articles about Logo. Briefly summarize them and tell whether any of these articles seem to be making unproved, unrealistically optimistic claims about the benefits of teaching this computer language.
2. Visit an educational computing lab (either in your college or in a public school) and ask for a demonstration of Logo. If you visit a public school, interview the teacher about his or her perceptions about the benefits and problems of teaching Logo to children.

SOME SUGGESTIONS FOR ADDITIONAL READING

Abelson, H. (1982). *Logo for the Apple II*. Peterborough, NH: BYTE/McGraw-Hill.

———, & deSessa, A. A. (1980). Turtle geometry: *The computer as a medium for exploring mathematics*. Cambridge, MA: MIT Press.

Bitter, G. B., & Watson, N. R. (1983). *Apple Logo primer*. Reston, VA: Reston Publishing Company.

Dale, E. (1984, September). Turtle toys and grid games. *Teaching and Computers, 2*, 56–58.

Harper, D. (1989). *Logo: Theory & practice*. Monterey, CA: Brooks/Cole.

Harvey, B. (1985). *Computer science Logo style: Intermediate programming*. Cambridge, MA: MIT Press.

———. (1986). *Computer science Logo style: Volume 2: Projects, styles, and techniques*. Cambridge, MA: MIT Press.

Lukas, G., & Lukas, J. (1986). *Logo: Principles, programming, & projects*. Monterey, CA: Brooks/Cole.

Watt, D. (1983). *Learning with Logo*. New York: McGraw-Hill.

Weir, S. (1987). *Cultivating minds: A Logo casebook*. New York: Harper & Row.

REFERENCES

Abelson, H., & diSessa, A. A. (1980). *Turtle geometry: The computer as a medium for exploring mathematics*. Cambridge, MA: MIT Press.

Becker, H. J. (1987). *The impact of computer use on children's learning: What research has shown and what it has not*. Baltimore, MD: Johns Hopkins University.

Black, J. B., Swan, K., & Schwartz, D. L. (1988). Developing thinking skills with computers. *Teachers College Record, 89*(3), 384–407.

Brekke, B., Johnson, L., & Williams, J. D. (1975). Conservation of weight with the motorically handicapped. *Journal of Special Education, 9*(4), 389–393.

Burton, J. K., & Magliaro, S. M. (1988). Computer programming and generalized problem-solving skills: In search of direction. *Computers in the Schools, 4* (3/4), 63–90.

Judd, D. H. (1983, March/April). Programming: An experience in creating a useful program or an experience in computer control. *Educational Computer*, pp. 20–21.

Krasnor, L. R., and Mitterer, J.O. (1984). Logo and the development of general problem-solving skills. *Alberta Journal of Educational Research, 30*(2), 133–144.

Kurland, D., & Pea, R. (1983, May). Children's mental models of recursive Logo programs. *Proceedings of the Fifth Annual Cognitive Science Society*, Rochester, NY.

Lerner, J. W. (1989). *Learning disabilities: Theories, diagnosis, and teaching strategies* (5th ed.). Boston: Houghton Mifflin.

Leron, U. (1985, February). Logo today: Vision and reality. *Computing Teacher, 12*(5), 26–34.

Maddux, C. (1989, February). Logo: Scientific dedication or religious fanaticism in the 1990's? *Educational Technology*, 18–23.

_____ & Johnson, D. L. (1988). *Logo: Methods and curriculum for teachers.* New York: Haworth Press.

Papert, S. (1980). *Mindstorms: Children, computers, and powerful ideas.* New York: Basic Books.

Pea, R. D. (1983). *Logo programming and problem solving* (Technical Report No. 12). New York: Bank Street College of Education, Center for Children and Technology.

_____ & Kurland, D. M. (1983a). *On the cognitive effects of learning computer programming* (Technical Report No. 9). New York: Bank Street College of Education, Center for Children and Technology.

_____ & _____ . (1983b). *Children's mental models of recursive Logo programming* (Technical Report No. 10). New York: Bank Street College of Education, Center for Children and Technology.

_____ & _____ (1983c). *On the cognitive prerequisites of learning computer programming* (Technical Report No. 18). New York: Bank Street College of Education, Center for Children and Technology.

_____ & _____ . (1984). *Logo programming and the development of planning skills* (Technical Report No. 16). New York: Bank Street College of Education, Center for Children and Technology.

Rieber, L. P. (1987). LOGO and its promise: A research report. *Educational Technology, 27*(2), 12–16.

Slesnick, T. (1984, March). Robots and kids: Classroom encounters. *Classroom Computer Learning*, pp. 54–59.

Wadsworth, B. J. (1989). *Piaget's theory of cognitive and affective development* (4th ed.). New York: Longman.

Making Choices and Looking Ahead

PART FOUR CONTAINS TWO chapters—one on evaluating educational software and a final chapter on the future of educational computing. In the evaluation chapter, a sample software evaluation form is presented, but users are encouraged to adapt the form to fit their specific needs.

The final chapter on the future is brief and it does not contain outlandish speculations about computing marvels to come. The future is difficult to predict, and this is particularly true in the fast-moving world of computing. Then, too, in this book we have tried to emphasize the importance of how computers are used, while de-emphasizing the importance of specific hardware developments. For these and other reasons, we have chosen not to indulge in what often amounts to the writing of science fiction, but to speculate only about those developments for which there is currently reasonable cause to predict school availability within a few years.

In this book, we have presented a number of problems and difficulties related to educational computing. We have even suggested that the field could fail if it is improperly developed. However, we are overjoyed to report that we believe that failure is becoming increasingly unlikely. We are daily becoming more optimistic about computers and education. We are encouraged by our vision of the future, because however the details of that vision differs from day to day, we agree that computers are here to stay, they are destined to help teachers teach and children learn, and the classroom of the twenty-first century will be a classroom where computers contribute materially to the enhancement and the celebration of our humanity. May we all work toward the rapid achievement of this, the most exciting and most desirable of all imaginable futures.

15

Evaluating Educational Software

GOALS AND OBJECTIVES

Goal: To become aware of the need for educational software review and to learn some facts and concepts useful in devising an evaluation process and form.

When you finish studying this chapter, you will be able to:

1. List at least one fact illustrating the need for educational software evaluation.
2. Write a short paragraph listing and explaining at least two reasons for the large gap between computer hardware quality and the quality of educational software.
3. Develop a short written passage in which you list and explain at least one short-term and one long-term solution to the problem of educational software quality.
4. List three ways to obtain software for preview.
5. Discuss at least one problem with relying on software reviews written by others.
6. Discuss at least one problem with relying on software evaluations you do yourself.
7. Tell why software reviews in popular magazines are sometimes biased or cursory.
8. Give at least two disadvantages to the use of formal evaluation forms.

KEY TERMS

CompuServe
courseware
EPIE

evaluation form
MicroSIFT
quality lag

One major problem in educational computing is the difficulty in finding good software. The problem of software quality has been pointed out in numerous articles and books dealing with educational computing issues and problems (Kinzer, Sherwood, & Bransford, 1986; Lillie, Hannum, & Stuck, 1989). Although quality is a problem, high-quality software is available to those who know how to identify it. Therefore, this chapter will be devoted to the topic of software evaluation.

We begin by establishing the need for good evaluation procedures, with an emphasis on the quality of current educational software. We go on to consider some reasons why much educational software has not been of the highest quality. The chapter then present short- and long-term solutions to this problem. Since most of these solutions involve formal software evaluation, the chapter presents information on how to find and interpret evaluations written by others, and we then move on to the topic of performing your own evaluations. A sample software evaluation form is presented, although we suggest that users should modify such forms to fit their own needs.

THE GROWING BODY OF EDUCATIONAL SOFTWARE

The need for developing methods of evaluating educational software (sometimes called courseware) can be appreciated in light of the fact that there today over 20,000 educational computer programs are available (Geisert and Futrell, 1990). Furthermore, nearly 2,000 new titles are appearing each year (Office of Technology Assessment, 1988). With such a large and growing number of programs on the market, the practice of ordering software sight unseen, with catalog descriptions accepted at face value, would be poor practice indeed.

THE QUALITY OF EDUCATIONAL SOFTWARE

Although software is improving rapidly, quality has been a problem since the beginning of the educational computer movement in the late 1970s and early 1980s. In 1983, the authors of this textbook wrote a series of computer-related mass-market books in paperback for Signet Press. Each book dealt with a different popular brand of personal computer, and since virtually nothing can be done with any computer without software, these little books were actually about software.

The book publisher provided us with offices, computers, and a staff of three assistants to telephone software distributors to request programs for review. As we began to review the extensive library of software that they provided, we were dismayed at the poor quality of most of it, particularly the educational software. We were especially surprised to find that a significant percentage of this software (about 20% to 30%) was technically flawed and would not even begin to run or would not run properly. A few of the remaining programs were excellent. However, the majority of the software we reviewed was so poorly conceived and executed that we agreed we could not recommend it for purchase.

Although our experience was informal, similar conclusions were reached as a result of more formal projects. That same year (1983) the Educational Products Information Exchange (**EPIE**) reviewed and rated most of the educational software then available. They reported that they were able to identify only 5% of the programs as "highly recommended" (Komoski, 1984).

Fortunately, educational software has been improving rapidly since the early 1980s. There are currently many excellent educational programs on the market. There are a number of reasons why software has improved. First, the problem has been widely acknowledged, with literally hundreds of articles over the last few years lamenting educational software quality. Because of wide acknowledgment, software houses have responded by improving quality. Although they still have a long way to go, they are making progress. Second, the field has matured, and there has been time for computer experts to learn about schools, curriculum, and how children think and learn. This knowledge is beginning to find its way into newer educational software, which is, consequently, much improved over earlier efforts.

Conversely, educators have begun to learn more about computers and their capabilities, and to think about how these capabilities can be used in education. Such educators talk to software developers and are beginning to influence them to improve their efforts. Researchers have begun to investigate the potential of computing, and reviewers have had time to survey past research, draw conclusions and generalizations, and make these reviews available to educators and software developers. Finally, educators have had time to outgrow their first uncritical infatuation with computers and are becoming more discriminating about educational computing applications. By purchasing better software and declining to purchase poorer software, they exert a positive influence on software development.

Even though software is improving, poor software quality is still a problem. Neill and Neill (1989) publish an extensive review of educational software entitled Only the Best: The Annual Guide to Highest-rated Educational Software for Preschool—Grade 12. In the 1990 edition, in which they reviewed 11,000 programs, they found large numbers of poor programs and identified only 7% as excellent.

The Office of Technology Assessment (1988), as part of their extensive study of interactive learning tools (conducted at the request of the House Committee on Education and Labor of the U.S. Congress), interviewed computer coordinators and other personnel in school districts and concluded that software quality is still a problem. Surprisingly, they found that technical or programming problems continue to plague educational software, and they concluded, "As educational software becomes more and more sophisticated, product reliability will become an increasingly important factor in schools' purchase decisions" (p. 135).

Similarly, Lockard, Abrams, and Many (1987) suggest that "Virtually any gathering of educators with computer interests will at some point prompt discussion of the appalling quality of courseware on the market" (p. 177). Willis (1987) concurs and suggests that "A distressingly large number of programs are poorly designed, some won't even work when you try to use them on your computer, and many are a waste of time and money" (p. 157).

WHY IS MUCH EDUCATIONAL SOFTWARE OF POOR QUALITY?

It is ironic that software quality is often seen as the major educational computing problem of the decade. The irony is that very modest progress has been made in improving software quality, while the quality of hardware has improved at a breakneck pace.

To dramatize this situation, we can draw an analogy to the use of popular stereo hardware and software. Suppose you were to obtain a selection of 40-year-old 78 rpm records and play them on modern, state of the art stereo equipment. Chances are you would be disappointed in the results. Although the situation is improving rapidly, this analogy holds for educational software compared to the hardware it runs on.

Why is there such a wide gap between hardware and software quality? Some disparity is natural and inevitable, since new capabilities must be built into hardware before software making use of that capability can be designed, produced, and marketed. This natural **quality lag** is evident in all software categories. However, the gap between hardware and educational software quality appears to be much wider than the gap in any other category.

There are many reasons why this is so. Lockard, Abrams, and Many (1987) identify a number of contributing causes, including (1) the lack of a theoretical base for most courseware, (2) an overemphasis on technical concerns such as graphics and sound and an underemphasis on educational concerns, (3) the application of old methods to the new computer medium (resulting in many programs that merely duplicate printed educational materials on the computer screen), and (4) the initial scarcity of educational programs and the desperation felt by educators who have consequently failed to demand high-quality programs.

Mandell and Mandell (1989) cite three causes including (1) the pressure educators felt to rush into computer education, resulting in frantic purchasing without a clear-cut plan, (2) scarcity of personnel with the expertise to select high-quality courseware, and (3) the initial scarcity of high quality educational computing software resulting from a rush by manufacturers to be the first to place a product on the market. This latter situation meant that educators were "left with little choice but to purchase inadequate software or let their computers sit idle" (p. 200).

Willis (1987) identifies many of these same contributors to the problem. In addition, he suggests that teachers experience difficulty in finding good educational software due to "the general lack of interest in educational software among computer retailers and software stores" (p. 157). He goes on to assert that, while hundreds of outstanding educational computer programs are available, very few retail stores carry more than 10 educational programs.

Another cause for the quality gap is that when microcomputers first appeared educational software was often authored by teacher-hobbyists who had good intentions, but who were novice programmers. Thus, much of the early software was simplistic or downright flawed (Geisert & Futrell, 1990). Some other early software authors were programming experts who knew little or nothing about schools, curriculum, or how children think and learn. Much of the software produced by these computer experts was technically slick, but had little educational relevance (Flake, McClintock, & Turner, 1990). Although many software developers today realize the importance of consulting experts in both education and computer science, some software is still developed without consideration of both technical and educational factors (Geisert & Futrell, 1990).

Another cause for poor-quality educational software is the high cost of developing a program versus the low potential profit. There is simply more potential profit in a piece of business software than in a piece of educational software. The Office of Technology Assessment (1988), in discussing capital limitations in educational software development, concluded that "The demand for software is too low to allow most publishers to recoup their development and marketing costs" (p. 143). This report goes on to state that "It is clear that software publishers face a severely fragmented demand that can seldom justify the level of investment necessary to create products" (p. 143). The report also suggest that software piracy contributes to the economic woes of software developers.

WHAT CAN BE DONE ABOUT THE PROBLEM OF SOFTWARE QUALITY?

We believe there are related short- and long-term answers to the problem of software quality.

Short-Term Solution

In the short term, educators should communicate directly with educational software producers. As Kinzer, Sherwood, and Bransford (1986) suggest, teachers have a responsibility to speak out, and software developers have a responsibility to listen and respond. These writers go on to suggest that teachers find or design a good evaluation form, use this form to evaluate whatever software they come into contact with, and send these evaluations to software producers. They also suggest that teachers seek out familiarity with existing programs by attending conferences where software demonstrations are held and by borrowing software from other teachers and schools. After filling out evaluation forms on such software, teachers should consider exchanging evaluations among themselves or among other schools and compiling evaluations to make a school- or district-level newsletter (Kinzer, Sherwood, & Bransford, 1986).

We have one further strategy to recommend. We suggest that teachers approach software selection more broadly than is common. That is, they should attempt to find the best instructional material to accomplish their educational objectives. Sometimes, then, this material will involve computers and sometimes it will not.

Long-Term Solution

In the long term, educators need only decline to purchase poor-quality software and refuse to recommend it for purchase. When software producers are convinced that they can realize a profit only if they produce high-quality, educationally relevant software, they will decline to produce any other kind. The rest of this chapter will concentrate on the long-term solution by presenting a rationale and a method for software evaluation.

Both the short- and the long-term solutions offered above require that software be expertly evaluated. Teachers can profit from software evaluation in two ways. First, they can find and read evaluations conducted by other educators. Second, they can conduct their own software evaluations. In many ways, most of this book is aimed at helping you to begin to develop the general ability to recognize excellent software when you see it. More specifically, many educators have found that a formal **evaluation form** can be helpful when evaluating software.

In the next section, we discuss how to find software evaluations written by others. We then discuss the use of formal evaluation forms to help you perform your own evaluations.

FINDING SOFTWARE EVALUATIONS WRITTEN BY OTHERS

There are many sources of educational software evaluations written by various individuals or groups. Pollard (1989) identifies 10 popular sources:

1. MicroSIFT
   Computer Technology Program
   Northwest Regional Educational Laboratory
   300 S.W. 6th Avenue
   Portland, OR 97204

2. The Educational Software Selector
   EPIE Institute Box 839
   Watermill, NY 11976

3. Computer Courseware Evaluations
   Learning Resources Distribution
   10410 121st St.
   Edmonton, Alberta T5N IL2
   Canada

4. Curriculum Software Guides
   (Contact an Apple computer education representative)

5. The Chime Newsletter
   Oklahoma State University
   108 Gunderson
   Stillwater, OK 74078-0146

6. Educational Software Preview Guide
   ICCE, University of Oregon
   1787 Agate St. Eugene, OR 97403

7. Micro
   Florida Center for Instructional Computing
   University of South Florida
   Tampa, FL 33620

8. Only the Best
   Education News Service
   PO Box 1789
   Carmichael, CA 95609

9. Software Reviews on File
   Facts on File, Inc
   460 Park Avenue South
   New York, NY 10016

10. Technology in the Curriculum
    California State Department of Education
    PO Box 271
    Sacramento, CA 95802

The two most popular national projects that compile software evaluations are the MicroSIFT Project (Microcomputer Software and Information for Teachers) at the Northwest Regional Educational Laboratory (see address above) and the EPIE Institute (Educational Products Information Exchange; see address above). In addition, educational agencies in many states either conduct their own software evaluations or act to disseminate evaluations conducted by others. Written evaluations can also be found in educational magazines or scholarly journals. Another source of software evaluations is formal research reports in academic journals.

MicroSIFT

Holznagel (1987) describes the process used by MicroSIFT:

> *Evaluations are completed according to a standard form that includes predefined criteria but also allows for open-ended comment. Each evaluation report is a composite of the opinion of three professionals: two teachers of the subject and level for which the material is intended, and one computer-education specialist. Reviewers are volunteers selected by a coordinator located at one of over two dozen education agencies participating in the SIFTnet evaluation network. A booklet, The Evaluator's Guide (Northwest Regional Educational Laboratory, 1983), describes completely the MicroSIFT evaluation criteria and their interpretation, and is available from the International Council for Computers in Education (ICCE). (p. 34)*

The EPIE Institute

EPIE, like MicroSIFT, uses a predetermined evaluation form that allows for evaluator comments. This project involves EPIE staff, Consumers Union staff, and personnel from a number of large public school districts. School district personnel are trained by EPIE staff members, and the evaluations are published in print format and in electronic database format that can be accessed through **CompuServe** (a telecommunications network). Stecher (1987) characterizes this database as "far more current than any printed guide to available software could ever be" (p. 182).

Efforts of the Various States

The Office of Technology Assessment (1988) surveyed all 50 states and the District of Columbia to determine what was being done about software evaluation at the state level. The survey revealed that efforts vary greatly, with some states collecting and evaluating software independently, some belonging to consortia, and some making available evaluations conducted by nongovernmental agencies. Teachers should contact their respective state education agencies to determine if software evaluation help is available.

Evaluations in Computing Magazines and Scholarly Journals

Software reviews are sometimes printed by computing magazines and scholarly journals, and these sources can be of help to teachers. Lockard, Abrams, and Many (1987) identify popular magazines such as *Electronic Learning*, *The Computing Teacher*, and *Classroom Computer Learning* as examples of magazines that frequently print reviews. We would add to the list such magazines as *Teaching and Computers* and *T.H.E. Journal*. In addition, School & Home Courseware, Inc. (301 West Mesa, Fresno, CA 93704) produces a loose-leaf product called *The Digest of Software Reviews: Education*. Included in the *Digest* is product information as well as summaries of published reviews. In addition, the editor marks certain programs as "Editor's Choice."

Some scholarly journals also print software reviews. Examples of such publications include *Computers in the Schools*, *Educational Technology*, the *Journal of Special Education Technology*, and the *Journal of Research on Computing Education*. In addition, many content-specific journals print reviews of software related to their subject area. For example, the *Journal of Learning Disabilities* sometimes prints reviews of programs intended for use by learning disabled individuals.

Formal Research Reports as Sources of Software Evaluations

Sometimes researchers conduct formal research studies on the efficacy of software. However, most of the time such research is directed at the effects of certain categories of software, rather than specific commercial programs.

PROBLEMS IN INTERPRETING SOFTWARE EVALUATIONS WRITTEN BY OTHERS

Reviews written by others can be helpful. Published reviews frequently provide essential information about hardware requirements, thus helping to reduce the number of programs a teacher needs to consider. A teacher with an Apple IIGS lab, for example, need not even consider software written only for MS-DOS-compatible machines. Such useful information (although not always accurate) can usually be obtained from published reviews.

However, we think some cautions are in order. In the first place, commercial magazines are supported by advertising. They are, therefore, sometimes hesitant to print negative reviews, especially if producers of reviewed software are major advertisers. Then, too, most commercial magazines obtain their reviews from one of two sources: (1) staff writers or (2) submissions from readers.

Reviews by staff writers are often superficial, primarily because such writers are pressed for time, are working under stringent deadlines, have many writing assignments besides the review, and base their evaluation on a cursory examination that may consist only of hurriedly booting the software and tinkering with it for 10 to 15 minutes. Reader submissions may suffer from the same superficial approach.

Reviews in scholarly journals are often of higher quality than those found in slick magazines. However, such reviews are generally written by faculty members at colleges and universities. Unfortunately, officials in higher education generally do not place much value on such reviews when it comes time for decisions about merit pay, tenure, or promotion. Therefore, many faculty members are not highly motivated to write such reviews or to invest a great deal of time or effort in them.

Geisert and Futrell (1990) sum up some of the problems in interpreting published reviews:

> First, the review is generally an opinion article—it is one person's view of the product. (Any reader of film or book reviews will know that one critic can pan what another will hail.) Second, there is nothing that guarantees you that a reviewer has ever used the program with its targeted user group (e.g., students) or is even minimally informed about such use. More likely, the reviewer simply looked at the program. Third, reviewers often can get caught up in the "bells and whistles" of a program (for example, startling graphics presentation) and overlook the question of how well the program would be likely to work with students. (p. 197)

Lockard, Abrams, and Many (1987) identify two problems with published reviews: (1) objectivity and (2) the time lag between the release of software and the appearance of published reviews. They conclude as follows:

> *Finally, any courseware product is of value only as it fits the need for which it is being considered. Effective evaluation requires assessment in light of the intended use for the package. Reviews tend to be one person's impression of the software and related materials, with no indication of how the product was used or what results were achieved. It is less common by far to find reviews reporting on actual classroom testing or reviews based on the experiences of several individuals with the package. Even the qualifications of the reviewers may not be given or may be impossible to assess. Thus, most reviews are best characterized as superficial and grossly inadequate as a basis for purchase decisions. (p. 184)*

We conclude this section with the following recommendation: published reviews are useful, should be consulted when available, but should never be the sole basis for purchase decisions.

PERFORMING YOUR OWN SOFTWARE EVALUATIONS

Much has been written about how to evaluate software. Nearly every educational computing book on the market has a chapter devoted to this topic. Evaluation of software can be thought of as consisting of two parts: (1) engaging in the evaluation process and (2) producing a product, usually a completed **evaluation form**.

The Evaluation Process

Unfortunately, no hard and fast rules have proved to lead to effective software evaluation procedures (Church and Bender, 1989). Very little research has been done on this topic. Bitter and Wighton (1987) describe one of the few efforts, in which 28 educational software evaluation agencies were surveyed and asked to rank a list of 22 criteria. Results were mixed, but there was a strong preference for emphasizing content-related criteria and de- emphasizing technical features such as graphics, animation, sound, and screen design.

Such a study is relevant, since one of the first steps in setting up an evaluation process is deciding what criteria are going to be considered important and desirable. After this decision is made, the criteria can be incorporated into an evaluation form.

As you might expect, there are many different ideas about what criteria should be used. Lockard, Abrams, and Many (1987) suggest that software should be evaluated against (1) intended use, (2) learning theory, and (3) specific criteria.

Evaluating against intended use requires that the teacher clearly define the learning objectives of the lesson in which the software might be used and then make a judgment as to whether the particular software can help achieve these objectives. Thus, this assessment is highly individualistic. This part of the evaluation can be facilitated if the software producers have done a good job of articulating the goals and objectives they had in mind when the software was produced. However, it is possible that a teacher would elect to use the software for some other important purposes.

Evaluation against learning theory requires that the evaluator understand such theory or theories. An example might be the evaluation of problem-solving software intended by the producers to teach skills that Piagetian developmental theory would characterize as formal operational thinking. Such software would probably not be reasonable for use in a second grade classroom, since children of that age level are probably not capable of such abstract thinking.

Lockard, Abrams, and Many (1987) suggest that evaluation against specific criteria might include consideration of variables in four major categories: (1) mechanical factors, (2) general criteria, (3) CAI-specific criteria, and (4) usability factors.

There are many other ways to categorize important criteria. Church and Bender (1989) suggest that the following be evaluated: (1) instructional content, (2) utilization of computer capabilities, (3) goals and objectives, (4) software presentation variables (pacing, ability levels, and the like), (5) product information, and (6) documentation. Lillie, Hannum, and Stuck (1989) recommend that attention be given to (1) instructional content, (2) instructional procedures, and (3) instructional management. We prefer to base evaluation on six similar criteria: (1) content, (2) mode of instruction, (3) management, (4) technical presentation, (5) documentation, and (6) ease of use.

Formal Evaluation Forms

Most authors suggest that a formal evaluation form be used, and examples of such forms abound. Holznagel (1987) has pointed out that most forms overlap considerably. We feel strongly that schools or school districts should adopt their own form. However, it is handy to have a form as an example or to use until a unique form can be adopted. Therefore, we have included a copy of our own software evaluation form in Figure 15.1. This form makes use of the six criteria listed at the end of the previous section.

Many other forms are available, and interested readers should consult any good computer education text for other examples. In addition,

```
                    SOFTWARE EVALUATION FORM

Name of Evaluator_____ Date _____

Title of Program _____

Title of Package _____

        Publisher _____

          Address _____

            Price _____ Subject area _____

Age/Grade _____

Goal(s) _____

        _____

        _____

    Objectives _____

               _____

               _____

               _____

Prerequisite Skills _____

                    _____

Instructional Purpose and Design

Type I _____      Type II _____

Operating System _____

Category (Circle one or more)

Drill and practice      Word Processing      Tutorial
Authoring               Simulation           Management
Problem solving         Assessment           Administrative
Computer language       Other _____

COMMENTS: _____

_____

_____


Recommended for purchase?    YES      NO
```

FIGURE 15.1   Software Evaluation Form

Rate the software using the following system:

1 - very strongly disagree   4 - agree
2 - strongly disagree   5 - strongly agree
3 - disagree   6 - very strongly agree
                    NA - not applicable

---

	disagree agree

CONTENT
1. Accurate/factual.   1 2 3 4 5 6 NA
2. Content is interesting for students.   1 2 3 4 5 6 NA
3. Content is educationally important.   1 2 3 4 5 6 NA
4. Content is appropriate for level of intended users.   1 2 3 4 5 6 NA
5. Prerequisite skills needed are realistic for
   intended users.   1 2 3 4 5 6 NA
6. Free of stereotypes/biases.   1 2 3 4 5 6 NA
7. Free of errors in grammar, spelling, etc.   1 2 3 4 5 6 NA
   Section Average (sum of ratings divided by number, excluding NAs) _____

MODE OF INSTRUCTION
1. New <u>vocabulary</u> is presented appropriately.   1 2 3 4 5 6 NA
2. New <u>concepts</u> are presented appropriately.   1 2 3 4 5 6 NA
3. Students can control pace.   1 2 3 4 5 6 NA
4. Students can control sequence.   1 2 3 4 5 6 NA
5. Program accommodates wide range of ability.   1 2 3 4 5 6 NA
6. Feedback is useful/appropriately stated.   1 2 3 4 5 6 NA
7. Program reflects knowledge of learning theory.   1 2 3 4 5 6 NA
   Section Average (sum of ratings divided by number, excluding NAs) _____

MANAGEMENT
1. Student records can be stored on a diskette.   1 2 3 4 5 6 NA
2. Stored records are useful and complete.   1 2 3 4 5 6 NA
3. Stored information is secure from unauthorized access.   1 2 3 4 5 6 NA
   Section Average (sum of ratings divided by number, excluding NAs) _____

TECHNICAL PRESENTATION
1. Graphics and sound (if used) are appropriate.   1 2 3 4 5 6 NA
2. Displays are uncluttered.   1 2 3 4 5 6 NA
3. Program is free of programming bugs.   1 2 3 4 5 6 NA
4. Menu items are understandable and descriptive.   1 2 3 4 5 6 NA
5. Program is appropriate in responses accepted
   as correct/incorrect.   1 2 3 4 5 6 NA
6. Directions make clear what type of response
   is solicited.   1 2 3 4 5 6 NA
7. Reading level is appropriate for intended users.   1 2 3 4 5 6 NA
   Section Average (sum of ratings divided by number, excluding NAs) _____

DOCUMENTATION
1. Hardware requirements are clear and complete.   1 2 3 4 5 6 NA
2. Program installation procedure is clear and complete.   1 2 3 4 5 6 NA
3. Goals and/or objectives are clearly stated.   1 2 3 4 5 6 NA
4. Prerequisite skills are clearly identified.   1 2 3 4 5 6 NA
5. Grade/age of intended users is clearly identified.   1 2 3 4 5 6 NA
6. Off-computer activities (if used) are appropriate.   1 2 3 4 5 6 NA
7. Documentation for students uses correct reading level.   1 2 3 4 5 6 NA
   Section Average (sum of ratings divided by number, excluding NAs) _____

FIGURE 15.1   Software Evaluation Form (*continued*)

```
EASE OF USE
1. Students can use program with minimal teacher help.    1 2 3 4 5 6  NA
2. On-screen directions are clear.                        1 2 3 4 5 6  NA
3. Directions can be skipped at option of user.           1 2 3 4 5 6  NA
4. Directions can be reviewed at any time.                1 2 3 4 5 6  NA
5. Students can review previous screens without
   restarting program.                                    1 2 3 4 5 6  NA
6. Students can exit the program at any time.             1 2 3 4 5 6  NA
7. Students can restart program where they stopped.       1 2 3 4 5 6  NA
   Section Average (sum of ratings divided by number, excluding NAs) __ __

       OPTIONAL OVERALL AVERAGE (Average of section averages) _____

(All calculations of section averages and overall average should be carried
out to two decimal places.)
```

FIGURE 15.1   Software Evaluation Form (*continued*)

Jones (1983) has compiled a booklet summarizing 10 different evaluation procedures and forms used in major projects.

Advantages and Disadvantages of Forms

Evaluation forms have both advantages and disadvantages. The advantage is that such forms provide a standard that many evaluators can use, thus making it easier to compare reviews by different people. Then, too, a form is essential for computer education beginners to provide needed structure and to ensure that important considerations are not ignored.

One disadvantage is the amount of time it takes to do a good job of filling out a form. Lockard, Abrams, and Many (1987) emphasize the time problem, especially in light of their excellent recommendation that evaluators should run the program at least three times: first as a better student might, then as a weaker student might, and finally as a test of how the program responds to completely inappropriate input. They further recommend that the form not be filled out until the evaluator has field tested the software with students.

Another disadvantage is that a single form is not likely to be the best form for every type of software or for all subjects at all grade levels. For example, the form we have presented in Figure 15.1 is not as good for evaluating tool software such as word processing programs or spreadsheets as it is for drill and practice software or simulations. Bitter (1989) addresses this problem by designing separate forms for evaluating programs in each of the following categories: (1) drill and practice, (2) tutorial, (3) simulation and problem solving, and (4) application software. (Interested readers will find these forms on pages 302—307 of his book.) A final disadvantage is the tendency for forms to become institutionalized and viewed as the final word.

Adapting Software Evaluation Forms

We believe that educators should take a flexible approach to the use of forms. In the first place, we think each school or school district should develop its own form that meets the needs of the particular settings in which software is used. Therefore, we think that individuals or committees charged with developing forms should take a look at a large number of forms and then modify them for their own purposes.

Holznagel (1987) lists a number of factors that may indicate that an existing form needs revision. He mentions differences in (1) the audience, (2) time constraints, (3) subject matter focus, and (4) emergence of new categories of software.

Obtaining Software for Evaluation

The suggestions discussed to this point require that teachers obtain software for evaluation prior to making a decision about purchasing. There are several ways to do this besides the ones already mentioned. Many software producers or distributors will provide software on a 30-day approval basis. We agree with Geisert and Futrell (1990), who recommend that educators should not buy programs that cannot either be examined before purchase or, if found unsatisfactory, returned after purchase.

Geisert and Futrell (1990) suggest that teachers write, rather than telephone, to request software for preview. They also recommend (1) using a school letterhead, (2) requesting only one or two titles at a time, (3) stating specific instructional goals for the software, (4) stating that you will be personally responsible for ensuring that the software is not illegally copied, (5) assuring timely return after preview, and (6) guaranteeing that you will supply a brief explanation if you decide not to purchase the software.

There are other ways to obtain software for preview. Sometimes libraries acquire software that can be checked out or used on premises. This is especially true of libraries or instructional materials centers located in colleges of education. Computer laboratories in colleges of education also frequently maintain educational software libraries that can be useful. Sometimes local software retailers will loan educational software or allow it to be previewed by teachers on premises. Another possibility is that district administrators may arrange for school or school district software fairs in which distributors set up booths and demonstrate their wares.

SUMMARY

Educational software quality is improving but continues to be a problem. A gap between hardware and software quality is to be expected in any field, but the gap in the field of education is particularly wide. Solutions to this problem include the need for teachers to communicate with software developers and to refuse to purchase software that lacks educational relevance.

It is possible to obtain published software evaluations. There are a number of national sources for such reviews, including magazines and journals. Problems with such reviews include superficial treatments, differing philosophies, the time lag between appearance of the software and availability of reviews, and a lack of field testing with students. Some states carry on evaluation projects.

Although published reviews are useful, software should always be personally reviewed before it is published. Such review usually involves the use of a standard evaluation form. Many such forms are available. Educators should develop their own form, using a variety of published forms as examples. An example of a form is provided, along with suggestions for when revision of a form is appropriate.

First-hand software evaluation requires that teachers obtain software and evaluate it. Software developers and distributors will usually either provide software on approval or permit return of the software if it is unsatisfactory. Educators should not purchase software that is not available under one of these options. Other sources of software for preview include libraries, conferences, and colleges of education.

LOOKING AHEAD

The final chapter of this book will deal with possible future developments in educational computing.

SOME QUESTIONS TO CONSIDER

1. What could the federal government do that might improve software quality?
2. What could individual school districts do that might improve software quality?
3. What categories of criteria would you incorporate in a software evaluation form of your own design? Why did you choose those categories?

RELATED ACTIVITIES

1. Call or write at least three commercial software companies and ask them about their preview and/or return policies for educators.
2. Use the sample evaluation form to evaluate at least two pieces of educational software. You may find such software in your college of

education computer lab, the main college library, the local school district, or at local software retail stores.

3. Produce your own software evaluation form emphasizing areas that you feel are most important.

REFERENCES

Bitter, G. (1989). *Microcomputers in education today*. Watsonville, CA: Mitchell Publishing.

Bitter, G., & Wighton, D. (1987). The most important criteria used by the education software evaluation consortium. *The Computing Teacher, 14*(6), 7–9.

Church, G., & Bender, M. (1989). *Teaching with computers: A curriculum for special educators*. Boston: College-Hill Press.

Flake, J. L, McClintock, C. E., & Turner, S. (1990). *Fundamentals of computer education*. Belmont, CA: Wadsworth.

Geisert, P. G., & Futrell, M. K. (1990). *Teachers, computers, and curriculum*. Boston: Allyn and Bacon.

Holznagel, D. C. (1987). Selecting software. In R. E. Bennett (ed.), *Planning and evaluating computer education programs*, pp. 25–42. Columbus, OH: Merrill.

Jones, N. B. (1983). *Evaluation of educational software: A guide to guides*. Austin, TX: Southwest Educational Development Laboratory.

Kinzer, C. K., Sherwood, R. D., & Bransford, J. D. (1986). *Computer strategies for education: Foundations and content-area applications*. Columbus, OH: Merrill.

Komoski, P. K. (1984, December). Educational computing: The burden of insuring quality. *Phi Delta Kappan*, pp. 244–248.

Lillie, D. L., Hannum, W. H., & Stuck, G. B. (1989). *Computers and effective instruction*. New York: Longman.

Lockard, J., Abrams, P. D., & Many, W. A. (1987). *Microcomputers for educators*. Boston: Little, Brown.

Mandell, C. J., & Mandell, S. L. (1989). *Computers in education today*. St. Paul, MN: West Publishing.

Neill, S. B., & Neill, G. W. (1989). *Only the best: The annual guide to highest-rated educational software for preschool—grade 12* (1990 edition). New York: R. R. Bowker.

Northwest Regional Educational Laboratory (1983). *Evaluator's guide for microcomputer-based instruction application*. Eugene, OR: International Council for Computers in Education.

Office of Technology Assessment (1988). *Power on! New tools for teaching and learning* (Publication No. 052-003-01125-5). Washington, DC: U.S. Government Printing Office.

Pollard, J. (1989, January). 10 top sources of reliable software information. *Learning*, pp. 64–65.

Stecher, B. (1987). Evaluating the outcomes of computer education programs. In R. E. Bennett (ed.), *Planning and evaluating computer education programs*, pp. 163-194. Columbus, OH: Merrill.

Willis, J. W. (1987). *Educational computing: A guide to practical applications*. Scottsdale, AZ: Gorsuch Scarisbrick.

16

The Future of Educational Computing

GOALS AND OBJECTIVES

Goal: To become aware of some of the possible future developments in educational computing, as well as some of the problems in Implementation of those developments.

When you finish studying this chapter, you will be able to:

1. Write a paragraph explaining the difference between technological and implementation possibilities.
2. Describe at least three possible innovations related to computers themselves.
3. List at least three advantages of optical disks over floppy diskettes.
4. Write a paragraph describing telestudying.
5. Define multimedia, interactive multimedia, and hypermedia.

KEY TERMS

authoring systems
CD-ROM
compatibility
distance education
futurists
hypermedia
implementation domain
Information Age, The
information technologies
interactive mulitmedia

mass storage
mulitmedia
optical disks
simulations
technical domain
telestudying
video discs
voice recognition
voice synthesis

Predicting the future is easy. Doing so accurately is difficult. Making accurate predictions about anything related to computing is particularly difficult, since changes in this field have occurred so rapidly. Bullough and Beatty (1987) dramatize this difficulty by pointing out that only 30 years ago, no one was predicting that many classrooms in the late 1980s would contain the equivalent of all the computer power available in the United States. in the 1950s.

Actually, this chapter will not constitute a prediction of the future as much as it will be an exploration of possibilities for the future. Whether these possibilities are taken advantage of or not will depend on your actions and the actions of other teachers like you. These possibilities lie in at least two separate domains.

The first domain is primarily technological. Judging by the developments of the last few decades, the possible hardware and software innovations for the future are nearly limitless. In fact, we are almost sure to underestimate future developments in this, the **technical domain.**

The second domain concerns how (or whether) educators will choose to make use of the technological improvements and changes that are bound to take place. Again judging by past developments, we may be tempted to overestimate developments in this, the **implementation domain.**

With regard to this latter point, we think it is clear that education has not, to date, taken full advantage of the considerable potential of computing. Geisert and Futrell (1990) make this point as follows:

> *The educational enterprise overall has not been enthralled at the idea of letting the microcomputer do those things at which it excels. In fact, a large portion of the educational world has seemed to view those functions an intrusive agent into the existing classroom patterns. Unlike the business world, where microcomputers were welcomed with open arms and put right to work, the machines were channeled to the sidelines of educational enterprise. I dare say they haven't made a dent in mainstream education. . . . Perhaps I'm being too negative here, but it seems to me that American school systems have been especially adept at making sure that new and potentially subversive ideas have been submerged into the traditional pattern, thus rendering them harmless. (pp. 317–318)*

While we agree that developments to this point support this pessimistic view, we believe that there are reasons to be much more optimistic about future developments in education. First, we believe that for the first time, computers have currently pervaded so many areas of daily life that educators will, in the future, be unable to block their entrance into schools, even if they were so inclined. Second, our world is being profoundly changed by technology and other forces, so that we are beginning to recognize that schools must alter their goals from those that have been in place for the last century or so. White and Hubbard (1988) make reference to this latter phenomenon:

> *There is realization that a postindustrial economy is now emerging that requires an educational system to prepare children and youth for the Information Age, where physical skills will be subordinated to levels of brain power beyond anything we have yet experienced. . . . Instead of educating a physically skillful, minimally literate, comparatively passive work force to execute routine tasks, educators are predicting that the population will need to be prepared to handle ambiguous situations and to have developed the ability to participate with others in decision making much more than at present. (pp. 181–182)*

While we agree with most of these points, we think the above passage is a bit exaggerated. Most educators would not agree that the educational goal of the past was to prepare "a physically skillful, minimally literate, comparatively passive work force to execute routine tasks." Most employers would not agree that such a work force was desirable or even minimally acceptable in the recent past.

Nor do we believe that there is reason to think that the future, either on or off the job, will present any more ambiguous situations than did the past. We would suggest that human events seem unambiguous only in retrospect, a fact that has led to the cliche that "hindsight is always 20/20" and to the expression "the good old days."

So-called futurists such as Toffler (1980) and Naisbitt (1982) seem to trade in such simplistic characterizations of the past. Such writers have been spectacularly successful in the popular book market. As historians, however, they often leave much to be desired. (We suspect that Abraham Lincoln did not find the problems of the Civil War and reconstruction unambiguous. We believe the same could be said for the average citizen living through this or any other period in our nation's history.)

Nevertheless, such simplistic analyses are based on at least a grain or two of truth. While it may be inaccurate, or at least misleading, to suggest that we are entering the Information Age, it is true that **information technologies** such as computing are becoming increasingly important and that such technologies are pervading virtually every aspect of our lives.

We believe that we are now confronting a very interesting and powerful fact: Computers are not going to go away! Whether we like them or not, they are becoming ubiquitous companions in business, industry, the military, homes, and all levels of government. Therefore, it is probably inevitable that they will soon become more commonplace in education.

Then, too, there is clearly an increasing emphasis on changing the goals of public education. Numerous commissions and agencies have reported on the state of education in this country, and all have recommended that education be reformed. It is generally agreed that schools should increase emphasis on critical thinking and problem solving, particularly in the areas of mathematics and science. To do so, educators of the future will need to increase their use of individualized instructional techniques. If we are to be successful in implementing individualized instruction, we will need new and better teaching tools. One very important tool will almost certainly be the computer.

POSSIBILITIES FOR THE FUTURE

In the remainder of this chapter, we discuss the future in terms of possibilities for both technological innovation and educational implementation.

Computers Themselves

One of the clearest technological trends is that computers are becoming smaller, cheaper, and more powerful. Although there must be a limit to all three variables, we cannot now know what those limits are likely to be. Computers continue to get cheaper. As they do, more and more schools acquire more and more of them. This will continue. It is conceivable that the day will come when every child has access to a school-based computer at any and all times of the day.

Whether this possible scenario becomes fact will depend on two things. First, prices must continue to decline, probably at least to the point that schools can acquire computers for the equivalent of $300 to $400 in 1990 money. We believe this will happen. Second, school funding must undergo radical reform. There are signs that this may take place. Courts are mandating changes, and there is widespread popular realization that inequities in funding result in inequities of opportunity and erosion of other fundamental democratic rights.

If all goes well, we expect that the day is not far off when every teacher will routinely use computers for some of the instruction in his or her subject area. This does not mean, however, that we expect to see the end of the school computer lab or the school educational computing expert. Even when and if computers are fully integrated into the teaching of every subject, there will still be a need for a specialist. The fact that English language skills or mathematics skills are integrated into various subjects has not eliminated the need for English or mathematics teachers.

School computers of the future will almost certainly be much smaller than they are now. Portable and battery-powered laptop computers are currently available. These will be improved and further miniaturized, particularly if expected improvements take place and result in smaller, more highly legible screens. We expect that the day is not far off when the only limit to miniaturization will be the size of the keyboard or other interactive input device.

Another possible development is a solution to the problem of lack of **compatibility** among different brands of microcomputers. Already, MS-DOS machine owners can purchase a special circuit board to allow their computer to run Apple II software. Although such circuit boards are today expensive and not without technical disadvantages, it is entirely possible that computers of the future will either conform to a single standard or be capable of running software intended for any major computer brand. (Already there are rumors of a future Macintosh computer that will have a color display and run Apple II, Macintosh, and MS-DOS software.) At the same time, the newest version of the Windows software from MicroSoft emulates the Macintosh operating system on MS-DOS-based computers. Clearly, we may expect more and more hardware and software compatibility.

We are often asked which computer company will win the hardware competition for the educational market. Although that remains unclear, there are today signs that a major change is approaching, especially for elementary school applications. Although the Apple IIe (followed by the related Apple IIGS) has been the most popular machine for such applications, Apple is moving rapidly away from this reliable, but antiquated standard. Only time will tell whether Apple will be able to continue its dominance of the elementary school market, either by succeeding with a revised Macintosh computer or with some new and yet unknown machine. However, we are becoming more pessimistic about Apple's chances. Management problems as well as plummeting prices of MS-DOS machines in the face of high Apple prices threaten Apple's dominance of the elementary market.

Memory and Mass Storage

The day is rapidly approaching when computers will have as much memory as needed or desired by the user. **Mass storage** devices of practically unlimited capacity and speed will also be available. Large capacity hard disk drives are currently available at declining prices and this trend will continue.

In the near future, however, we believe that mass storage technology will be completely revised (more likely, it will be revised several times). Currently, the most promising development involves the use of **optical disks** for mass storage. This technology makes extremely large storage possible.

Most current applications involve the use of such disks to store vast amounts of data that can then be loaded into computer memory. This type of application is called **CD-ROM** (compact disk, read only memory). As the term implies, data can be loaded from the optical disk to the computer, but the user cannot store data on the disk. However, this technology is advancing rapidly and there are already a few machines that can both read and write data on an optical disk. For example, the NEXT computer makes use of a 5 $\frac{1}{4}$ -inch read/write/erasable optical disk. This disk can store 256 megabytes (256 million bytes) of data. This computer also has a built-in CD-ROM unit that stores the entire collected works of William Shakespeare!

To appreciate the great capacity of optical disks, we must be aware that the first floppy diskettes stored only 100 kilobytes (100,000 bytes) of data. Optical disks with the capacity to store over 600 megabytes of data are currently available.

Optical disks have other advantages, also. Bitter (1989) sums these up as follows:

> *Optical disks are small and lightweight; they are impervious to dust, heat, and normal handling; they have a lower error rate than magnetic tape storage; they can store digitized data from image, audio, text, and graphics sources; and they are easily duplicated by mechanical stamping. With such capabilities, the entire curriculum for a class could be contained on one small, rugged, easy-to-store optical disk. (p. 347)*

In addition, optical disks, unlike floppy disks, do not wear out since they are read by a low-power laser beam, rather than by physical contact.

In the future, teachers will have the ability to author their own interactive software, or purchase commercial software that integrates **video disks** and computers making full use of motion and sound. Video disks are optical disks with the capacity for storing huge amounts of auditory and visual material. For example, a single optical disk can store over 100,000 slides that can be accessed almost instantly. Fully animated material such as that currently found on video tapes can also be stored on video disks, and a video disk player can be coordinated with, and controlled by a computer based on interactive responses made by a user.

The great speed and capacity of optical disks give them great potential for a number of applications such as the study of geography. One such project consists of thousands of slides of Aspen, Colorado. The software that makes use of this disk makes it possible for students to tour Aspen in any way they choose. Other obvious applications would be a tour of the Smithsonian or other museums via video discs containing digital slides or films made on location.

One thing holding up great educational progress in the use of optical disks is the difficulty of selecting, controlling, and sequencing such large amounts of data. In other words, our ability to store data is already beginning to exceed our ability to make intelligent use of that data. The development of simple, flexible **authoring systems** will help to solve this data management problem.

Telecommunications

We believe that telecommunications has a great, but nearly untapped educational potential. For example, the technology exists that could make libraries obsolete. If all printed material was converted to electronic storage and made available to anyone with a computer, a modem, and a telephone, students could access any published material in the world from their homes or classrooms. Although we doubt that the collected published work of humanity will ever be stored in a single electronic database, many specialized databases exist today and many more will be added in the near future.

Favaro (1986) presents an interesting potential educational application of telecommunications called **telestudying.** This application would be implemented in order to solve the age-old problem of persuading students to complete homework assignments. According to Favaro (1986), homework has always been considered an onerous task because it is solitary, boring, and inefficient in terms of feedback. Favaro suggests that telecommunications could make it possible for a computer to be on call 24 hours a day to check, monitor, and interact with students who have a computer and who are engaged in home study:

> *A telecommunications-based homework center can provide practice exercises, extra help, and interactive homework correction to any remote location. Schools could provide the services (called on-line services) without the expense of keeping rooms open, paying staff extra hours, or making it seem like punishment to children who could just as easily do the work at home. (Favaro, 1986, pp. 183–184)*

Telecommunications also has great potential for **distance education.** Via their classroom computers, students in rural settings could, communicate with students, teachers, or anyone with the proper equipment anywhere in the world. They could also have access to the finest library collections.

Robots

Robots will probably become increasingly prevalent in schools of the future. As industry makes more and more use of robots in manufacturing, students will need to know more about them to prepare for the world of work. In addition, robots could perform some routine or dangerous work in the schools, such as acting as lab assistants and handling acids or other dangerous material.

Software

Perhaps we can expect the greatest improvements in the area of educational software. As machines become more and more sophisticated, software will also tend to become better and more sophisticated. Making predictions about future educational software is very difficult. However, some general types of software we feel are certain to improve greatly.

We think that authoring systems will become much simpler and more flexible. There are already packages that allow beginners to draw graphics on the screen using a mouse and/or touch-sensitive screens. The software then generates the programming code necessary to re-create the designs. Other packages allow musicians to play music while the software generates the corresponding written notes. Other software may act as research assistants and will be directed to search various databases for desired information (Bitter, 1989).

Software making use of other media, sometimes called **multimedia**, will become common. Currently, such software may employ videocassette players, slide projectors, videodisk players, or other equipment.

Another area that will be more fully exploited in the future is **simulations**. The military already makes good use of sophisticated simulations. Education has been slow to follow, primarily because the hardware and software needed for advanced simulations have been too expensive for schools. However, as equipment prices fall, excellent simulations should become common in schools.

Prosthetic Devices for the Handicapped

Great progress has already been made in this area, and even greater progress is on the near horizon. Already, there is hardware and software that reads print aloud for blind individuals or that make written and oral communication possible for individuals who cannot speak. **Voice synthesis** (production) and **voice recognition** are improving daily. The best voice synthesis devices today are hardly distinguishable from human speech, although they remain very expensive. Speech synthesis and recognition will continue to improve and prices will continue to decline. A problem that must be solved, however, is who will pay for these devices.

Hypermedia, Interactive Multimedia, and Nonlinear Information

Hypermedia and **interactive multimedia** are two popular topics in education today. The two terms have somewhat different meanings, but the underlying philosophies overlap. The concepts and technology they represent are thus lumped together in many discussions. In fact, many of the best examples of innovative instructional technology today are both hypermedia and multimedia.

The meaning of the term interactive multimedia is relatively straightforward. A good example of interactive multimedia is Exploring Chemistry, a package for IBM computers that was developed by Dr. Loretta Jones and Stanley Smith at the University of Illinois. Designed for use in college-level general chemistry classes, the program combines expository text displayed on the computer's screen with video clips from a laser disk. Students get some information from reading screen displays, but much of what they learn comes from conducting simulated experiments. Exploring Chemistry uses IBM's InfoWindow display which is touch sensitive. Students choose experiments and set the parameters for those experiments through the keyboard and by touching options on the screen. Then the experiment, as they have designed it, is shown on the screen. The video images come from the laser disk and they show real experiments instead of computer graphic simulations of experiments. The results of the experiment are also displayed and students can compare the actual results with the results they predicted.

Exploring Chemistry is interactive because it involves students directly in the action of the lesson. The decisions a student makes determine what happens next in the lesson. It involves multimedia because students work with several media including computer text, computer graphics, and video from the laser disk.

Exploring Chemistry is not, however, hypermedia. The lessons of Exploring Chemistry have been planned and sequenced by the developers. Lessons begin at a particular point and progress logically through a series of steps to a conclusion. Students are involved and they make decisions that determine what happens next, but the structure of the lesson is predetermined and relatively linear. Linear lessons have a definite structure, a sequence. Standard textbooks, lectures, and articles in magazines and journals are all linear. It is logical to begin at a particular point and follow a set path through the information. Most instructional material available today has a linear structure.

Hypermedia is not linear. Students using hypermedia instructional materials are not required to follow a particular pattern. Hypermedia provides the student with options that allow them to create their own paths through the material. For example, The Surface Anatomy of Birds, a hypermedia instructional package developed by Patrick Lynch at the Yale School of Medicine, begins with a screen like the one in Figure 16.1.

Students can begin their exploration of bird anatomy by pointing to any of several terms on the left side of the screen with their mouse pointer and clicking (pressing the switch on their mouse). Each term is a button. Students can, for example, click the word Flight to get information on flight. They can also click anywhere on the image of the bird and

FIGURE 16.1   Surface anatomy of a bird.

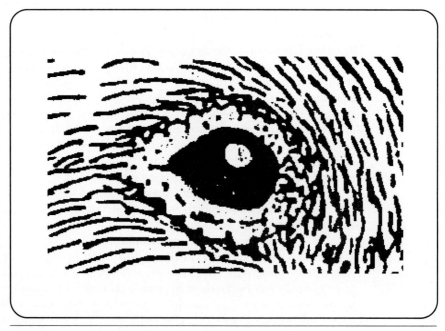

FIGURE 16.2   A sample of what the student would see on the computer screen after clicking the eye.

get information on that aspect of the bird's anatomy. Clicking the eye, for example, takes the student to a close up of the eye (see Figure 16.2).

There are a number of buttons on this screen. Click the page icon (image) on the left and detailed information is provided on the eye. Click the image of the laser disk to see video about eye anatomy. Students can also click the center of the eye and see a cutaway view of eye anatomy which also has buttons that can be clicked for even more detailed information. The Surface Anatomy of Birds is hypermedia because students decide how they will proceed through the information in this program. One student might, for example, work through all the information on the eye, while another might not even look at the information on the eye. Another might spend time on the general information without exploring any facet of bird anatomy in detail.

The nonlinear aspect of hypermedia is also illustrated in a program called Culture 1.0, which is subtitled A HyperMedia Guide to Western Civilization. This hypermedia instructional package allows students to explore different eras of Western civilization, from the Greco-Roman period through the twentieth Century. Students can click the period they want to explore and then select the topic they want to explore (history, literature, art, music, or religion and philosophy) and the country (England, France, Germany/Netherlands/Spain, or Italy). Students have access to essays on many different topics as well as pictures of well-known people, art, and sculpture. Culture 1.0 runs on the Macintosh computer and also takes advantage of the computer's built-in speech and music features to provide synthesized speech and excerpts of music from the different periods.

If tutorial and drill and practice software represents the current expression of behavioral learning theory, then hypermedia is an expression of developmental and cognitive theories such as Piaget's. Hypermedia requires students to be active learners, but it also requires students to make decisions about what they will learn and the learning paths they take through the material. A book edited by Ambron and Hooper (1990), is an excellent overview of current thinking on both hypermedia and multimedia.

Hypermedia is not one type of instructional software, however. It is more like a family of learning alternatives that share some common elements but can also be very different (Florin, 1990). Worldview, for example, is a hypermedia atlas of the world. It could be considered a very rich database that can be explored along many different paths. Florin describes *The Living Constitution* as an "interactive documentary." It deals with the topic of federalism through a series of video clips that shows how the federal government and the state government of Mississippi dealt with the admission of James Meridith to the University of Mississippi.

Another type of hypermedia is the annotated movie. For example, Florin describes the development of a hypermedia instructional program based on the movie "Life Story," which describes Watson and Crick's discovery of the structure of DNA:

> *An annotated movie's storyline is the major feature of the information landscape, through which it flows like a stream. . . . We chose to represent it with a plot map shaped like a double helix. . . . One strand retraces the story of Jim Watson and Francis Crick at Cambridge's Cavendish Lab in England. The other strand follows the parallel storyline of another team of researchers, Rosalind Franklin and Maurice Wilkins, at King's College in London. Both stories intertwine throughout the drama. . . . The round buttons along each strand represent key scenes in the drama; you can click on any of them to jump directly to that scene, which can then be played back at the touch of a button. (Florin, 1990, pp. 40–41)*

Once students have viewed a scene that interests them, they can explore the topic in several different ways. Clicking one of the main characters, for example, might produce a stage whisper that provides more information about that character, as well as directions to click a button to see a BBC interview of the scientist. When Rosalind Franklin is working with an X-ray diffraction camera, clicking it provides information on how it works.

Thus far, hypermedia has been discussed as a product that can be used in flexible ways by students. Many hypermedia products are just that. However, a significant thrust in hypermedia development is the creation of hypermedia by students. For example, Ambron (1990) described how elementary school students in one California school used The Visual Almanac, a videodisk of 7,000 still images and video clips, to create multimedia compositions. One student, for example, created a report on animals that included text, pictures, and video of animals. With the growing availability of electronic encyclopedias, future term papers, reports, and themes may be multimedia compositions in which the information is expressed in text as well as many other media.

Hypermedia is still in its infancy, but it represents a powerful concept that is likely to play a major role in education.

We could continue to speculate about future developments. Suffice it to say that technological potential is virtually unlimited. We suspect that 10 years from now the speculations in this chapter will seem almost childishly naive compared to actual developments.

As we mentioned in the beginning of this chapter, the extent to which the remarkable technology of the present and future is intelligently implemented in education will depend on the actions of teachers everywhere. We can count on technology to continue its rapid advancement. Whether or not we, as teachers, are flexible and creative enough to take advantage of this unprecedented opportunity remains to be seen. We like the following quote by Raymond Nickerson (1988):

> *It seems clear that technology has the potential to affect education in significant ways in the foreseeable future. How that potential will be realized, and whether education will be better as a consequence, remain to be seen. . . . The answers to these questions are, to a large degree, within our control. The future, and in particular the future of education, will be what we make it. Technology is expanding the possibilities; human choice will determine the actualities. (p. 29)*

We hope this book has helped to clarify some of the possibilities and assisted you in deciding what your professional choices will be.

SUMMARY

Future developments in educational computing will depend on technological progress, which will probably be startling in its sophistication. It will also depend on how educators choose to implement the new technology. In the past, technological progress has far outstripped progress in educational implementation.

Although many educators are pessimistic about the future of educational computing, we find two reasons for optimism. First, computers are so commonplace in every walk of life that it is probably inevitable that they become commonplace in schools. Second, we believe that the goals of schooling will change and that realization of these new goals will require the intelligent implementation of computers.

In the future, computers will continue to become smaller, cheaper, and more powerful. More and more computers will be acquired by schools. If prices continue to decline and if school funding practices are reformed, all students may have access to their own school computer for the entire day. All teachers may eventually use computers to help them teach, although there will probably always be a place for a computer specialist. Laptop and portable computers will become commonplace, with miniaturization limited only by keyboard and screen size. Compatibility problems will likely be solved.

Memory and mass storage will become, for all practical purposes, unlimited. Optical disks will play an important role.

Telecommunications will become a valuable educational tool for linking students with other students, other teachers, and general and specialized databases. Robots will begin playing a role in education.

Software will improve greatly. Authoring systems will become simple and powerful and will permit the writing of multimedia programs. Simulations will advance greatly.

Gains will continue to be made in prosthetic devices for the handicapped. Communication devices including speech synthesis and recognition hold great promise.

Hypermedia and interactive media are two exciting new developments in education that will likely play increasingly important future roles.

SOME QUESTIONS TO CONSIDER

1. Do you believe that technology has set the stage for a reevaluation of the goals of schooling? If so, tell how you think the goals should change.
2. Do you believe that we are entering an Information Age? Tell why or why not.
3. What are the important variables that will determine whether or not technologies of the future will be implemented in education?

RELATED ACTIVITIES

1. Interview three people who have leadership roles in three different occupations, including teaching. Ask what they see as the future of computing in their respective fields. Compare and contrast their responses.
2. Do some reading on various plans to restructure educational funding. Which of these do you think are most likely to actually take place and why?
3. Visit a computer retail store and ask to be shown the smallest laptop or notebook computers. Write a paper on what you were shown.

REFERENCES

Ambron, S. (1990) Multimedia composition: Is it similar to writing, painting, and composing music? Or is it something else altogether? In S. Ambron and K. Hooper (Eds.). *Learning with Interactive Multimedia,* pp. 69-84. Redmond, WA: Microsoft Press.

_____ & Hooper, K. (eds.) (1990). *Learning with interactive multimedia.* Redmond, WA: Microsoft Press.

Bitter, G. G. (1989). *Microcomputers in education today.* Watsonville, CA: Mitchell Publishing Inc.

Bullough, R. V., & Beatty, L. F. (1987). *Classroom applications of microcomputers.* Columbus, OH: Merrill.

Favaro, P. J. (1986). *Educator's guide to microcomputers and learning.* Englewood Cliffs, NJ: Prentice-Hall.

Florin, F. (1990). Information landscapes. In S. Ambron and K. Hooper (eds.) *Learning with interactive multimedia,* pp. 27–50. Redmond, WA: Microsoft Press.

Geisert, P. G., & Futrell, M. K. (1990). *Teachers, computers, and curriculum.* Boston: Allyn and Bacon.

Naisbitt, J. (1982). *Megatrends.* New York: Warner Books.

Nickerson, R. S. (1988). Technology in education in 2020: Thinking about the not-distant future. In J. J. Hirschbuhl & R. M. Konet(eds.), *Computers in education* (4th ed.), pp. 25-29. Guilford, CN: Dushkin Publishing Group.

Toffler, A. (1980). *The third wave.* New York: Morrow.

White, C. S., & Hubbard, G. (1988). *Computers and education.* New York: Macmillan.

SOFTWARE RESOURCES APPENDIX

Accolade
550 S. Winchester Dr., Suite 200
San Jose, CA 95128
800-245-7744

Addison-Wesley Publishing Co.
2725 Sand Hill Rd.
Menlo Park, CA 94025
415-854-0300

Advance Ideas, Inc.
2902 San Pablo Ave.
Berkeley, CA 94702
415-526-9100

Aldus
411 1st Ave. So.
Seattle, WA 98104
206-441-866

Alfred Publishing Co., Inc.
P.O. Box 10003
Van Nuys, CA 91410
818-891-5999

American School Publishers
P.O. Box 408
Hightstown, NJ 08520
800-843-8855

ARS NOVA
Box 637
Kirkland, WA 98083
800-445-4866

Ashton-Tate
20101 Hamilton Ave.
Torrance, CA 90502-1341
213-329-8000

Baudville
5380 52nd St. SE
Grand Rapids, MI 49512
616-698-0888

Beagle Bros.
6215 Ferris Square Suite 100
San Diego, CA 92121
619-452-5500

Bergwall Electronic Publishers
106 Charles Lindbergh Blvd.
Uniondale, NY 11553
516-222-1111

BLS Tutorsystems, Inc.
Woodmill Corporate Center
5153 W. Woodmill Dr., Suite 18
Wilmington, DE 19808
800-545-7766

Borland International
1800 Green Hills Rd.
Scotts Valley, CA 95067
408-438-8400

Broderbund Software
17 Paul Drive
San Rafael, CA 94903
415-492-320

Bytes of Learning, Inc.
150 Consumers Rd., Suite 202
Willowdale, Ont, M2J 1P9 Canada
416-495-9913

C.C. Publications
P.O. Box 23699
Tigard, OR 97223
800-547-4800

Cherry Software
Box 390 Westchester Ave.
Pound Ridge, NY 10576
800-672-6002

COMPress/Division of Queue, Inc.
338 Commerce Dr.
Fairfield, CT 06430
800-232-2224

Compu-Teach
78 Olive St.
New Haven, CT 06511
800-448-3224

Computer Systems Research, Inc.
Avon Park South
40 Darling Dr.
Avon, CT 06001
800-922-1190

CONDUIT
University of Iowa
Oakdale Campus
Iowa City, IA 52242
800-365-9774

Coronado Publishers, Inc.
1250 Sixth Ave.
San Diego, CA 92101
800-237-2665

D.C. Heath & Co.
125 Spring St.
Lexington, MA 02173
617-860-1348

Data Command
P.O. Box 548
Kankakee, IL 60901
815-933-7735

Data Transforms
616 Washington
Denver, CO 80203
303-832-1501

Davidson & Associates
3135 Kashiwa St.
Torrance, CA 90505
800-545-7677

DesignWare, Inc.
345 4th St.
San Francisco, CA 94107
415-546-1866

Developmental Learning Materials
One DLM Park
Allen, TX 75002
214-248-6300

Didatech Software
3812 William St.
Burnaby, B.C. V5C 3H9 Canada
800-665-0667

Educational Activities, Inc.
P.O. Box 293
Freeport, NY 11520
516-223-4666

Educational Materials &
Equipment
P.O. Box 2805
Danbury, CT 06813
203-798-2050

Educational Resources
1550 Executive Dr.
Elgin, IL 60123
800-624-2926

EduSoft
P.O. Box 2560
Berkley, CA 94702
800-338-7638

Edutech
P.O. Box 51755
Pacific Grove, CA 93950
408-372-8100

EduTech, Inc.
1927 Culvert Rd.
Rochester, NY 14609
716-482-3151

Electronic Learning Systems, Inc.
2630 NW 39th Ave.
Ganesville, FL 32605
800-443-7971

EMC Publishing
300 York Ave.
St. Paul, MN 55101
612-771-1555

Eureka
Lawrence Hall of Science
University of California
Berkley, CA 94720
415-642-1016

Focus Media
839 Stewart Ave.
Garden City, NY 11530
516-794-8900

Gamco Industries
P.O. Box 1911
Big Spring, TX 79721
915-267-6327

Gessler Educational Software
55 W. 13th St.
New York, NY 10011
212-627-0099

Great Wave Software
5353 Scotts Valley Dr.
Scotts Valley, CA 95066
408-438-1990

Grolier Electronic Publishing
Sherman Turnpike
Danbury, CT 06816
203-797-3500

Hartley Courseware, Inc.
133 Bridge St.
Dimondale, MI 48821
517-646-6458

High Technology Software Products
P.O. Box 60406
Oklahoma City, OK 73416
405-848-0480

Holt, Rinehart and Winston
383 Madison Ave.
New York, NY 10017
212-614-3300

IBM
PC Software Department
System Product
1 Culver Rd.
Dayton, NJ 08810
800-222-7257

Hyper Glot Software Co.
505 Forest Hills Blvd.
Knoxville, TN 37919
800-726-5087

Innovative Data Design
2280 Bates Ave., Suite A
Concord, CA 94520
415-680-6818

Instructional/Communications
  Technology
10 Stepar Pl.
Huntington Station, NY 11746
516-549-3000

Interactive
36 Beechmont Crescent
Gloucester, Ontario, Canada K1B 4A8
613-830-0380

JMH Software of Minnesota, Inc.
P.O. Box 41308
Minneapolis, MN 55447
612-424-5464

Johnson Institute
7151 Metro Blvd.
Minneapolis, MN 55439-2122
612-944-0511

K-12 Micromedia Publishing
P.O. Box 677
6 Arrow Rd.
Ramsey, NJ 07446
800-922-0401

Krell Software
Flowerfield Bldg. #7, Suite 1D
St. James, NY 11780
516-584-7900

Langenschiedt Publishers, Inc.
46-35 54th Rd.
Maspeth, NY 11378
718-784-0055

Learning Company, The
6493 Kaiser Dr.
Fremont, CA 94555
415-792-2101

Lingo Fun, Inc.
P.O. Box 486
Westerville, OH 43081
614-882-8258

Logo Computer Systems, Inc.
P.O. Box 162
Highgate Springs, VT 05460
800-321-5646

Logo Publications
7 Conifer Cres.
London, Ontario, Canada N6K 2V3
519-657-9334

Lotus Development Corp.
55 Cambridge Parkway
Cambridge, MA 02142
617-577-8500

Marblesoft
21805 Zumbrota NE
Cedar, MN 55011
612-434-3704

Marshware
P.O. Box 8082
Shawnee Mission, KS 66208
816-523-1059

MCE
1800 S. 35th
Galesburg, MI 49053
616-665-7075

MECC
3490 Lexington Ave. North
St. Paul, MN 55126
612-481-3550

MICRO-ED, Inc.
P.O. Box 24750
Edina, MN 55424
612-929-2242

Microsoft Corp.
1 Microsoft Way
Redmond, WA 98052-6399
206-882-8080

Microtech Consulting Company, Inc.
909 W. 23rd
Cedar Falls, IA 50613
800-383-7446

Midwest Software
22500 Orchard Lake Rd.
Farmington, MI 48336
313-477-0897

Milliken Publishing Co.
P.O. Box 21579
St. Louis, Mo 63132
314-9914220

Mobius Corp.
405 N. Henry St.
Alexandria, VA 22314
703-684-2911

New Centry Education Corp.
220 Old Brunswick Rd.
Piscataway, NJ 08854
800-833-6232

Quality Educational Designs
P.O. Box 12486
Portland, OR 97212
503-287-8137

Quantum Technology
30153 Arena Dr.
Evergreen, CO 80439
303-674-9651

Queue, Inc.
338 Commerce Dr.
Fairfield, CT 06430
203-335-0906

Realtime Learning Systems
2700 Conneticut Ave. NW
Washington, D.C. 20008-5330
800-832-2472

Research Design Associates
10 Boulevard Ave.
Greenlawn, NY 11740
516-754-5280

Scholastic, Inc.
730 Broadway
New York City, NY 10003
800-548-1604

Scholastic Software
P.O. Box 7502
Jefferson City, MO 65102
800-541-5513

Scott, Foresman & Co.
1900 East Lake Ave.
Glenview, IL 60025
708-729-3000

Selective Software
903 Pacific Ave.
Santa Cruz, CA 95060
800-423-3556

Sensible Software
335 E. Big Beaver, Suite 127
Troy, MI 48083
313-528-1950

Skills Bank Corp.
825-D Hammonds Ferry Rd.
Linthicum, MD 21090-1301
800-451-5726

Society for Visual Education, Inc.
1345 Diversey Parkway
Chicago, IL 60614
312-525-1500

South Coast Writing Project
Graduate School of Education
University of California, Santa Barbara
Santa Barbara, CA 93106
805-961-4422

South-Western Publishing Co.
5101 Madison Rd.
Cincinnati, OH 45227
513-271-8811

Strategic Simulations, Inc.
675 Almanor Ave., Suite 20
Sunnyvale, CA 94086
408-737-6800

Sunburst Communications, Inc.
39 Washington Ave.
Pleasantville, NY 10570
800-628-8897

Tapestry Learning
4300 Stockton Dr. N.
Little Rock, AK 72117
800-323-7577

Teacher Support Software
1035 N.W. 57th
Gainesville, FL 32605
800-228-2871

Teach Yourself by Computer
349 W. Commercial, Suite 1000
East Rochester, NY 14445
716-381-5450

Temporal Acuity Products, Inc.
300 120th Ave., NE, Bldg.#1
Bellevue, WA 98005
206-462-1007

Terrapin Software, Inc.
400 Riverside St.
Portland, ME 04103
207-878-8200

Tom Snyder Productions
90 Sherman St.
Cambridge, MA 02140
617-876-4433

True Basic Inc.
12 Commerce Ave.
West Lebanon, NH 03784-9758
800-872-2742

Unicorn Engineering, Inc.
5221 Central Ave., Suite 205
Richmond, CA 94804
415-528-0670

Univeral Technical Systems, Inc.
1220 Rock St.
Rockford, IL 61101
815-963-2220

Vernier Software
2920 S.W. 89th St.
Portland, OR 9722
503-297-5317

Wadsworth Electronic Publishing
Co.
10 Davis Dr.
Belmont, CA 94002
415-595-2350

Weekly Reader Software/Optimum
Resource 10 Station Place
Norfolk, CT 06058
800-327-1473

William K. Bradford Publishing Co.
P.O. Box 1355, Dept. EL
Concord, MA 01742
800-421-2009

WordPerfect Corp.
1555 N. Technology Way
Orem, UT 84057
800-451-5151

Wordstar International, Corp.
P.O. Box 6113
Novato, CA 94948
415-382-0606

World Book, Inc.
Merchandise Mart Plaza
Chicago, IL 60654
800-621-8202

INDEX

A

abstract environment, 179
academic learning time, 193, 200
adapter, 68
Adaptive Firmware Card, 213,
    221, 222
administrative software, 21, 30,
    31
advocates, 1, 4, 8, 10, 11, 17
affective domain, 251, 265
affective learning, 267
affective qualities, 95, 108
affective variables, 251, 262
Aiken, H., 48
Alliance for Technology Access,
    224
analogy, 231, 233, 235
analysis, 251, 253, 258
Analytical Engine, 44, 45, 46, 47
anthropologist, 5, 6, 16
anthropomorphize, 155
Apple Computer, 53, 54
Apple Macintosh, 54, 56, 60, 73
application, 251, 258, 266
applications software, 44, 55, 56,
    73

artificial intelligence, 267, 270,
    95, 108
Assembly Language, 156, 157
assessment software, 21, 30, 40
attitudes, 5, 6, 15
authoring systems, 311, 317, 318,
    323
automatic programming, 153,
    157

B

Babbage, Charles, 43, 44, 45, 46,
    47, 73, 74
backlash, 1, 3, 9, 10, 11, 14, 17,
    21, 22, 267, 275, 278
backup copy, 81, 83
Bank Street, 208, 210
Bank Street Studies, 267, 277
BASIC, 2, 153, 158, 166
behaviorism, 95, 99, 102, 110
behaviors, 5
beliefs, 5, 7
binary number system, 45, 46
binary system, 44, 45
bit, 44

Bloom's taxonomy, 251, 252, 257, 258, 259, 264
Boole, George, 43, 48, 49, 74
Boolean logic, 49, 50
booting the system, 153, 169
branching programs, 96, 97, 99
Bruner, Jerome, 179
bug, 50
business environment, 4
byte, 44, 62, 64

C

CAD, 55, 59
California Technology Project, 146
card readers, 60, 61
cashless society, 81
cathode ray tube, 66
CD-ROM, 64, 65, 74, 311, 316
CGA, 68
chip, 48, 52, 53, 61, 74
chunking, 96, 103
classroom communication environments, 193, 202
classrooms, open, 11
COBOL, 153, 157, 161
cognitive amplifier, 267, 276, 278, 286
cognitive domain, 251, 258, 264, 265
cognitivism, 96, 99, 101, 102, 110
collaboration, 193, 203, 206, 211
Colossus, 48, 73
command driven, 193, 198
comment category feature, 231, 239
communication skills, 10
compatibility, 311, 315, 323
compatible, 231, 237, 240, 247
comprehension, 251, 255, 258, 266
CompuServe, 224, 294, 124, 144, 145, 147, 301

computer equity, 76, 79, 80, 89
computer ethics, 81, 91
computer languages, 153, 155, 157, 169, 171
computer literacy, 75, 76, 77, 78, 89, 91, 92
computer networking, 86
computer operating systems, 165, 166, 171, 226
computer simulations, 21, 35
computer virus, 83
computer-assisted instruction, 117
computer-managed instruction, 30, 116, 117, 120, 128
computerized accounting program, 131, 139
computerized scheduling programs, 131, 136
computerized scoring, 96, 106, 110
computing entrepreneurs, 84
concrete environment, 179
concrete thinking, 258
concretizing the abstract, 267
copy program, 83
copy protected, 83
courseware, 86, 294, 296, 297, 299, 301, 303
CPU, 44, 61, 73
Crowder, Norman, 97, 112
curriculum, 18, 19, 41, 76, 77, 85, 91
curriculum integration, 85, 86, 89, 90
cursor, 57, 58, 59, 60, 193, 196, 198

D

database, 233
database management, 21, 32, 33, 40, 78, 89

debugging, 263
decoded, 213, 219
deductive, 99
degree of control, 153, 154
demodulation, 115, 123
desktop publishing, 131, 134
Dewey, John, 179
dictionary, 196, 207
difference engine, 44, 45, 46
differential, 267, 271
diphones, 213, 216
discipline tracking, 131, 137, 143
discovery learning, 267, 272, 274, 280
disk drive, 44, 62, 64, 66
distance education, 311, 317
domain specificity, 251, 256
domain specific software, 251
"doomsday key", 56
DOS, 153, 166, 168, 171
dot-matrix printer, 69, 70, 72
downloading, 116, 124
draft quality, 44, 69
drill and practice, 93, 95, 96, 100, 101, 102, 103, 104, 105, 110, 111
drill and practice software, 21, 25, 26, 28, 29

E

ease of use, 153, 154
education subculture, 4, 7, 12
educational innovations, 11, 13, 17
Educational Products Information Exchange, 295, 300
educational software, 44, 54, 55
educational television, 11
efficacy, 3, 10, 12, 13
EGA, 68
Electric Pages, 131, 144, 147
electronic bulletin board, 82, 83, 116, 122, 124, 126, 129
electronic database, 231, 232, 233, 234, 235, 249
electronic information utilities, 147
electronic mail, 132, 143, 145, 146, 147, 148
electronic memory, 231, 243
electronic signals, 213, 219
electronic spreadsheets, 21, 32, 33, 96, 106
encoded, 213, 219
ENIAC, 50, 54
EPIE, 294, 295, 299, 300
ERIC, 143, 149
Euclidean point, 286
evaluation, 252, 258
evaluation form, 291, 293, 294, 298, 299, 300, 303, 304, 305, 306, 307, 308, 309, 310
Everest syndrome, 116, 126, 127
executive skills, 252, 255
expert systems, 21, 30, 96, 108, 109

F

factual knowledge, 252, 258
field, 231, 235, 239, 248, 249
file, 231, 233, 234, 235
filing, 232, 233, 234, 236, 237
floppy disk, 62, 64
forecasting, 231, 244
formal operational thinking, 253, 258, 267, 272, 276
formatting, 153, 170
FORTRAN, 153, 157, 158
forums, 132, 144, 145
frames, 97
FrEdWriter, 209
free-form style, 231, 239
full screen editing, 193, 198
functional learning, 193, 202

function keys, 57
future, 311, 312, 313, 314, 315, 316, 317, 318, 322, 323, 324, 325
futurists, 311, 313

G

game paddles, 59
GC EduNET, 132, 144, 146
GEnie, 124
gradebook program, 132, 136
grammar, new, 11
graphics, 179, 267, 273
graphics software, 21, 39
graphics tablets, 59
grid, 231, 241

H

hacker, 83
hacking, 81
halt key, 56
handicapped, 213, 214, 215, 216, 217, 218, 221, 222, 223, 224, 225, 226, 227, 228
Handicapped Education Exchange, 146
hard disk drives, 64, 73
hard masters, 75, 80
hardware, 43, 44, 54, 56, 73, 74
hierarchy, 252, 258
high-level languages, 153, 156, 157
higher-order thinking skills, 21, 23, 252, 255, 257, 258, 261, 263, 266
Hollerith, Herman, 43, 47, 73
Hopper, Grace, 50
HOTS, 21, 23, 252, 255, 257, 258, 261, 263, 266

human error, 7
hype, 116, 126, 128
hypermedia, 311, 318, 319, 321, 322, 324

I

IBM-compatible computer, 54, 60, 62, 66
icon driven, 193, 198
idea processor, 194, 206, 207, 210, 252, 260
IDEAL, 252, 254, 264, 265
ILS approach, 115, 121
implementation domain, 311, 312
import/export capability, 193, 198
individual educational program, 109
individualized instruction, 116, 118
inductive, 99
information age, 311, 313, 324
information management, 116, 118, 119, 120
information technologies, 311, 313
information utilities, 116, 124, 125
information utility, 213, 224
ink jet printer, 70, 71
input devices, 56, 58, 59, 60, 66, 73
instructional simulation, 173, 177, 184
integrated circuit, 43, 48, 50, 51, 52, 61, 62, 73, 74
integrated learning system, 119
integrated software spreadsheet cells, 231
interactive multimedia, 311, 318, 319, 324
interactive programs, 268, 282

inventory management
    programs, 139
ISTE, 144, 145

J

Jobs, Steve, 53, 54
joysticks, 58, 59, 60

K

Kelman, P., 162
keyboard, 56, 57, 58, 59, 66, 73
Kneller, G. F., 5, 7, 19
Kriegspiel, 173, 175

L

LAN, 66
languages, 154, 155, 156, 157,
    158, 160, 162, 165, 171
laser disc, 65, 66
laser printer, 44, 71, 72, 73
leadership roles, 132, 133, 148
learning initiative, 132, 145
Leibnitz, Gottfried, 45, 73
light pen, 59, 214, 217
linear program, 96, 97, 99
LISP, 268, 273
list processing, 268, 273, 274,
    277, 279, 281
local area network, 66, 86
Logo, 3, 10, 19, 21, 28, 35, 151,
    153, 160, 163, 164, 165, 171,
    267, 268, 269, 270, 271, 272,
    273, 274, 275, 276, 277, 278,
    279, 280, 281, 282, 283, 284,
    286, 287, 288
Logo list, 268, 282
Logo turtle, 268, 273, 274, 286
Logo word, 268, 282
Lovelace, Ada, 44, 45, 74

lower-order thinking skills, 258,
    261
low-level languages, 157

M

machine language, 153, 155, 156,
    157, 169
macro, 214, 219
mail, 54, 66
mainframe, 66
management system, 87, 88
management tasks, 131, 132,
    133, 134, 137, 147
mass media, 6
mass storage, 311, 315, 323
mastery learning, 116, 118
math, new, 11
mathophobia, 267, 268, 273, 274,
    278
MECC, 239, 248, 250
media, 23, 24, 39
megabyte, 62
memory, 44, 47, 56, 62, 64, 73
mental rigor, 268, 276
menu driven, 194, 208
menu options, 231, 239
meta-analysis, 21, 32, 96, 105,
    110, 112
metacognition, 194, 201, 268, 277
metacognitive skills, 252
microelectronic techniques, 61
microprocessor, 53
MicroSIFT, 294, 299, 300
mnemonic system, 154
modem, 116, 123, 129, 132, 144,
    146
modulation, 116, 123
module, 116, 117, 139, 140, 142
Molnar, Andrew, 76, 92
motor impairment, 213, 214, 215,
    217
mouse, 59, 60

multimedia, 311, 318, 319, 321,
322, 323, 324
music box, 43, 44, 45, 46

N

national economic necessity, 77,
78
National Logo Exchange, The,
275
Nation at Risk, A, 75, 77, 91, 92
network manager, 76, 88
new grammar, 11
new math, 11
nondomain specific software, 251,
252

O

on-line catalog, 132, 143
on-line database, 132, 143
on-line service, 214, 224, 225, 317
open classrooms, 11
operating systems, 153, 154, 165,
166, 169, 170, 171
optical character readers, 61
optical disks, 311, 315, 316, 323
output devices, 66, 73

P

PALS program, 65
panacea, 86
Papert, Seymour, 267, 270, 271,
272, 273, 274, 275, 279, 280,
286, 288, 289
Pascal, 154, 158, 159, 172
Pascal, Blaise, 43, 44, 45
passive involvement, 24
pattern recognition, 103
PC Serial A.I.D., 222
PC Truant, 136

pendulum syndrome, 3
peripheral devices, 214, 226
peripherals, 66, 73
Piaget, Jean, 270, 272, 273, 286,
288, 289
PILOT, 160
piracy, 297
pixel, 68
PLATO, 103
play, 173, 175, 180, 181, 182, 183,
186, 188, 190
plotters, 66
point in space, 268, 274, 286
Polya, 251, 252, 254, 266
Prab Command, 219
Prentke-Romich, 222
presentation software, 22, 39
Pressey, Sidney, 96, 97, 103, 110,
112
prevocational necessity, 76, 77
principals, 8
print formatting, 194, 198
printer, 66, 68, 69, 70
problem solving, 251, 252, 253,
254, 255, 256, 257, 258, 259,
260, 261, 262, 263, 264, 265
problem-solving software, 22, 37,
40
program, 50, 54, 55, 62, 65
programmed instruction, 95, 96,
97, 98, 99, 100, 101, 110,
111, 113, 116, 118
programming, 154, 155, 156, 157,
158, 159, 160, 162, 163, 164,
165, 168, 172
programming language, 22, 34,
35, 40
prosthesis, 214
prosthetic aids, 22, 39, 40
prosthetic devices, 213, 214, 215,
216, 221, 223, 224, 225, 227,
228
PSInet, 132, 145, 146
psychological theory, 12
psychomotor domain, 252, 258

Q

quality gap, 297
quality lag, 294, 296

R

rack and pinion calculators, 46
RAM, 44, 62, 154, 167, 168
real and fantasy environments, 173
real environment, 184
records, 231, 233, 234, 235, 236, 238, 239
referent, 38
reinforcement, 96, 97, 98, 100
remediation, 30
Resources in Computer Education, 187
revolutionaries, 6
robots, 317, 323
ROM, 44, 62, 154, 167
rote computational habit, 252, 260
rote memory, 26, 28, 40

S

scanner, 60
scanning device, 214, 221
SchoolLINK, 132, 146
science teacher's network, 132, 146
Scully, John, 53
search and replace, 194, 198
Sell Bicycles, 173, 175
Sell Lemonade, 173, 175, 184
semiconductor, 50, 51, 52
sense of audience, 193, 194, 202, 210
serial port, 214, 222
SIGs, 144
simulations, 173, 174, 175, 176,

177, 178, 179, 181, 182, 183, 184, 185, 186, 188, 189, 190, 191, 311, 318, 319, 323, 329
site license, 82, 83, 87
Skinner, B. F., 8
socialization, 184
soft mastery, 75, 76, 80
software, 3, 9, 14, 15, 16, 54, 55
software piracy, 82, 83
solid character impact, 69
sorting information, 231, 236
spaghetti program, 154, 159
special input device, 214, 217
special interest groups, 132
spelling checker program, 194, 196
spreadsheet, 231, 232, 238, 241, 242
spreadsheet formulas, 232, 242
spreadsheet software, 76, 78
standardized tests, 30
Stanford Project, 96, 103
structured, 163
structured problems, 96, 109
Student Information Management System, 135
stylus, 59
subconscious theories, 12
switches, 214, 218, 219, 222
symbol manipulation, 156, 232
synthesis, 252, 258
synthesized speech, 214, 216, 223
SYSOP, 124
systems operator, 116

T

Tandy/Radio Shack, 53, 54
task analysis, 96, 97, 98
teacher-link, 132, 146
teaching machines, 95, 96, 97, 98, 99, 100, 101, 102, 103, 110, 111, 112, 113

team teaching, 11

technical domain, 311, 312

technology gap, 78

telecommunications, 22, 39, 115, 116, 122, 123, 124, 125, 126, 127, 128, 129, 132, 144, 145, 146, 147, 148

teleconferencing, 132, 143, 144, 145, 146, 147,1 48

telestudying, 311, 317

template, 59, 232, 238, 240, 241, 246, 247, 248

thesaurus, 194, 198, 207, 208, 209

Thorndike, Edward L., 97

TIMS, 141

Top Management Decision Simulation, 175

touch screen, 217

Trackball, 60

transfer, 252, 253, 256, 257, 260, 262, 263, 264, 268, 271, 276, 277, 279, 287

TRS-80 Model One, 54

Turing, Alan, 43, 44, 48, 73, 74

turtle graphics, 268, 274, 277

tutorial programs, 96, 102, 104, 105

tutorial software, 22, 29

Type I, 21, 22, 23, 24, 25, 26, 27, 28, 29, 30, 31, 39, 40, 41

Type II, 21, 22, 23, 24, 25, 26, 27, 29, 30, 31, 32, 33, 34, 36, 37, 38, 39, 40, 41

U

Underwood, K. E., 5, 20

unstructured problems, 95, 96, 109, 110

user friendly, 232

U.S. Office of Technology Assessment, 9

V

vacuum tubes, 43, 50, 73

variable, 268, 271, 272, 273, 282, 283, 284, 285, 286

VGA, 68

vibration, 214, 219

video discs, 311, 316

voice recognition, 311, 318

voice synthesis, 311, 318

voice-control keyboard, 214, 219

von Neumann, John, 48, 74

W

Webb & Sherman, 5

Windows, 194, 199, 201, 227

WISC-R, 108

word processing, 15, 16, 17, 22, 27, 30, 31, 32, 33, 39, 40, 78, 80, 89, 193, 194, 195, 196, 197, 198, 199, 200, 201, 202, 203, 204, 205, 206, 208, 209, 210, 211

word wraparound, 194, 196, 198

Wozniak, Steve, 53, 54, 74

Z

Zuse, Konrad, 48

Credits:

Figures 3.1, 3.2, 3.3, and 3.4 courtesy of Smithsonian Institution.
Figure 3.5 courtesy of Mostek.
Figure 3.6 courtesy of Apple Computer Corporation.
Figure 3.7 Courtesy of Scholastic.
Figure 3.8 courtesy of Key Tronic. (Photo by Robert Barrows Photography.)
Figure 3.9 courtesy of Polytel.
Figure 3.10 courtesy of FTG Data Systems.
Figures 3.11 and 3.12 courtesy of Logitech OEM Products.
Figure 3.13 courtesy of Toshiba.
Figure 3.14 courtesy of TDK.
Figure 3.15 courtesy of Seagate.
Figure 3.16 courtesy of Sony.
Figure 3.17 courtesy of Phillips.
Figure 3.18 courtesy of Thomson.
Figure 3.19 courtesy of Seikosha.
Figure 3.20 courtesy of Diablo.
Figure 3.21 courtesy of Sharp.
Figure 3.22 courtesy of Rikoh.
Figure 3.23 courtesy of TurboRes Typeshop.
Figures 8.1 and 8.2 courtesy of Charles Crume, Technical Consultant, University of Nevada Computing Center.
Figures 11.1, 11.2, 11.3, 11.4, and 11.5 courtesy of Nevada Technology Center.
Figure 14.1 reprinted courtesy of Charles Crume, Technical Consultant, University of Nevada Computing Center.